DSA®
DRIVING STANDARDS AGENCY
SAFE DRIVING FOR LIFE™

The **OFFICIAL DSA GUIDE** to
DRIVING
the essential skills

London: TSO

Written and compiled by the Learning Materials Section of The Driving Standards Agency (DSA).

First edition Crown copyright 1992
Second edition Crown copyright 1997
Third edition Crown copyright 1999
Fourth edition Crown copyright 2001
Fifth edition Crown copyright 2005
Sixth edition Crown copyright 2007
Seventh edition Crown copyright 2011
Third impression 2011

ISBN 978 0 11 553134 7

A CIP catalogue record for this book is available from the British Library

Other titles in the Driving Skills series

The Official DSA Theory Test for Car Drivers
The Official DSA Theory Test for Car Drivers (CD-ROM)
The Official DSA Guide to Learning to Drive
Prepare for your Practical Driving Test (DVD)
DSA Driving Theory Quiz (DVD)
The Official Highway Code Interactive CD-ROM

The Official DSA Theory Test iPhone App
The Official DSA Theory Test Kit iPhone App

The Official DSA Guide to Riding – the essential skills
The Official DSA Theory Test for Motorcyclists
The Official DSA Theory Test for Motorcyclists (CD-ROM)
The Official DSA Guide to Learning to Ride
Better Biking – the official DSA training aid (DVD)

The Official DSA Guide to Driving Buses and Coaches
The Official DSA Guide to Driving Goods Vehicles
The Official DSA Theory Test for Drivers of Large Vehicles
The Official DSA Theory Test for Drivers of Large Vehicles (CD-ROM)
Driver CPC – the official DSA guide for professional bus and coach drivers
Driver CPC – the official DSA guide for professional goods vehicle drivers

The Official DSA Guide to Tractor and Specialist Vehicle Driving Tests
The Official DSA Guide to Hazard Perception (DVD)

Every effort has been made to ensure that the information contained in this publication is accurate at the time of going to press. The Stationery Office cannot be held responsible for any inaccuracies. Information in this book is for guidance only.

All metric and imperial conversions in this book are approximate.

75% recycled
This book is printed on 75% recycled paper

Find us online

Information and services about:

- car drivers
- motorcyclists
- driving licences
- driving tests
- towing a caravan or trailer
- medical rules
- driving for a living
- online services

Visit **direct.gov.uk/motoring**

If you need to contact us

If you can't find the answer to your question online and you need information about DSA's service standards, complaints procedures, out-of-pocket expenses or for other matters, visit **direct.gov.uk/contactdsa**

Or you can call us on **0300 200 1122**

You can also find contact details for other motoring agencies like DVLA at **direct.gov.uk/motoringcontacts**

The Driving Standards Agency (DSA) is an executive agency of the Department for Transport. You'll see its logo at theory and practical test centres.

DSA aims to promote road safety through the advancement of driving standards, by

- establishing and developing high standards and best practice in driving and riding on the road; before people start to drive, as they learn, and after they pass their test
- ensuring high standards of instruction for different types of driver and rider
- conducting the statutory theory and practical tests efficiently, fairly and consistently across the country
- providing a centre of excellence for driver training and driving standards
- developing a range of publications and publicity material designed to promote safe driving for life.

The Driving Standards Agency recognises and values its customers. It will treat all its customers with respect, and deliver its services in an objective, polite and fair way.

dft.gov.uk/dsa

The Driver and Vehicle Agency (DVA) is an executive agency within the Department of the Environment for Northern Ireland.

Its primary aim is to promote and improve road safety through the advancement of driving standards and implementation of the government's policies for improving the mechanical standards of vehicles.

dvani.gov.uk

Contents

section **one**
THE DRIVER

This section covers
- Attitude
- Good habits
- Health
- Learner drivers
- New drivers
- Older drivers
- Disabled drivers

A message from the chief driving examiner

Each year thousands of men, women and children are killed or seriously injured on roads in Great Britain. The majority of the crashes that result in these deaths and injuries are the result of human error. This makes it vital that every driver understands the responsibility that driving a car brings with it and the importance of making safety their overriding priority.

Safe driving is all about developing the right attitude and approach, and combining this with a sound knowledge of defensive driving techniques. It means not only driving with courtesy and consideration for everyone else, but also being prepared to make allowances for the mistakes of others.

The increasing volume of traffic on our roads today means you'll often find yourself driving in crowded conditions on all types of road. By adopting the correct attitude and taking pride in your driving, you'll ensure that this convenient means of transport remains both safe and enjoyable.

The predecessor to this book, *The Official Driving Manual*, has long been recognised as an essential reference book for every motorist, regardless of experience, and for instructors too. This latest edition has been updated to take account of changes in legislation, roads, vehicles and driving techniques and procedures. Read this book carefully – and put into practice the advice it gives. Above all, make sure your aim is *'safe driving for life'*.

Trevor Wedge

Trevor Wedge

Chief driving examiner and director for safer driving

Attitude

No matter how good, how fast, how expensive or how efficient your vehicle is, it's you, **the driver**, who determines whether it's a safe means of transport.

Driver skill and driver attitude are two key areas which determine your approach behind the wheel.

There is, after all, a lot of enjoyment and satisfaction to be gained from showing not only your skill and ability but also courtesy and consideration to those around you. Apart from the reward of a nod or smile in appreciation, you'll have the added satisfaction of knowing you are making our roads that much safer.

The right attitude and behaviour are the key factors to becoming a good driver. A good driver isn't a perfect driver; it's very doubtful whether such a driver exists. Nevertheless, apart from skill and experience, which only come with time, a good driver needs

- responsibility
- concentration
- anticipation
- patience
- confidence.

Together, these qualities go to make up what is generally known as the driver's attitude. It is attitude which, in turn, influences driver behaviour.

Remember, it's a fact that nearly all road traffic incidents are caused, to some degree, by the driver. Reducing them is the responsibility of every driver.

Developing the right attitude and behaviour will come more easily to some drivers than others, but these attributes are so important to safe driving that it's vital for every driver to make the effort to keep working on them. Take pride in your driving and remember that, even if you have been driving for years, there's always something to learn.

Responsibility

As a responsible driver, you must always be concerned for the safety of

- yourself
- your passengers
- all other road users.

Yourself See pages 17–19.

Your passengers Be aware of any particular needs of your passengers, for example, if they have mobility problems or are suffering from an illness that might require additional attention. Be aware also of your responsibilities regarding the use of seat belts by your passengers (see page 39).

Other road users Be tolerant; remember that everyone is entitled to use the road. This may mean making allowances for other road users from time to time, particularly the most vulnerable, such as

- children and older people
- people with disabilities
- cyclists and motorcyclists
- people in charge of animals.

Look around you, and plan your actions well ahead to avoid causing danger or inconvenience. In this way you can avoid the temptation to act hastily – perhaps with dire consequences.

Be responsible by recognising your own limitations and those of others.

Remember, the responsibility for safe driving rests with you.

Concentration

To be able to drive safely in today's traffic conditions, you must have 100% concentration.

If you let your mind wander, even for a moment, the risk of making a mistake is increased enormously, and mistakes frequently lead to incidents.

Avoid driving if you're

- feeling tired or unwell
- thinking about something else
- upset or annoyed
- suffering stress of any kind.

If you have to drive under any of these conditions, try to give yourself more time to react.

Concentration is the key to anticipation and is helped by having

- good vision
- good hearing
- good health
- self-discipline.

If you have any in-vehicle system such as satellite navigation, congestion warning or vehicle management system, don't let these divert your attention from your driving or reduce your concentration. Restrict any visual or manual interaction with the system to an absolute minimum. In the interests of safety, you should find an appropriate, safe and legal place to stop before making any adjustments.

While on the move don't

- make or answer phone calls or texts
- use iPods or generic MP3 players
- look at road maps or route guidance and navigation systems
- try to tune the radio or change CDs
- let conversation distract you (an argument with your passengers can be particularly distracting)
- listen to loud music or use headphones of any kind, as these can mask other sounds
- be distracted by eating, drinking (even non-alcoholic drinks) or smoking.

In addition, don't

- stick non-essential stickers on the windows of your vehicle; they can restrict your view
- hang objects in your vehicle (eg dolls, dice, etc) where they might distract you and restrict your view.

Passengers Passengers can be a major source of distraction, particularly if they have been drinking or taking drugs. However it can also be distracting even if they are just talking to you, using a mobile phone or moving around unnecessarily.

Mobile phones

You **MUST NOT** use a hand-held mobile phone, or other similar device, when driving, except to call 999 or 112 in a genuine emergency when it is unsafe or impractical to stop.

Using any phone or microphone, even if it is hands-free, can also divert your attention from the road. It is far safer not to use any phone while driving.

Find a safe place to stop before making a call. Use voicemail to receive calls and make regular stops to retrieve messages.

Driving requires all of your attention, all of the time.

These rules apply even if you're not driving but are supervising a learner driver.

Anticipation

Anticipation in driving means planning well ahead and acting promptly to deal with the changes going on around you. It should, with experience, become almost an automatic reaction. It's the hallmark of a good driver.

You need to continually question the actions of other road users.

If you plan ahead and try to anticipate the actions of others, you can

- avoid being taken by surprise
- prevent some hazards developing
- save fuel by anticipating situations early so that you can plan your approach and therefore keep moving when it is safe to do so
- take early evasive action with regard to those hazards that do develop.

Anticipation and good planning are essential to developing defensive driving techniques (see page 201).

Patience

It's said that patience is a virtue, and this is certainly true when you're driving.

Sadly, incompetence, bad manners and aggression seem to be commonplace on our roads, but there is no excuse for this type of behaviour when driving.

You shouldn't let bad driving behaviour by other road users lead to conflict. If you do, you're well on the way to an incident.

Be prepared to make allowances for someone else's mistakes. In everyone's interest, try to ignore their behaviour.

Don't

- drive in a spirit of retaliation or competition
- use aggressive language or gestures
- try to teach another road user a lesson, even if they have caused you inconvenience.

Do

- keep calm
- show restraint
- use sound judgement.

There's no better lesson than a good example.

Learner drivers Be patient if the vehicle ahead of you is being driven by a learner. They may not be as skilful at anticipating and responding to events as a more experienced driver.

> **Remember,** not every vehicle showing L plates (D plates in Wales) is fitted with dual controls, and the person accompanying the driver might not be a professional.

Don't

- drive up close behind
- rev the engine
- become impatient if the other vehicle is slow to move off, anticipate that they might stall
- overtake only to cut in again sharply.

Expect a learner to make mistakes and allow for them. Don't harass them; learners may not take the action you expect. Remember that it takes them longer to do things. Don't forget we were all learners once.

Drivers who have recently passed their test may be displaying a green 'P' plate or other warning sign.

Older drivers Although they have the experience, the reactions of older drivers may be slower than those of younger drivers. Make allowances for this.

Confidence

This is all part of a driver's attitude and is closely related to

- skill
- judgement
- experience.

New drivers will naturally be unsure of themselves, but confidence will grow with experience.

A good driver will avoid being over-confident as this only leads to carelessness.

Good habits

Good habits and thoughtful behaviour can help ensure that both you and your passengers arrive safely.

If you're upset by the bad behaviour of another driver, try not to react. If necessary, slow down to calm down, even if you feel like making a more aggressive response. Consider stopping to take a break. While you're upset you're vulnerable. Your powers of concentration, anticipation and observation are likely to be much reduced, making a road traffic incident is much more likely.

Be prepared to make allowances for someone else's mistakes.

> **Remember,** your actions can affect the actions of other drivers. Lack of consideration can have dangerous consequences. Obey the rules set out in The Highway Code.

Relax

- Give yourself plenty of time.
- Make yourself comfortable.
- Keep your mind on your driving.

The better you feel, the easier your journey will be.

Consideration

It helps other drivers if you don't try to dominate the road. So don't

- cut across the path of other vehicles
- rush through traffic
- change your mind at the last minute
- use aggressive language or gestures.

Calm down

Irritation and anger, for whatever reason, are dangerous. They can cause mistakes, and mistakes lead to incidents.

If you're angry, take time to compose yourself before a journey. Don't jump into your vehicle when you're angry or annoyed. Wait until you've calmed down. The chance of an incident is too great to risk driving under such pressure.

Plan your journey

- Give yourself plenty of time for your journey. Hurrying leads to mistakes, and mistakes lead to incidents.
- If it's a long journey, plan enough time for breaks and refreshment.
- If you have a satellite navigation system, programme it before you start your journey. Don't rely on it exclusively as it may have out-of-date or incomplete information at any given time.
- Use road and street maps before you set out, or check your route from the internet.
- Planning your journey to take the best route can also help you save fuel.

Getting lost can also lead to frustration and loss of concentration. Avoid rush hours around major cities if you can. Before you set out, check **direct.gov.uk/trafficinfo** for an online journey planner, live traffic updates and an iPhone app from the Highways Agency. You could also listen to local and national radio for news of roadworks and traffic congestion.

The weather

The weather is an important factor when you're driving. If it's really bad, it might be best to postpone your trip or use public transport. Always try to avoid driving in thick fog or icy conditions. It's a much greater strain, and the risk of a road traffic incident is far higher.

Many drivers run into difficulties in very bad weather. Follow the weather forecasts and general advice to drivers through local and national media.

Animals

- Keep animals under control.
- Don't allow animals loose in the vehicle.
- Don't leave animals in a vehicle for any length of time, especially in hot weather.
- Never allow animals loose on the public road – they can cause incidents.

Driving close to home

Many incidents happen close to home on regular daily or routine journeys. If you drive to work every day, don't leave yourself the bare minimum of time to get there. More haste, less speed.

Don't let familiarity with your home area and surroundings lead you to start taking risks simply because you feel you know every detail. Remember that strangers won't have the benefit of local knowledge, so they might drive more cautiously than you feel they should.

Health

Your eyesight

You must be able to read in good daylight, with glasses or contact lenses if you wear them, a motor vehicle number plate from a distance of 20 metres (about 66 feet). This is about five car lengths. Older-style number plates should be read from a distance of 20.5 metres (about 67 feet).

Fitness to drive

You must

- be medically fit to drive
- understand that some medicines should not be taken if you intend to drive
- notify the Driver and Vehicle Licensing Agency (DVLA), Swansea (DVA in Northern Ireland) if your health is likely to affect your ability to drive, either now or, because of a worsening condition, in the future.

Don't drive if you're feeling tired or unwell. Even a cold can make it unsafe for you to drive. If you find you're losing concentration or not feeling well, keep your speed down and give yourself more time to react.

Physical fitness and mobility are also important. Make sure that you have full control of your vehicle at all times.

Remember that

- a twisted ankle can reduce pedal (including brake) control
- a stiff neck can make it difficult to look behind when reversing or checking blind spots.

Alcohol

Alcohol will seriously reduce your judgement and ability to drive safely. You must be aware that

- to drive with alcohol in your blood is extremely dangerous, and carries severe penalties if you drive or attempt to drive while over the legal limit
- if you drink in the evening, you might still be over the legal limit and unfit to drive the following morning.

Alcohol may remain in the body for around 24–48 hours. Your ability to react quickly may be reduced and the effects may still be evident the next morning. Your body tissues actually need up to 48 hours to recover. The only safe limit, ever, is a zero limit.

You **MUST NOT** drive if your breath alcohol level is higher than 35 µg/100 ml (equivalent to a blood alcohol level of 80 mg/100 ml).

> **Remember,** be safe! If you drink, don't drive! If you drive, don't drink!

Drugs

Illegal drugs Driving when you're under the influence of illegal drugs is an offence. You must not take any of the drugs that are generally accepted as 'banned substances' while driving or before you intend to drive.

Unlike alcohol (the effects of which last for about 24–48 hours), the effects of drugs can be unpredictable and you may not be aware of them. The direct effects of some drugs can last up to 72 hours.

The effects can be even more serious than alcohol, and may result in a fatal or serious road traffic incident.

Medicines Check any medicine you're taking to see if it affects your ability to drive. Even medicines for coughs and hay fever can make you drowsy. Read the label and follow any recommendations given. Consult your doctor or pharmacist if you're not sure. If still in doubt, **don't drive.**

After a shock A shock or bereavement can badly upset your concentration. In this situation, avoid driving altogether.

Are you comfortable? Make sure you're feeling comfortable. Wear sensible clothing for driving, especially on a long journey.

Shoes Shoes are particularly important. High heels and slippery soles can be dangerous on the pedals. Shoes that are too wide, or that easily fall off, can be just as dangerous.

It's a good idea to keep a suitable pair of shoes in your vehicle, just for driving.

Fatigue

Driving while you are tired increases your risk of being involved in a collision.

Don't begin a journey if you feel tired – make sure you get a good night's sleep before starting a long journey.

Try to avoid driving between midnight and 7.00 am because this is when the 'body clock' is in a daily trough.

If you begin to feel sleepy, stop in a safe place before you get to the stage of 'fighting sleep'. Sleep can come upon you more quickly than you would imagine. You **MUST NOT** stop on the hard shoulder of a motorway to rest.

If it's not possible to stop immediately, open a window for fresh air. Stop as soon as it's safe and legal to do so.

The most effective ways to counter sleepiness are caffeine and a short nap. The combination of a caffeinated drink (for example, two cups of caffeinated coffee), followed by a short nap of up to 15 minutes, is particularly effective. This is because caffeine takes 20–30 minutes to be absorbed and act on the brain, hence the opportunity for a nap.

On a motorway, pull in at the nearest service area or leave the motorway. **DO NOT** pull up on the hard shoulder just to rest.

Don't drive for too long without taking a break. Your concentration will be much better if you plan regular stops for rest and refreshments. It is recommended that you take a break of at least 15 minutes after every two hours of driving. This is especially important at night.

Learner drivers

Attitude is critical to a new driver's approach, both to their own driving and to the actions and mistakes of other road users.

If you're a novice, you need to use your sense of responsibility, patience and courtesy to develop the skills necessary to become a good driver.

A great deal of what you'll learn will depend on your instructor.

Planned tuition

A planned approach to learning is essential, particularly in the early stages.

Each lesson should be matched to your needs and abilities. There are no short cuts to becoming a good defensive driver (see page 201).

Who should teach you?

The best way to learn is by having

- regular planned lessons with a good professional instructor
- as much practice as possible.

Once you understand the basics, it's a good idea to combine professional instruction with as much practice as you can with relatives and friends.

If you pay someone for tuition, they must be an approved driving instructor (ADI) (car) or a trainee licence holder.

Approved driving instructor (car)

An ADI must

- pass a rigorous three-part examination to qualify
- have their name entered on the register held by DSA
- display a green ADI identification certificate on the windscreen of the tuition vehicle
- reach and maintain the standards required by DSA.

Some trainee instructors who have not yet completed the qualifying examination are granted a trainee licence to enable them to gain instructional experience.

This is a pink identification certificate which must be displayed on the windscreen of the tuition vehicle.

How to choose an ADI

- Ask friends and relatives.
- Choose an instructor
  - who has a good reputation
  - who is reliable and punctual
  - whose vehicle suits you.
- Visit **direct.gov.uk** for more information on ADI grading.

Take advice from your ADI on

- all aspects of driving
- what books to read or what DVDs, downloads, CD-ROMs and apps are available
- when you'll be ready for the driving test
- how to practise.

The official syllabus

If you learn with an ADI, make sure they cover the official syllabus fully. See the book *The Official DSA Guide to Learning to Drive*. The syllabus is also shown in the Driver's Record. The Driver's Record, which also helps you to monitor your progress, is available from your ADI or downloadable from **direct.gov.uk/driversrecord**

Since October 2010, all practical driving tests have included a period of independent driving. This assesses your ability to drive on your own while making decisions for yourself without instruction. The examiner will be looking for evidence that you have the required skills, knowledge and attitude to be a safe driver.

This new section is an important element, because driving on your own is precisely what you will be able to do as soon as you have passed your driving test. The section will last for around 10 minutes, during which you will be asked to

- drive following traffic signs to a destination **OR**
- drive following a series of verbal directions

or a combination of both.

Accompanying a learner

If you're accompanying a learner, you should try to encourage confidence. It's also important not to put them in a situation that requires more skill than they can be expected to show.

Don't let them try to run before they can walk. Overestimating a learner's skill could lead to disturbing incidents for both the learner and other road users. This can set back the learner's progress and also be dangerous. Be aware that anyone supervising a learner must

- be at least 21 years of age
- have held for at least three years (and still hold) a full EC/EEA licence for the category of vehicle being driven.

The book *The Official DSA Guide to Learning to Drive* includes a section which will assist you in understanding what a learner driver needs to practise and will alert you to the hazards you may encounter when accompanying a learner driver.

Learning by example

The inexperienced often learn by example. They should, therefore

- be shown how to drive with quiet confidence

- have examples of bad driving explained and not excused

- be discouraged from developing bad habits and using excuses such as, 'Everyone else does it, so why shouldn't I?'

- learn from the good example you demonstrate.

Taking on too much The enthusiastic learner should be very careful not to take on too much.

Over-confidence can lead to carelessness, risk-taking and, sometimes, tragic incidents.

The training vehicle A vehicle being driven by a learner must display L plates (or D plates in Wales), which should be removed or covered at all other times.

If you own a car or intend to buy one, it might be best to find a driving school that uses a similar model.

At a later stage, it might also be possible to have lessons in your own car. Avoid using a different vehicle for practice in the early stages. The controls and feel of the car will be so different that it might hinder rather than assist progress.

Avoid fixing L plates (D plates) to the windscreen or back window; they restrict your view.

New drivers

Young and inexperienced drivers are more vulnerable on the roads. They can often be involved in incidents early in their driving careers, sometimes tragically so. Such incidents can usually be attributed to

- the natural exuberance of youth
- immaturity; an inability to cope with the serious nature of driving
- showing off to friends; 'egging on' by passengers looking for excitement
- competitive behaviour, racing and so on
- lack of experience and judgement, especially when driving 'high-performance' cars
- being over-confident of their own ability.

If you are a new driver, avoid

- driving too fast; speed can kill
- reckless driving; drive with consideration and care
- showing off; if you want to impress your friends, show them how safe a driver you are
- being 'wound up'; keep calm, learn to ignore the stupidity of others
- an aggressive attitude and behaviour; again, stay calm and safe
- loud music; this could interfere with your concentration or with your hearing at a critical moment
- driving beyond your capabilities; always leave yourself a safety margin
- being distracted by passengers.

Above all, be responsible and always show courtesy and consideration to other road users. Your life, and the lives of others, could depend on it!

False perceptions Many younger drivers wrongly believe that fast reactions and the ability to handle their vehicle will make them a good and safe driver. They fail to recognise that driving skill alone will not prevent road traffic incidents.

Having the right attitude and a sound knowledge of defensive driving techniques is essential.

Pass Plus New drivers can take further training after they have passed their test.

Remember, be safe: don't take risks!

The Pass Plus scheme has been created by DSA for new drivers who would like to improve their basic skills and safely widen their driving experience. If you take the Pass Plus course, you may also receive reduced insurance premiums.

Ask your ADI for details of the scheme or visit **direct.gov.uk/passplus** for more information.

Advanced driving courses Other organisations offer courses in advanced driving techniques. These are listed on page 365.

Older drivers

Although experienced, older drivers can also be vulnerable, but for different reasons. The natural and gradual deterioration in physical fitness and ability that comes with age can seriously affect judgement and concentration.

If you are an older driver, be responsible and

- have your eyesight checked regularly, including your night vision

- don't drive if you feel unwell

- take care when judging the speed of oncoming traffic at junctions. If in doubt, wait. Don't make hasty manoeuvres. Look, assess and decide before you act

- keep concentrating on your driving – always!

- find a safe place to stop and rest if you feel tired

- keep up to date with the changes to rules and regulations – for example, new road markings and signs. Study the current edition of The Highway Code and put the advice it gives into practice

- take extra care – your reactions might not be as quick as they used to be.

Remember, recognise your own limitations and don't take risks.

Disabled drivers

Advances in modern technology offer many more disabled people the chance to drive, and all standard vehicles can be modified for a disabled driver.

Many cars are available with automatic transmission and power-assisted steering to help the disabled driver.

Modifications

These can include

- hand controls for braking and acceleration
- steering and secondary control aids
- left-foot accelerator conversions
- clutch conversions
- parking brake devices
- additional car mirrors
- seat belt modifications
- harnesses
- special seating
- wheelchair stowage equipment.

For the more severely disabled driver

- joystick and foot steering; a four-way joystick can now be used to steer, accelerate and brake
- infra-red remote control systems which enable a driver to enter a vehicle and drive from a wheelchair with complete independence.

Assessment

Driving assessment centres for disabled persons are available to

- test driving ability
- give advice on the sort of controls and adaptations needed to drive safely and in comfort.

A list of some mobility centres is given on page 366, although this is not exhaustive. Visit **mobility-centres.org.uk/find_a_ centre** for a complete list. You could also visit **motability.co.uk** for information about financing modifications and adaptations.

The major motoring organisations and some motor manufacturers offer special services for disabled drivers.

Parking concessions

Severely disabled persons might qualify for parking concessions. Contact your local authority to apply for the Blue Badge scheme or visit **direct.gov.uk/bluebadge** or more information.

section **two**

THE DRIVER AND THE LAW

This section covers

- Your driving licence
- Insurance
- Vehicle registration certificate (V5C)
- Vehicle excise duty
- Vehicle test certificate
- Roadworthiness
- The Highway Code
- Seat belts
- Loading your vehicle

Your driving licence

Driving any vehicle carries with it legal requirements, and you must satisfy some of these before you begin to drive on the public road. Others apply after you start to drive.

For the category of vehicle you intend to drive, you **MUST** have one of the following

- a valid provisional driving licence
- a valid full driving licence

or, in certain circumstances

- a signed, valid International Driving Permit (IDP)
- a full driving licence issued outside the UK.

Your age

You **MUST** be at least 17 years of age to drive a car. As an exception, if you're receiving Higher Rate Disability Living Allowance, you can start driving at 16.

Provisional licence

Driving licences are issued by the Driver and Vehicle Licensing Agency (DVLA) (or DVA in Northern Ireland). The application form (D1) can be obtained from any licence-issuing post office. Alternatively you can apply for a provisional licence online at **direct.gov.uk/drivinglicence**

These forms need to be sent to the appropriate office as detailed on the form. You must enclose the required passport-type photographs as all provisional licences now issued are photocard licences.

When you receive your provisional licence, check that all details are correct.

L plates (D plates in Wales) You **MUST** display L plates (D plates) which conform to legal specifications, and which are clearly visible from both in front of the vehicle and from behind the vehicle.

If the vehicle is **NOT** being driven by a learner driver, the L plates (D plates) should be removed or covered.

Your accompanying driver You **MUST** be accompanied by a driver who is at least 21 years old and who holds a full EC/EEA licence for that type of car (manual or automatic) and has held one for at least the last three years.

Motorways Holders of provisional car and motorcycle licences are not allowed to drive on a motorway.

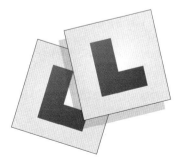

Full licence

To obtain your full licence you **MUST** pass a theory test, followed by a practical test for the category of vehicle you wish to drive. You will then be able to drive unaccompanied and on a motorway. Your car licence also allows you to drive a light van of up to 3.5 tonnes maximum laden weight, but different speed limits apply to vans over 2 tonnes maximum laden weight (see page 106).

Photocard licences

Since 1998 photocard licences have been issued to anyone applying for a new or replacement licence. This is made up of two parts: the licence and the counterpart. If you have been issued with a photocard licence, you must always be able to produce the counterpart if requested by a police officer.

Changes to your driving licence

If you change your name and/or address, you must complete the details on your licence and send it to: DVLA, Swansea, SA99 1BN (DVA in NI) or you can do this online at **direct.gov.uk/driverinfo**

Visitors and new residents

Visitors If you're a visitor to the UK, you're allowed to drive on your current licence or permit for up to a year after your latest entry into the country.

New residents If you come to live in Britain you may drive for up to one year on your foreign licence.

If you come from certain designated countries, you may exchange your licence for a British one within five years of becoming a resident. However, if your full EC/EEA licence remains valid, you need not exchange it but may drive until you reach the age at which British renewal becomes necessary.

If you come from a country outside the EC/EEA (or from a non-designated country) you can obtain a full British licence by applying for a British provisional licence and passing a British driving test.

Further information can be found in leaflet D100 (available from main post offices) or factsheet 'Driving in Great Britain as a visitor or new resident' (available from DVLA on **0870 240 0009**) or from **direct.gov.uk/motoringleaflets**

Insurance

You would be very irresponsible to drive without insurance. It's illegal and, should you cause injury to anyone or damage to property, it could be expensive and result in criminal prosecution.

Uninsured drivers can now be detected by the police and roadside Automatic Number Plate Recognition (ANPR) cameras as they are linked to the Motor Insurance Database. The penalties for uninsured drivers include

- a fine of up to £5000
- 6–8 penalty points on your licence
- possible disqualification
- your vehicle can be seized by the police, taken away and crushed.

Before you take a vehicle on public roads, buy insurance cover. You can arrange this with an insurance company, a broker or via a comparison website.

Types of insurance

Third-party cover This is the legal minimum and the cheapest insurance cover. The third party is anyone you might injure or whose property you might damage. You're not covered for damage to your vehicle or injury to yourself.

Third-party, fire and theft This is the same as third-party, except that it also covers you against your vehicle being stolen or damaged by fire.

Comprehensive This is the best type of insurance, but the most expensive. Apart from covering other persons and property for injury and damage, it also covers damage to your vehicle.

The cost of insurance

This varies, depending on

- your age; the younger you are, the more it will cost, especially if you're under 25
- whether you have completed the Pass Plus scheme
- how long you've been driving
- the make and power of your vehicle
- where you live and keep your car overnight
- how you intend to use your vehicle
- any court convictions and fixed penalty offences
- any no-claims discount you have earned.

It can also vary from one insurer to another, so it pays to shop around.

You must answer all questions on the insurance application honestly as, in the event of a claim, your policy could be worthless if the insurance company discovers that you have not told the truth. They then have the right to void the policy which would leave you open to prosecution for being uninsured. For example, a young person is committing fraud if they state that an older, more experienced driver is the main user of their vehicle to reduce the cost of their cover. This is known as 'fronting' and insurance companies look out for it.

What's insured

This also varies from company to company. Read your insurance policy carefully and ask your insurer or broker if you're in any doubt. Otherwise you might have difficulties when you claim.

If you do make a claim, you'll often have to pay around the first £250 of the cost yourself – this is called the 'excess', and can double for young and inexperienced drivers.

Buy the best policy you can afford. It could be the cheapest in the long run.

Remember, when you drive someone else's vehicle, check your insurance cover. You're probably only covered for third party risks. You might not be covered at all!

The certificate of insurance

This short and simple document shows
- who's insured to drive the vehicle
- the vehicle covered
- the period of cover
- what the vehicle can and cannot be used for
- whether there is cover to drive other vehicles.

Sometimes a broker will give you a temporary certificate or 'cover note' while you're waiting for the certificate. A cover note normally lasts for one month.

Showing your certificate Keep the certificate safe and produce it
- if the police ask you to
- when you renew your vehicle excise licence at a post office
- if you're involved in an incident.

The policy document This contains the full details of the contract between you and the insurance company and how to claim. Insurance companies also supply a summary of cover showing the main cover, terms and conditions. If there's anything you don't understand, ask your broker or the insurance company to explain.

New legislation is to be introduced which means that it will be an offence to keep an uninsured vehicle, rather than just to drive when uninsured. Continuous Insurance Enforcement (CIE) will complement and run alongside existing roadside enforcement. Drivers will be notified in writing that their vehicle appears to be uninsured. If they fail to insure the vehicle they will be fined. If the vehicle still remains uninsured, it could be seized and destroyed. Vehicles with a valid Statutory Off-Road Notification (SORN) will not be required to be insured.

Incidents

If you're involved in an incident, you may need to give your insurance details; see page 297.

Vehicle registration certificate (V5C)

A vehicle registration certificate (V5C), also known as a logbook, contains information about the vehicle. It shows

- the name and address of the vehicle's registered keeper
- information about the vehicle, including the make, model and engine size
- the date the vehicle was first registered.

The registered keeper is the person who is responsible for taxing the vehicle, although they may not be the legal owner. If you are the registered keeper of a vehicle, it is your responsibility to keep the details of your V5C up to date. You must tell DVLA when

- you change address
- you change name
- you change any of the details of your vehicle (eg colour)
- you no longer have the vehicle.

You can update your V5C by filling in the relevant section and sending the whole form to DVLA, who will issue a new V5C. Informing DVLA ensures your V11 (tax reminder) is sent to the correct address, enabling you to tax your vehicle.

When a vehicle is sold, both the seller and the buyer must complete and sign the V5C and the seller must send the relevant part of the V5C to DVLA. The seller is still responsible for the vehicle until they have received a disposal acknowledgement letter from DVLA.

You can get more information about the V5C on the form itself, or from **direct.gov.uk/v5c**

If you lose or mislay your V5C, you can request a replacement from DVLA, although a fee may be charged.

Remember:

- the registered keeper is responsible for informing DVLA in the event of any changes to their name, address, or details of the vehicle
- the registered keeper must notify DVLA when they no longer have a vehicle
- the V5C is not proof of ownership.

Vehicle excise duty

This is often called car tax or vehicle licensing. You can buy a tax disc (vehicle licence) for 6 or 12 months. The tax disc must be displayed on the vehicle. Any vehicle exempt from duty must display a 'Nil' tax disc. A tax disc must not be transferred to another vehicle.

The registered keeper of a vehicle (the person named on DVLA's record) remains responsible for taxing a vehicle or making a SORN (until that liability is formally transferred to a new keeper).

The keeper needs to inform DVLA when the vehicle is off the road, or has been sold, transferred, scrapped or exported; otherwise they remain liable for taxing it. Once DVLA has been notified about a sale or transfer or that the vehicle is off-road, it will issue an acknowledgement letter, which should be kept as proof that the vehicle record has been changed.

If you don't relicense your vehicle

Keepers who fail to relicense their vehicle (or declare SORN) will incur an automatic penalty. DVLA will carry out a computer check each month to identify those vehicles without a valid tax disc. Although it is no longer necessary for the vehicle to be seen on a public road before a penalty is issued, on-road enforcement will still continue.

To apply for your tax disc

To ensure your tax disc is up to date

- fill in the relevant section of the renewal reminder form V11, or
- apply for a new tax disc by filling in form V10. You will also need to produce your vehicle registration certificate (or the tear-off slip V5C/2 if within two months of date of purchase).

In both cases, take the completed form to a licence-issuing post office to obtain your tax disc. You will also need to produce

- a valid certificate of insurance
- an MOT certificate if the vehicle is over three years old (some vehicles may be covered by other requirements).

Alternatively, you can apply online at **taxdisc.direct.gov.uk**

Telephone 0300 123 4321
Minicom 0300 790 6201.

Statutory Off-Road Notification

If you don't intend to use or keep the vehicle on a public road, you can declare SORN so that you don't have to pay road tax. Your SORN declaration is valid for 12 months (provided the vehicle is kept off-road). Failure to renew (or relicense) it will incur a penalty.

You can declare SORN by

- filling in the relevant section of your renewal reminder form V11 and taking it to a licence-issuing post office branch
- calling **0300 790 6801**, if you are the registered keeper
- filling in a SORN declaration form V890 and sending it to DVLA. These forms are available from all DVLA local offices, licence-issuing post offices or by downloading from **dvla.gov.uk**
- making a declaration on 'application for refund' forms V14 and V33 if you are also applying for a refund and the vehicle is to remain in your possession.

Alternatively, you can apply online at **taxdisc.direct.gov.uk**

Telephone 0300 123 4321
Minicom 0300 790 6201.

Vehicle test certificate

The MOT test applies to all motor vehicles three years old and over.*

The purpose of the MOT test is to ensure that your vehicle's key safety and environmental systems and components meet the required minimum legal standards.

The test must be carried out every year by a vehicle testing station appointed by the Vehicle Operator Services Agency (VOSA), an executive agency of the Department for Transport.

For details of VOSA's MOT text reminder service, see **direct.gov.uk/MOT**

Vehicles which must be tested

If your vehicle is more than three years old* you must have a current MOT test certificate. You won't be able to renew your vehicle excise licence without it.

*Note

Certain vehicles, including the following, must be tested one year after registration and annually thereafter

- large goods vehicles (LGVs) over 3.5 tonnes gross weight
- passenger-carrying vehicles (PCVs) with more than eight seats
- ambulances
- taxis.

Remember, you can have your vehicle tested as much as one month before the current certificate runs out. The expiry date of the new certificate will be one year after the expiry date of the old one.

Failure

If your vehicle fails its MOT and you want to continue to use it, you must make arrangements to have the necessary repairs carried out without delay. The vehicle must pass a retest before it's used on the road, except when

- driving it away from the testing station after failing the test
- driving to have the repairs carried out
- driving to an MOT test appointment booked in advance.

Even in these circumstances you can still be prosecuted if your car is not roadworthy under the various regulations governing its construction and use. In addition, check that your insurance cover remains valid.

You can go online at **direct.gov.uk/MOT** to check your vehicle's MOT status and history.

Appeals

If you consider the vehicle has been incorrectly failed, you have the right to appeal. Information on how to appeal may be obtained at vehicle testing stations.

Your certificate

An MOT test certificate is not a guarantee that the vehicle will remain roadworthy and comply with the minimum standards of the certificate. Neither does it imply that the engine and transmission systems are in good condition – these items are not critical to safety and are not covered by the MOT test.

Fees

Ask any vehicle testing station about the current test and retest fees.

Exhaust emission limits

Remember, the test includes a strict exhaust emission test. This means your engine must be correctly tuned and adjusted.

There are prescribed emission limits for vehicles with petrol engines registered after 1975 and the MOT test will check that these limits are not exceeded.

Roadworthiness

You must ensure that the vehicle you intend to drive

- is legally roadworthy
- has a current vehicle test certificate (MOT) if over the prescribed age
- is properly licensed and has the correct tax disc displayed.

The braking system Your brakes must be in good and efficient working order and correctly adjusted, including the parking brake (also known as the handbrake).

Tyres All tyres on the vehicle **MUST** meet current requirements (see pages 279 and 314).

Lights/indicators All lights, including lenses and reflectors, must be in working order, even during daylight hours.

Exhaust A silencer must be fitted which reduces noise to an acceptable level.

For cars and light goods vehicles, exhaust emissions must not exceed the prescribed limits. Any MOT testing station will be able to tell you the limits for your vehicle.

For best fuel economy, have the engine tuned according to the manufacturer's recommendations.

Instruments and equipment Appropriate mirrors must be fitted.

All instruments and equipment must be in good working order, including

- speedometer
- horn
- windscreen wipers and washers.

Vehicle modifications

Some vehicle modifications, such as heavily tinted windows, may restrict vision. Others may potentially endanger pedestrians, as in the case of bull bars.

Disability modifications If your vehicle has been adapted for your disability, make sure that the modifications don't affect the safe control of the vehicle.

The Highway Code

The Highway Code contains essential advice for all road users.

A set of rules

Its purpose is to prevent road traffic incidents by ensuring that we all adopt the same rules when we use the road.

Road traffic law has developed over the years into a comprehensive set of rules, many with underpinning legislation. Use of **MUST** or **MUST NOT** in red within a rule indicates that direct legislation applies, and a reference to that legislation also appears beneath the rule.

If you disobey these rules you are committing a criminal offence. The Highway Code explains these rules as simply as possible and helps to make sure they are fully understood.

Road traffic law changes from time to time, and so do the penalties for breaking it. Make sure you keep up to date. The Highway Code is updated fairly frequently, and you should study and apply the contents of the current edition.

Road signs and signals

You **MUST** know and comply with

- all traffic signs and road markings
- signals given by police officers, traffic wardens, school crossing wardens, Highways Agency traffic officers, Vehicle and Operator Services Agency officials and any other authorised person (eg road workers operating 'stop/go' boards)
- traffic signals at
  - junctions and crossroads
  - roadworks
  - narrow bridges
  - pedestrian crossings
  - fire and ambulance stations*
  - level crossings*
  - tramway (light rail transit) crossings.

*usually red flashing lights

Road safety

In everyday driving, you need to follow the rules set down in The Highway Code for your own safety and that of all road users.

Even if you're an experienced driver, you need to know The Highway Code thoroughly and apply it in your everyday driving.

You **MUST NOT** drive

- dangerously
- without due care and attention
- without reasonable consideration for other road users.

Although not all the rules in The Highway Code are legal requirements, they can be used in court proceedings to establish liability and support prosecutions under the Traffic Acts.

Look on The Highway Code as an aid to safe driving. **Don't** look on it as a restriction.

The Highway Code is available as a book or an interactive CD-ROM as well as in British Sign Language.

Seat belts

Seat belts save lives and reduce the risk of injury. Unless you're exempt, you must wear a seat belt if one is available.

The following table summarises the legal requirements for the wearing of seat belts. It is important that seat belts are always correctly adjusted and are comfortable, with both the lap belt, and the diagonal belt where available, protecting the body.

The driver is responsible for ensuring that all children under 14 years of age wear seat belts or use an approved child restraint.

	Front seat all vehicles	Rear seat cars and small minibuses*
Driver	Seat belt **MUST** be worn if fitted	–
Child under 3 years old	Correct child restraint **MUST** be used	Correct child restraint **MUST** be used*
Child from 3rd birthday up to 1.35m in height (or 12th birthday, whichever they reach first)	Correct child restraint **MUST** be used	Correct child restraint **MUST** be used where seat belts fitted**
Child over 1.35m (approx 4ft 5ins) **in height, or 12 or 13 years**	Adult seat belt **MUST** be worn if available	Adult seat belt **MUST** be worn if available
Adult passengers aged 14 years and over	Seat belt **MUST** be worn if available	Seat belt **MUST** be worn if available

* If the correct child restraint is not available in a taxi, the child may travel unrestrained.

** If the correct child restraint is not available in a licensed taxi or private hire vehicle, or for reasons of unexpected necessity over a short distance, or where two occupied child restraints prevent fitment of a third, then an adult seat belt **MUST** be worn.

Carrying children

A child restraint appropriate to the child's weight and size **MUST** be used when carrying children under 1.35 metres tall. Types of restraint include

- baby seat
- child seat
- booster seat
- booster cushion.

Child seat restraints **MUST** be correctly fitted in accordance with the manufacturer's instructions. If in doubt, seek specialist advice.

Adults **MUST NOT** put one seat belt around both themselves and an infant on their lap. This does not comply with the law and could result in severe internal, and/or fatal, crush injuries to the child in the event of a crash.

When carrying children you should also ensure that

- they are kept under control
- child safety door locks are used, where fitted
- they do not sit behind the rear seats in an estate car or hatchback, unless a special child seat has been fitted.

Airbags

Rear-facing child seats **MUST NOT** be used in a seat protected by an airbag. In a collision, the airbag would hit the child seat with such a force that the child would almost certainly receive serious or fatal injuries.

Loading your vehicle

It is your responsibility as a driver to ensure that your vehicle is not overloaded.

Never exceed the weight limits for your vehicle as this can be dangerous. It will also mean that your vehicle uses more fuel as the engine has to work harder.

You **MUST** also ensure that any load

- is fastened securely
- does not obscure your view
- does not stick out dangerously.

Make sure that any objects or animals you carry are secured safely.

- Dogs should be strapped in with a special car harness or travel behind a grille. Other animals should be carried in cages or special carry-boxes which should be secured with the seat belt.
- Make sure packages are securely stored, preferably in the boot of the vehicle where they should be strapped down or wedged in to stop them moving around.

If you do need to carry packages inside the car make sure that they will not move if you have to brake or turn suddenly. In particular

- strap down any large or heavy object with the seat belt
- don't put anything on the parcel shelf or anywhere that it would obstruct your vision
- it is probably safest to carry small items on the floor, but make sure they don't get into the footwell and impede your use of the pedals.

Any load will have an effect on the handling of your car, so

- you need to allow a greater stopping distance when carrying a heavy load
- you may need to adjust your headlights and inflate your tyres more to take account of the load
- you should ensure that you distribute the weight evenly as any change to the centre of gravity will affect the braking and steering.

Consider fitting

- a specially designed roof box to carry bulky items. This is streamlined to save fuel as well as securing the load more safely
- special cycle racks on top of or behind the car to carry cycles more securely (if they are fitted behind the car make sure that the number plates and lights are not obscured).

THE CONTROLS

This section covers

- Driving position
- The hand controls
- The foot controls
- Switches
- Other controls

Driving position

You must adopt a suitable driving position before you can use the controls on the car safely.

You must be able to

- reach and use each control easily and comfortably; for example, you should be able to operate the clutch pedal without stretching your left leg

- control the vehicle by keeping a suitable grip on the steering wheel; your arms should be relaxed and not restricted at the elbows

- see the road ahead clearly.

Driving seat adjustment

You must make sure that the seat is adjusted to suit you. Most driving seats can be adjusted for

- 'rake' – the angle of the seat back

- position – the seat will move forwards or backwards.

Sometimes, especially on larger vehicles, the driving seat will also adjust for height.

Driver and front passengers should avoid sitting too close to the steering wheel or dashboard.

If someone else has been driving the vehicle, make sure you make any adjustments before you start to drive.

Never adjust your seat while the vehicle is moving.

Remember, after adjusting your seat, make sure it's firmly locked in position. Listen for, or feel for, the locking mechanism engaging. An insecure driving seat is dangerous.

As soon as you're seated, check that the vehicle is secure by ensuring the parking brake is applied.

Steering column adjustment

On some vehicles, you can adjust the angle of tilt of the steering column to suit you.

When making this adjustment, take care not to allow the steering wheel to interfere with your view of the instrument panel. Also, make sure you secure the locking mechanism after any adjustment.

Never attempt to adjust your steering column angle while the vehicle is moving.

Head restraint adjustment

Head restraints are provided to protect against neck and spine injuries, commonly referred to as whiplash.

For maximum protection, correct head restraint adjustment is vital – but all too easy to overlook.

The head restraints should be adjusted so that the rigid part of the head restraint is

- at least as high as the eyes or top of the ears
- as close to the back of the head as is comfortable.

An incorrectly adjusted head restraint offers little or no protection against whiplash injuries.

Don't remove the head restraints; they are fitted for your safety and can save you from more serious injuries in the event of an incident.

Remember, it's a head restraint not a head rest.

Seat belt adjustment

Adjust the seat belt properly. Place the lap belt as low as possible over the hips. Ensure the shoulder belt lies on the chest and over the shoulder.

Many cars are now fitted with height adjusters for the diagonal strap. The diagonal strap should be adjusted to lie centrally over the shoulder and away from the neck. Adjust the strap so that it lies in contact with your shoulder and slopes up and back to the anchorage point.

The hand controls

The positions of some of the controls, such as indicators, light switches and windscreen wipers, vary from model to model.

Before you drive an unfamiliar vehicle, you should get to know the positions of all the controls. You should never have to fumble or look down for them when you're driving.

Keep your eyes on the road.

The steering wheel

The steering wheel should normally be controlled with both hands.

Function The steering wheel controls the direction in which you want the vehicle to travel.

It controls the steering mechanism, which turns

- the front wheels in most vehicles
- all four wheels in vehicles with four-wheel steering – limited to a small number of models.

How to use the steering wheel For best control

- keep both hands on the wheel, unless you're changing gear or working another control with one hand. Return that hand to the wheel immediately you have finished the task
- avoid resting your arm on the door, which can restrict your movement
- grip the wheel firmly, but not too tightly; when the vehicle is moving you need very little effort to turn the wheel.

Remember, never take both hands off the wheel when the vehicle is moving.

Steering lock* This is the angle through which the front wheels turn when you turn the steering wheel: this can be either 'right lock' or 'left lock'.

Turning the steering wheel as far as it will go is called 'full lock'. The amount of lock varies from vehicle to vehicle.

Small cars will generally turn in a smaller circle than larger vehicles. Taxi cabs are an obvious exception as they have a very small turning circle.

* Not to be confused with the steering column locking mechanism which engages when the ignition key is removed on most modern vehicles as an anti-theft device.

Steering

You should

- place your hands on the steering wheel in a position that's comfortable and which gives you full control
- keep your movements steady and smooth
- turn the steering wheel to turn a corner at the correct time.

Oversteer and understeer Vehicles vary in how they behave when turning at various road speeds.

Some respond more than you would expect in relation to the amount of turn you give the wheel (oversteer). Some respond less (understeer).

You must get to know the characteristics of your vehicle before you drive in traffic, and drive extra carefully until you're familiar with its behaviour.

Power-assisted steering Most vehicles now have power-assisted steering (PAS). This makes steering easier – particularly for drivers with weakness in their limbs.

PAS reduces driver steering effort and gives a lighter feel to the steering.

On some vehicles the amount of power assistance reduces with increased speed.

PAS is most useful at low speeds, such as manoeuvring in a tight corner or parking.

With PAS the steering feels light and you can easily turn the wheel too much, especially if you're used to driving a vehicle not fitted with it.

'Dry' steering When you are manoeuvring, try to avoid turning the steering wheel when the vehicle is stationary. This is known as 'dry' steering and may cause

- damage to the tyres
- excess wear in the steering mechanism.

This applies whether you have PAS or not.

Power-assisted steering helps to manoeuvre the car more easily, especially when turning a tight corner or parking.

The gear lever

The gear lever is normally to the left of the driving seat, either on the floor or on a raised console.

A few cars have the gear lever protruding from the instrument panel, and a few have a gear lever on the steering column.

Function The gear lever enables you to change from one gear to another.

The gearbox

The gearbox contains the gears, which control the relationship between engine speed and road speed.

First gear provides the greatest force at the driving wheels and is normally the one you use to get the vehicle moving.

As you speed up, you change up to the higher gears, each one giving you less gear force but more road speed. Top gear provides the least force, but usually has the widest range of speeds. Using as high a gear as possible for speed and road traffic conditions saves fuel.

Most modern cars have five or six forward gears, while heavier vehicles often have many more.

As well as the five or six forward gears, there is also a reverse gear.

In neutral, no gear is engaged.

The clutch links the engine to the road wheels through the gearbox and allows the gradual connection of the engine to the wheels.

Four-wheel drive vehicles may have a double gearbox with high- and low-ratio ranges, which effectively double the number of available gears to eight or ten. The lower range is normally used off-road.

Gear positions

Most cars have five-speed or six-speed gearboxes. The first four gears normally form an 'H', while reverse and fifth form an additional 'I'. Many cars are designed so that you cannot move straight from fifth to reverse gear, and the gear lever automatically springs back into neutral when no gear is engaged. This tendency of the gear stick to line up with particular gears is known as bias. Third and fourth gears are often lined up.

Some older cars have four-speed gearboxes. These have the gears in an 'H', with reverse extended on the left or right.

Avoid looking down at the gear lever

You should have a mental picture of the gear layout. This will enable you to change gear without looking at the diagram on top of the gear lever. Your eyes should be on the road.

With practice, changing gear becomes second-nature.

For automatic transmission systems, see section 22.

The parking brake

Sometimes the parking brake is referred to as the handbrake.

Position The parking brake lever is normally floor-mounted just behind the gear lever. In some vehicles, it is just under the instrument panel, while on some other models the parking brake is applied by operating an additional pedal.

Function The parking brake holds the vehicle still when it has stopped.

In most cars the parking brake operates on the rear wheels only. If it's applied while the vehicle is moving, there's a real danger of locking the braked wheels and skidding.

The parking brake shouldn't be used to stop a moving vehicle, except in an emergency such as footbrake failure – very unlikely with dual-circuit braking systems.

> **Remember,** when you leave your vehicle parked on a gradient, even in your own drive, always make sure that the parking brake is fully on. Many serious incidents have been caused by failure to do this.

Applying Generally, you should press the button on top of the parking brake lever and pull the lever fully upwards. Then release the button. The parking brake will engage in the 'on' position.

However some manufacturers recommend that you don't press the button in while pulling the lever up. Refer to your vehicle handbook to check the correct procedure for your vehicle.

Releasing Pull the lever up slightly and press the button in to release the ratchet. Then, keeping the button in, move the lever to the 'off' position.

On some vehicles, instead of pressing a button, the parking brake is released by twisting the hand grip.

Electronic parking brake Some modern vehicles are fitted with an electronic parking brake which is operated with a switch or button and releases automatically when you drive off.

The foot controls

The accelerator/gas pedal

This is operated by the right foot and is positioned on the extreme right of the group of three pedals.

Function The accelerator controls the rate at which the mixture of fuel and air is supplied to the engine. The name 'gas pedal' is derived from 'gasoline', the American word for petrol.

Petrol engines A carburettor mixes the fuel with air which is then drawn into the engine.

Many modern cars have an electronic fuel injection system instead of a carburettor.

Diesel engines A high-pressure fuel injector delivers the fuel into the cylinders. This is known as a compression-ignition engine.

In both engine types The more you press the accelerator, the more fuel goes to the engine, the more power is generated and the higher the engine speed.

Getting to know the right amount of pressure to put on the accelerator takes practice. Accelerating fiercely also wastes fuel and creates noise.

When moving off, you need just the right amount. Too little, and the engine stalls. Too much, and the vehicle can surge forward.

The footbrake

The right foot operates the footbrake as well as the accelerator. You shouldn't need to use both controls at the same time.

The footbrake is the middle of the group of three pedals, so the right foot can travel smoothly and quickly from one to the other.

Function The footbrake is to slow down or stop the vehicle.

Using the footbrake The more pressure you put on the footbrake, the more the vehicle will slow down.

Slowing down under control isn't just a matter of slamming the footbrake on as hard as you can. As with the other foot controls, using the footbrake needs practice.

Press the footbrake with the ball of your foot. Use enough pressure to slow the wheels without allowing them to lock.

Progressive braking In normal circumstances, always press lightly on the brake pedal to begin with and gradually press harder as the brakes begin to act. This is known as progressive braking, and will give maximum control as well as smoother stopping.

Dual-circuit braking Modern cars are equipped with dual-circuit braking systems. These systems ensure that, in the rare event of a braking system failure, there remains some braking available when the brake pedal is pressed. Under these conditions it may be necessary to push the brake pedal harder than normal.

Anti-lock braking system Many cars either have an anti-lock braking system (ABS) fitted or have it available as an option.

If ABS is fitted it activates automatically. It prevents the wheels from locking so that you can continue to steer the vehicle while braking. You should refer to the vehicle handbook for details of the manufacturer's recommended method of use.

ABS is only a driver aid; it doesn't help the vehicle to stop more quickly. Nor does it remove the need for good driving practices such as anticipating events and assessing road conditions. You still need to plan well ahead and brake smoothly and progressively.

The clutch

The clutch pedal is operated by the left foot and is on the left of the group of three pedals.

Function The clutch is the connection between the engine and the gearbox. It's a connection over which the driver has control, but which requires practice in its use.

How it works In its simplest form, the clutch is made up of two plates. One is connected to the engine and rotates all the time the engine is running. The other is linked to the gearbox and rotates only when it's held against the first plate by springs.

When you press the clutch pedal, you force the plates apart, breaking the drive connection.

In neutral, even though both plates are touching, the wheels do not turn because no gear is engaged.

The 'biting point' The point of engagement, when the two plates begin to make contact and the load on the engine increases, is known as the 'biting point'.

You'll learn with practice to judge the biting point exactly. You'll feel it, and hear it because the engine speed will drop slightly.

The feel of the clutch will vary with different vehicles. Also, as the clutch plates begin to wear, the biting point may change.

Clutch control Being able to sense the biting point is a crucial part of clutch control.

The other important part is allowing the clutch plates to engage fully and smoothly. If the plates come together too suddenly, the engine can stall or the vehicle may jerk out of control.

Good clutch control only comes with practice, and is essential when moving off or changing gear.

Switches

Sidelights and headlights

Position On many vehicles, the lighting controls are on a stalk at the side of the steering column.

This stalk normally has three positions

1 off

2 sidelights (or dim–dip), rear and number plate lights

3 headlights (main or dipped beam) and the dip control. On some vehicles the dip control is a separate switch.

Some vehicles have 'dim–dip' headlights, which come on as the sidelights are switched on. It's impossible to drive these vehicles with only the sidelights switched on. The sidelights normally work without the ignition being switched on.

Use This is covered in section 13.

Fog lights

Fog lights should work only when the sidelights or headlights are on. Modern vehicles must be fitted with at least one rear fog light. Front fog lights are often fitted as an option.

Position Since they're only used in bad weather, the fog light switches are usually on the instrument panel rather than on the steering column.

Use You must only use fog lights when visibility is seriously reduced, ie 100 metres (328 feet) or less. You must not use fog lights in any other circumstances, because they can dazzle and distract other drivers.

Normally a warning light (usually blue) shows when the headlights are on main beam.

A warning light will show when the rear fog lights are on.

Direction indicator

Position The direction indicator switch is usually on a stalk which may be on either side of the steering column.

Function The direction indicators enable you to show other road users which direction you intend to take. Correct use of the direction indicators is vital to safe driving.

Self-cancelling indicator switches might not cancel after a slight change of direction.

Always check that the signal has been cancelled. You can do this by checking the

* repeater warning light
* audible warning, usually a ticking noise when the indicators are flashing.

Use You should be able to operate the direction indicators without taking your hand off the steering wheel.

Hazard warning lights

Position The position of this switch varies. Some vehicles have it on the steering column, others on the instrument panel. It's usually

- within easy reach of the driver's hands
- clearly marked to prevent accidental use.

Use Hazard warning lights should be used to warn other road users when you're temporarily obstructing traffic; for example, when

- you have broken down
- you have to slow down quickly on a motorway or unrestricted dual carriageway, because of a hazard ahead. Only use them long enough to ensure that your warning has been seen.

Don't use them to excuse stopping in a restricted area, such as on double yellow lines, regardless of how brief your stop.

A warning light will flash when the hazard warning lights are in use. Don't forget to switch them off before moving away!

Because the lights flash at the same rate as normal indicators, if another driver is unable to see both sides of your vehicle, the hazard warning lights could be mistaken for a turning or moving out signal.

Windscreen washers and wipers

Position The windscreen washer and wiper controls are usually on stalks mounted on the steering column. You should be able to find the controls without taking your eyes off the road.

On most vehicles, the same stalk controls both the washers and wipers. Both are essential in bad weather.

Where they are provided, rear washers and wipers have separate controls. Some vehicles may be fitted with miniature washers and wipers to keep the headlights clear.

Function The windscreen washers and wipers are to keep the windscreen clear of rain, spray, snow or fog.

Use washers before wipers Use your washers first to wet the surface before you switch on your windscreen wipers. Wiping a dry windscreen can cause scratches to the screen as well as shortening the life of the wiper blades.

Avoiding excessive dirt build-up can also help to stop scratches on your windscreen. Tiny bits of grit can scratch the surface and make driving at night very difficult.

Wash your windscreen regularly with a sponge and plenty of water. Wash the wiper blades as well.

Regular checks Check the fluid containers regularly, and keep them topped up.

You can use additives to prevent smearing, assist cleaning and, especially in the winter, to prevent icing up.

Wiper blades Wiper blades are vital to your safety. Replace them when they become worn or ineffective.

Horn

Position On most vehicles, the horn switch is either

- on the steering wheel
- on the outer end of the stalk which controls the direction indicators.

Function The horn is to warn other road users of your presence.

Use Use it to tell other road users you're there, if this is necessary.

Aggressive sounding of the horn is dangerous. It can distract and alarm other road users.

You must not sound your horn (unless there's a danger from another vehicle), when your vehicle is stationary or when driving in a built-up area between 11.30 pm and 7.00 am.

Heated windscreen and rear window

Most cars have heated rear windows, and some have heated front windscreens as well.

Function The front and rear windscreen heaters are to keep the windscreen and rear window clear of

- internal condensation
- frost and ice on the outside.

Use They should be used as necessary to keep your windscreen and rear window clear, especially in wet and cold conditions.

Demister Once the engine has warmed up, you can set the controls to direct warm air to the windscreen and, on some vehicles, the front side windows.

The fan control can be set to boost the warm air flow.

Ignition switch and starter

Position Usually positioned on the steering column.

Before operating the starter Make sure that

- the parking brake is on
- the gear lever is in neutral.

On most vehicles, the ignition and starter are incorporated in the same switch and operated by the ignition key. Some vehicles have a separate starter button.

On most vehicles, an anti-theft device is incorporated into the ignition switch and operated by the ignition key. The mechanism locks the steering column, so slight movement may need to be applied to the steering wheel while turning the ignition key to release it.

The first position This operates some of the electrical equipment, such as the radio.

The second position This switches on the ignition, instrument panel and gauges. A red ignition warning light will usually show when the key reaches this position.

The third position This operates the starter.

The direction indicators, and on some vehicles the headlights, will only operate when the ignition is switched on.

Use The starter is usually operated by turning the ignition key to its maximum. As soon as the engine starts, release the key. Don't operate the starter when the engine is running. This can damage the starter motor and the engagement mechanism.

Being towed When the vehicle is being towed, the anti-theft device locking the steering column must be released by inserting the ignition key and ensuring that the steering wheel is free to move (unless a suspended tow is being used).

Remember, without the ignition being switched on, the steering will be heavy and the brakes will not work as well as normal.

Other controls

Instrument panel

For detailed information and guidance on this, see your vehicle handbook.

The main visual aids on the instrument panel are

- speedometer: to tell you how quickly the vehicle is travelling in miles and kilometres per hour. It's usually a dial, with a needle showing the speed, but it may be a digital display
- direction indicator repeater light(s)
- fuel gauge
- high-beam indicator light (usually blue)
- rev counter (on some vehicles), to tell you the engine speed in revolutions per minute (rpm)
- warming-up coil indicator lamp (on diesel engines)
- temperature gauge (may be a warning light).

Cruise control

This is a device, usually electronic, which enables the driver to select and maintain a safe speed on the open road.

Use cruise control on your vehicle if it is fitted. The sophisticated electronics in the engine management system precisely measure the amount of fuel the engine needs to work most efficiently for a given speed. If you use this where you can it may cut down on your fuel consumption.

It relieves the driver of the physical effort involved in keeping an even pressure on the accelerator pedal for long periods. It's only suitable where continual changes of speed are unlikely to be required.

Normal control can be resumed immediately should the need arise. In most cases this happens as soon as the driver uses the accelerator, clutch or the footbrake.

The visual aids are grouped on the instrument panel directly in front of the driving seat.

Warning lights

Function These lights help you to

- drive safely
- monitor the performance of the engine
- protect your engine and other equipment against damage
- see the functions selected.

Types of light There are many different types of light that may be fitted, including

- oil pressure (often amber). This shows if the oil is dangerously low or isn't circulating as it should be. This should light up as you turn the ignition on, but go out as the engine starts
- ignition warning light (usually red). If this comes on when the engine is running, it shows you have a problem with the electrical charging system
- ABS. This should light up as you turn the ignition on and may not go out until the car is travelling at 5–10 mph
- brake condition warning light

- water temperature, if the engine is overheating (it can be a gauge)
- doors open or boot lid unlocked
- 'Parking brake applied' light
- four-way hazard flashers
- rear fog light warning light
- rear window heater indicator light
- seat belt warning lights
- fog/head/side lights indicator light.

Choke

All vehicles with petrol engines have some form of choke. This reduces the amount of air in the air/fuel mixture, and helps to start the engine from cold. Most cars have an automatic choke but some older cars may have a manual choke. The further you pull the control out, the richer the mixture. You must push in the control as soon as the engine warms up.

A pre-heating device is incorporated in some vehicles with diesel engines. The starter should only be operated when the indicator light goes out (where fitted).

Oil pressure

Brake condition

Doors open

Seat belt

section **four**

MIRRORS

This section covers

- Mirrors
- Adjusting mirrors
- Using mirrors
- Blind spots
- The mirrors and hazards
- MSM routine

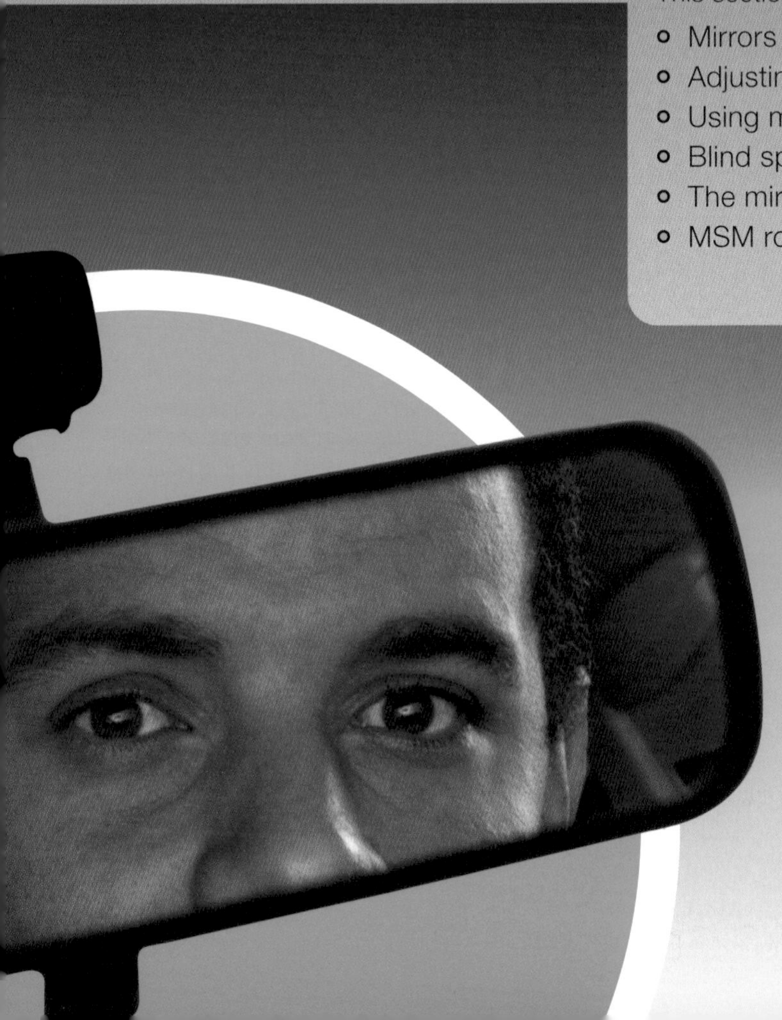

Mirrors

Using the mirrors has to be part of a basic Mirrors – Signal – Manoeuvre (MSM) routine. You must always know how your driving is likely to affect traffic behind you.

The MSM routine includes interpreting what you see in the mirrors and acting appropriately. Regular and sensible use of the mirrors is an essential element of safe driving.

You should make the MSM routine an integral part of your driving.

Modern cars are required to have an offside (driver's side) mirror fitted, as well as an interior mirror. However, most vehicles have three driving mirrors

- an interior mirror
- two exterior mirrors; one on the nearside (left-hand) door and one on the offside (right-hand) door.

Vans and other vehicles with a restricted view to the rear must have an exterior mirror on each side.

Function

Your mirrors

- give you a view of the road behind and to the sides
- enable you to keep up to date with what's happening behind and to the sides of your vehicle
- help you to make safe and sensible decisions, based on the position and speed of other traffic.

Defensive driving

A driving mirror is often referred to as the driver's third eye.

Mirrors are one of the keys to defensive driving. Always use them to keep up to date with what's behind and to the sides of your vehicle.

Remember, don't just look into your mirrors; act safely and sensibly on what you see.

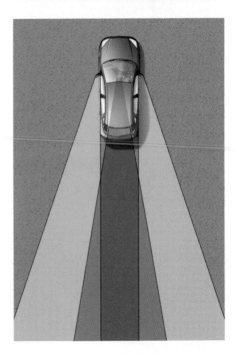

The view covered by your interior and exterior mirrors.

Flat mirrors

Most interior and some exterior door mirrors have flat glass.

Flat mirrors don't distort the picture of the road behind. This makes it easier to judge the speed and distance of traffic behind you.

Convex mirrors

Many exterior mirrors have convex glass, which

- is slightly curved
- gives a wider field of vision.

This makes accurate judgement of speed and position of vehicles behind you more difficult.

A vehicle behind seems smaller in a convex mirror, so it could be closer than you think.

Some cars may have 'split' mirrors which give wider vision.

Extended arm mirrors

If you're towing a caravan or a wide trailer, fit side mirrors with extended arms to enable you to see past the caravan or trailer.

Your interior mirror cannot be used when you're towing a caravan, because your view of the road behind is usually blocked.

Adjusting mirrors

Before moving off, make sure all mirrors are clean and adjusted to give you the best possible view of the road behind.

While in your normal driving position, adjust your mirrors so that you require the minimum of head movement to get a good view of traffic behind.

Always check your view as part of your 'cockpit drill' (see page 75).

When adjusting mirrors, grip them at the edge to avoid getting fingermarks on the surface. Fingermarks can distort and blur the view in the mirror.

Interior mirror

Adjust your interior mirror so that you get the best possible view through the rear window, especially to the offside, without moving your head.

Exterior mirrors

Adjust your exterior mirrors

- to give the best view behind
- so that the side of the vehicle is only just visible.

Don't adjust the mirrors while you're driving. Do it before you move off, or at any time your vehicle is stationary.

Check when you get into your vehicle that they've not been knocked out of position.

Remember to check that your exterior mirrors are still positioned correctly after you have been through a car wash.

Keep your exterior mirrors clean, and before you move off, ensure they are clear of frost and condensation.

Electric mirrors

Many vehicles have door mirrors which can be adjusted electrically using switches inside the vehicle.

Some of them have a heating element to keep them clear of frost and condensation.

Anti-dazzle mirrors

The interior mirror usually has an anti-dazzle position. When driving at night, you can use this to prevent dazzle or distraction by the lights of traffic behind you. You'll still be able to see the lights, but the dazzle will be greatly reduced.

Remember to reset the mirror for normal use.

Using mirrors

Using your driving mirrors regularly and sensibly is vital to good driving.

Learning to judge the speed and distance of vehicles behind you takes time.

Try the following exercise when your vehicle is stationary.

- Compare the different impressions you get when you view vehicles through the interior mirror and the exterior mirror. The vehicles may seem smaller in the exterior mirror. Then look over your shoulder to get the real view.

- Also while you're stationary, look for blind spots. These are the areas that your mirrors don't always show you, which are explained on page 67.

Which mirror to use

Your use of the mirrors should be linked to the manoeuvre you intend to make and the type of vehicle you're driving.

Normally you should always use the interior mirror first, followed by the exterior ones.

Your use of the exterior mirrors will depend on the manoeuvre and the situation. For example, before turning left in slow-moving traffic, your nearside exterior mirror will help you to look for cyclists filtering on your left.

When to use your mirrors

You should always

- use your mirrors in good time, that is, well before you
  - approach a hazard
  - slow down, change lane or begin any manoeuvre
- act sensibly on what you see
- begin the MSM routine early (see page 70).

Always use your mirrors before

- moving off
- signalling
- changing direction or lane, turning left, right or overtaking
- slowing down or stopping
- opening your car door.

This is one of the few driving rules that is not subject to any exception or qualification, other than in an emergency.

What's behind you? Ask yourself

- how close is traffic behind you?
- how fast is it moving?
- what is it doing?
- is the manoeuvre safe?

It's also important to use the mirrors early enough to allow other road users time to react to any signal you need to give. Use your mirrors to check their reaction.

Blind spots

A blind spot is the area that cannot be seen either when using normal forward vision or when using the mirrors. The main blind spots are

- the area between what you see as you look forward and what you see in your exterior mirror
- the area obscured by the bodywork of the vehicle when you look in your mirrors. Vehicles of different shapes have different blind spots.

You should be aware that some 4x4s have very large blind spots – they can obscure a group of pedestrians, a motorcyclist or a small car.

Exterior mirrors help reduce blind spots, but remember that mirrors will not show you everything behind you. You can buy auxiliary mirrors to mount on the surface of your exterior mirrors. These give an even wider angle of vision and go some way to reducing blind spots, but won't entirely eliminate them.

Even though you have used your mirrors, always look round over your right shoulder to check the blind spot before you move off.

Check your mirrors.

Check your blind spot.

Checking blind spots on the move

On occasions it will be necessary to check blind spots while you are on the move. These blind spots will be to either side and should not require you to look round, but rather to give a quick sideways glance.

Looking right round to check blind spots on the move is unnecessary and dangerous, especially when driving at high speeds; in the time it takes you'll lose touch with what's happening in front.

Regular and sensible use of the mirrors will keep you up to date with what's happening behind. You will, however, still need to know when a glance into the blind spots is needed.

Take a quick sideways glance

- before changing lanes
- before joining a motorway or dual carriageway from a slip road
- before manoeuvring in situations where traffic is merging from the left or right.

Defensive driving

Recognise where other drivers' blind areas will be and avoid remaining in them longer than necessary. This is particularly important when overtaking large vehicles.

The mirrors and hazards

A hazard is any situation which involves you in some risk or danger. Hazards may cause you to slow down or change course.

When approaching a hazard, you should use your mirrors and be prepared to change speed and/or direction.

Hazards include

- bends in the road
- junctions
- pedestrian crossings
- roadworks
- livestock on the road.

Always check your mirrors in good time, and before you change direction, to decide

- whether a signal is necessary
- whether it's safe to change speed or direction.

Keeping up to date

Keep up to date with the position and speed of traffic behind you.

Good drivers should always know as much about the conditions behind as they know about the situation ahead.

Traffic positions change rapidly on some roads. Frequent glances in mirrors keep you up to date with what's behind. How frequently you do this depends on road and traffic conditions.

Driving on high-speed roads

When driving on motorways or dual carriageways, check your mirrors earlier than you would on ordinary roads.

The higher speeds are more difficult to judge and situations develop more quickly.

MSM routine

Regardless of your driving experience, you **must** make the Mirrors – Signal – Manoeuvre (MSM) routine an integral part of your driving.

Remember this routine

- **MIRRORS** – check the speed and position of traffic behind you
- **SIGNAL** – consider whether a signal is necessary. If it is, signal your intention to change course or slow down clearly and in good time
- **MANOEUVRE** – a manoeuvre is any change of speed or position.

Manoeuvre

This is broken down into

P – Position

S – Speed

L – Look

Position Your vehicle must always be in the correct position for the manoeuvre. When a change of direction is required, move into position in good time.

Speed Ensure that the vehicle is travelling at the appropriate speed and in a suitable gear to complete the manoeuvre safely.

Look The 'look' phase consists of four elements (**LADA**).

- **L**ooking – What can you see?
- **A**ssessing – What are your options?
- **D**eciding – Depending on what you see.
- **A**cting – Either continue or wait.

Using MSM

Always use the MSM routine before

- moving off
- signalling
- changing direction
    - turning left or right
    - overtaking or changing lanes
- slowing down or stopping.

Never

- signal without checking mirrors first
- rely solely on mirrors when you're reversing. Keep looking around to watch for other road users
- assume that, because you have signalled, you can carry out the intended manoeuvre safely. Check to be sure, because other road users might not
    - have seen your signal
    - understand your intention.

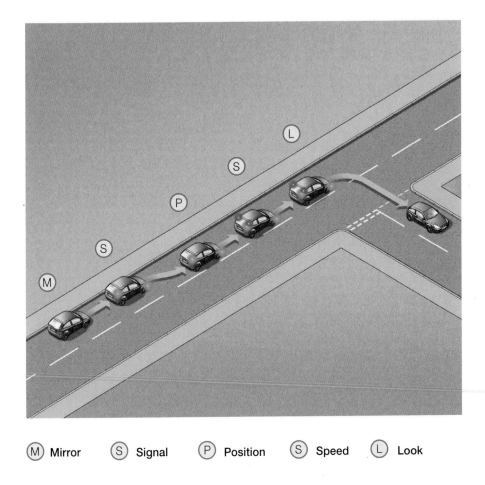

(M) Mirror   (S) Signal   (P) Position   (S) Speed   (L) Look

section **five**

STARTING TO DRIVE

This section covers

- Getting started
- Vehicle checks
- Starting the engine
- Moving off
- Braking
- Stopping in an emergency
- Skidding
- The parking brake
- Steering
- Changing gear
- Signalling
- Moving off at an angle
- Moving off on hills

Getting started

Before you drive on busy roads and in traffic, you should master the basic techniques of starting, moving off and stopping. You must have full control of your vehicle at all times. This involves

- a good working knowledge of the various controls
- being able to coordinate hand and foot controls together.

In addition you need to have

- an understanding of the rules of the road
- respect for the needs of other road users
- a basic knowledge of your vehicle, to enable you to check it to make sure that everything is working correctly and that it is safe before setting out.

Driving isn't just a matter of starting the engine and moving off.

Vehicle checks

You should first of all check your vehicle to make sure it's safe and ready for the road.

Everyday checks

Make a habit of checking daily that

- the windscreen, windows and mirrors are clean
- all lights (including brake lights and indicators) are working; replace any dead bulbs immediately (it's a good idea to carry spare fuses and bulbs)
- the brakes are working; **don't drive with faulty brakes**.

Periodic checks

These checks are both for safety and good vehicle maintenance.

Check and top up if necessary

- engine oil
- water level in the radiator or expansion tank
- brake fluid level

- battery; top up with distilled water if necessary (some batteries are maintenance-free and don't need topping up)
- windscreen and rear window washer bottles.

You should also check tyres and make sure they are

- legal; they must have the correct tread depth and be free of dangerous cuts and defects
- at the right pressure.

How often you make the checks depends on how much you drive. Consult your vehicle handbook. If you drive a lot, you may need to do these every day.

Basic maintenance

Further information about basic maintenance can be found in section 14.

Regular servicing

Have your vehicle regularly serviced. The vehicle handbook will tell you when servicing is recommended.

Having your vehicle serviced according to its maintenance schedule helps the engine work more efficiently, so saving fuel and reducing the effect on the environment by cutting emissions.

Cockpit drill

Make these checks for the safety of yourself, your passengers and other road users.

Every time you get into your vehicle, check that

- all doors are properly closed and the parking brake is on
- the driving seat is in the best position, and you can see clearly in all directions and reach **all** the controls comfortably
- the head restraint is in the correct position
- the mirrors are clean and correctly adjusted
- you and your passengers have seat belts on
- check the parking brake again and that the gear lever is in neutral (if you're driving an automatic, that the gear lever is in 'P' or 'N')
- you have enough fuel before starting your journey.

Driving a vehicle unfamiliar to you

Before you start your journey, make sure you know and understand the vehicle's

- controls; where they are and how they work
- size; width, height and weight
- handling; front, rear or four-wheel drive
- brakes; whether ABS brakes are fitted.

Starting the engine

After you've made the preliminary checks and you're settled comfortably in the driving seat, begin the drill for starting the engine.

- Check the parking brake is on by trying to pull it on slightly further.

- Check that the gear lever is in neutral (or 'P' or 'N' if driving an automatic).

- Pull the choke out if your vehicle has one. Most vehicles have an automatic choke.

- Switch on the ignition by turning the key. The ignition and oil pressure light, if fitted, will come on. Other warning lights should also come on. With a diesel engine you might have to wait for a glow plug lamp to go out.

- Operate the starter by turning the key further, or use the separate starter switch, if one is fitted.

- Release the starter key or switch as soon as the engine begins running; otherwise the starter could be damaged. Do not operate the starter if the engine is already running.

You might find it necessary to use the accelerator a little as you operate the starter. The amount will depend on the make and model of your vehicle.

If the engine fails to start

If the engine fails to start first time

- release the key or switch
- wait a moment
- try again.

When the engine starts

You may need to press the accelerator slightly to help the engine keep running.

The engine should now be idling ('ticking over').

The ignition and oil pressure warning lights should go out when the engine is running. If either light stays on, switch off the engine and have the fault checked. Never drive a vehicle with the oil pressure warning light showing – it could damage the engine.

If your vehicle has a manual choke, push it in as the engine warms up. Don't drive with the choke out any longer than necessary. This wastes fuel, causes wear to the engine and can be dangerous, especially with automatic transmission.

Move off as soon as possible after starting the engine. Allowing the engine to warm up while you are stationary wastes fuel and causes pollution.

Moving off

With your left foot, press the clutch pedal fully down and hold it there.

Move the gear lever into first gear. If it won't engage, move the gear lever to neutral then let out the clutch and repeat the first two steps.

You should prepare to move off only if you'll be able to do so safely.

- With your right foot, press the accelerator slightly and hold it steady.

- Slowly and smoothly, let up the clutch pedal until you hear the engine noise change slightly. This change means the clutch is at the biting point. With experience, you'll be able to feel the biting point.

- Hold the clutch steady in this position.

- Now make your final safety checks, use your mirrors and look over your right shoulder to check the blind spot.

- Decide if a signal is necessary. The timing of any signal is crucial. Avoid waiting unduly with the clutch at biting point.

- If it's safe to move off, be ready to release the parking brake.

- Look round again if necessary and keep an eye on your mirrors.

- When you're sure it's safe and convenient to move off, release the parking brake and at the same time, let the clutch pedal come up a little more. The vehicle will begin to move. Tight clutch control is needed, so keep the clutch pedal just above the biting point.

- Gradually depress the accelerator for more speed and let the clutch come up smoothly, then take your left foot off the clutch pedal. Accelerating fiercely wastes fuel.

Biting point The 'biting point' is when the clutch plates start to engage. You must be able to find this point confidently when you bring up the clutch pedal. Although you can press the pedal down quickly, you must not let it come up too fast. Practise finding the biting point until you become familiar with it.

Although this process is the same for all vehicles with manual gear boxes, there can be slight variations in how different vehicles feel, and sound, when at the biting point. If you have to use a different vehicle on occasions while learning, take a few minutes to practise finding its biting point first, before driving on the roads.

This advice also applies after you have passed your test, whenever you have to drive an unfamiliar vehicle.

Practice makes perfect Getting these steps in the right order is difficult at first. Choose a quiet, level road to practise starting, moving off, and stopping.

Don't

- signal and move out regardless
- sit with the signal showing when you can't move out safely.

Defensive driving

- Check all round before moving off.
- Signal if necessary.
- Don't move out into the path of oncoming traffic.
- Don't rush.

Braking

Safe and controlled braking is vital in good driving. Try to slow down gradually and smoothly.

Anticipation

If you anticipate properly, you'll seldom need to brake fiercely.

Good anticipation will give you time to brake progressively over a longer distance.

Late, harsh braking is a sign of poor anticipation and of reduced safety margins.

Braking and steering

Braking shifts the balance of weight of the vehicle forward and makes steering more difficult.

If you have to brake hard, try to do so when you're travelling in a straight line.

You should consider

- the safety and peace of mind of everyone concerned, including your passengers
- wear and tear on brakes, tyres and suspension
- vehicles behind you whose brakes might not be as powerful as yours.

Avoid braking on bends

Braking on a bend can have serious consequences.

The weight of the vehicle is thrown outwards as well as forwards. The front tyre on the outside of the curve will be overloaded and the vehicle could be thrown into a severe skid.

Road surface conditions can have a big effect in these situations. Watch for uneven, loose or slippery surfaces.

Remember, the greater your speed when you brake

- the more difficult it is to control the vehicle
- the greater the distance you need to stop the vehicle.

Think ahead

Think well ahead to avoid the need for harsh, uncontrolled braking.

You should never drive too fast or too close to the vehicle in front. Other drivers might be affected by your actions.

Always use your mirrors before braking and give yourself plenty of space.

Consider

- your own speed of reaction
- the mechanical condition of your vehicle – brakes, steering and suspension
- the type, condition and pressure of your tyres
- the size and weight of your vehicle and its load
- the gradient of the road
- whether the road has a camber or bend
- the weather and visibility
- the road surface. Is it rough, smooth, loose, wet, muddy, or covered with wet leaves, ice or snow?

Five rules for good braking

- Anticipate. Think and look well ahead.
- Know your own limitations and those of your vehicle.
- Take note of the state of the road and its surface.
- Give yourself plenty of time and distance to brake progressively.
- Avoid the risk of skidding, rather than trying to control it.

Defensive driving

If the vehicle behind is too close, slow down gradually to increase your distance from the vehicle ahead so that you can avoid having to brake suddenly.

Stopping

The drill for stopping is always the same, except in an emergency. You must learn it thoroughly from the beginning.

The amount of pressure you need to apply to the footbrake depends on

- your speed
- how quickly you need to stop.

To stop you should

- use the mirrors
- decide whether you need to signal your intention to stop
- signal if necessary

Check your mirrors before braking.

- take your foot off the accelerator. The engine will slow down
- push down the brake pedal lightly with your right foot and then more firmly (see progressive braking later in this section and on page 52)
- press the clutch pedal right down with the left foot just before the vehicle stops. This disengages the engine from the driving wheels and prevents stalling. Don't do it too soon: the engine helps with braking
- ease the pressure off the footbrake just as the vehicle stops
- apply the parking brake
- put the gear lever into neutral
- take both feet off the pedals.

Changing down before you stop When stopping normally, you can stop in the gear that you are in; you don't necessarily have to change down. However, your vehicle should always be in the right gear for the road speed and conditions.

Brake after you have checked your mirrors.

Progressive braking

This is a safe driving technique, which

- allows other drivers time to react
- prevents locked wheels
- prevents skidding
- saves wear and tear on brakes, tyres and suspension
- saves fuel
- is more comfortable for your passengers.

To brake progressively

- put light pressure on the brake at first
- gradually increase the pressure as required to stop the vehicle
- when the vehicle has almost stopped, ease off the pressure so that the vehicle stops smoothly. There should be little or no pressure as the vehicle actually stops.

Practise Choose a particular point at which you would like to stop. See how near to it you can get.

It's better to stop short of the mark rather than overshoot it. You can always ease off the brakes and run forward a bit more.

Stopping at the kerb needs practice too. Aim to stop reasonably close to the kerb without hitting it.

Both hands should be on the steering wheel.

Stopping in an emergency

In normal conditions, a good driver should not need to brake really hard.

However, emergencies can happen – for instance, when a child runs into the road in front of you – so you must know how to stop quickly under control. Stopping in an emergency increases the risk of skidding.

Remember, even when stopping quickly, follow the rule of progressive braking – pushing the brake pedal harder as the vehicle slows down.

A quick reaction is crucial in an emergency. The sooner you start braking, the sooner you will stop!

Practise the following routine

- Keep both hands on the steering wheel. You need as much control as possible.

- Avoid braking so hard that you lock any of the wheels. A skid sideways or a wheel sliding may cause serious loss of control.

- Don't touch the clutch pedal until just before you stop. This helps with your braking and stability.

- Don't touch the parking brake. Most parking brakes work on the back wheels only. Extra braking here can cause skidding.

Note
This routine is not necessarily correct if you have ABS brakes. Refer to your vehicle handbook.

Unless you're moving off again straight away, put the parking brake on and the gear lever into neutral.

Practise braking to judge the correct pressure and remember to take into account road and weather conditions.

If the road is dry you should apply firm pressure, but on a wet road or loose surface you should avoid using too much. This means you'll need to reduce speed and increase your separation distance from the vehicle in front.

When braking in an emergency

- Don't signal – you need both hands to control the steering.
- Don't make a special point of looking in the mirror – you should know what's behind anyway.
- Stop as quickly and safely as possible, keeping your vehicle under full control.
- Look all round before moving off again.

Defensive driving

- Try to avoid the emergency arising
  - look well ahead
  - watch for children playing
  - remember school times
  - look out for pedestrians
  - look for clues, such as reflections.
- Always drive at such a speed that you can stop safely in the distance you can see to be clear. If it's not clear, slow down.
- Prepare for the unexpected.

Anti-lock braking systems

If your vehicle is fitted with ABS brakes, the system activates automatically under conditions of harsh braking.

ABS employs wheel-speed sensors to anticipate when a wheel is about to lock under extreme braking. Just before the wheels begin to lock, the system releases the brakes momentarily before automatically reapplying them. This cycle is repeated several times a second to maximise braking performance, sending a pulsing sensation through the brake pedal. You may find this a little disconcerting the first time it occurs and you may be tempted to respond by relaxing the pressure on the brake pedal. However it is important that maximum pressure is maintained.

ABS does not necessarily reduce your stopping distance but because the wheels are prevented from locking you can continue to steer; something you would not be able to do if the wheels were locked. Reducing the pressure or pumping the brake pedal reduces the effectiveness of the system. The pressure on the brake pedal must be maintained until the hazard is safely avoided.

Knowing ABS will help you stop safely should not encourage you to drive less carefully. ABS cannot overcome the laws of physics; it's still possible for one or more of the tyres to skid because of

- poor road contact
- surface water
- loose road surface.

ABS will enhance your skills, **not** replace them.

Check the vehicle handbook for the correct use of ABS on your particular vehicle.

Skidding

Three important factors cause a skid. In order of importance, they are

- the driver
- the vehicle
- the road conditions.

Skids don't just happen. They're caused by a driver asking too much of the vehicle for the amount of grip the tyres have on the road at that time.

A skid happens when you change speed or direction so suddenly that your tyres cannot keep their grip on the road.

There's an increased risk of skidding as you

- slow down
- speed up
- turn a corner or round a bend
- drive uphill or downhill.

The risk increases on a slippery road surface.

Skids caused by braking

Harsh and uncontrolled braking is one of the chief causes of skidding. Brakes have their greatest stopping power when they're nearly, but not quite, locked.

The weight of the car is thrown forward, and the heavier the braking the more weight goes to the front and the less there is on the rear wheels.

The less the weight on the rear wheels, the more likely they are to lock.

Skidding on dry roads Skids can happen on dry roads, even with good tyres, if you brake harshly.

All the weight is thrown forward and it's impossible to keep the vehicle straight. It begins to swing and only has to touch something to be in danger of turning over.

Anti-lock brakes Anti-lock systems help you to continue steering while braking, but on wet or slippery roads this will be less effective. The brakes are only as good as the tyre grip on the road.

Do not assume that a car with anti-lock brakes will stop in a shorter distance.

Skids caused by steering

These are caused by steering too sharply for the speed at which you are travelling.

Skids caused by acceleration

Sudden or harsh acceleration whilst cornering, particularly in the lower gears, may cause the driving wheels to spin on the road surface. Unless you ease off the accelerator very quickly, the vehicle could go into a skid because of the wheelspin.

Skids caused by braking and steering

If you combine incorrect braking with incorrect steering, you're asking for trouble.

You're bound to skid if your tyres are only just gripping while you're cornering and you start braking.

You could also skid if you're braking when you start cornering.

Don't expect your tyres to do the impossible.

The answer is simple: adjust your speed to the conditions and give yourself plenty of space. If the road is wet or icy, the amount of grip your tyres have is much less.

Avoiding skids

There's no better protection against skids than driving in a way that will avoid them. Skids are caused by drivers; they don't just happen. Take the following advice.

- On very slippery surfaces your stopping distance can be as much as **10 times** longer than on a dry road.
- Look out for signs of slippery roads. Any wet road, even in summer, is likely to be slippery. Be wary of rain, ice, packed snow, frost in shady places, wet mud, loose surfaces and wet leaves. Diesel and oil spillages will also make the road slippery, as will patches of new tarmac.

- If you suspect the road is slippery, keep your speed down. Your brakes will not get you out of trouble when your tyre grip is poor. Brakes are far more likely to get you into trouble.
- Use engine braking. Change down in good time but be very careful with the accelerator and clutch, particularly in very slippery conditions. They can cause skids too!
- Keep your vehicle in good condition
  - brakes that snatch or pull unevenly are dangerous on slippery roads
  - an accelerator pedal linkage which is jerky can lead to wheelspin.

Anti-skid technology

Electronic stability control (ESC), sometimes known as Electronic Stability Program (ESP®), allows the vehicle to turn exactly where the driver expects and remain under control – providing the speed of the vehicle is not excessive for the situation.

ESC cannot overcome the laws of physics; if the driver is travelling too fast there is still a risk of losing control. Drivers still have a responsibility to be able to pull up and stop in the distance they can see to be clear and safe.

The system comprises the functions of ABS and traction control system, and aims to prevent a vehicle from skidding sideways.

Its key benefits are
- continued alertness, becoming active when vehicle skidding is imminent
- detecting the risk of a skid at an early stage, even before braking
- comparing the driver's steering intention with actual travel direction (25 times per second)
- selective braking intervention so that the vehicle reacts as the driver intends, thus reducing engine power to restore vehicle stability.

ESC is becoming more widely available in new cars in the UK, but it is still the case that very few smaller new cars have the system fitted.

Dealing with skids

If your car is skidding there are a number of things you should do.
- Release the brake pedal fully. Drivers often instinctively do the opposite, keeping their right foot hard down on the brake pedal throughout the skid. This makes matters worse, so keep off the brakes. If you have ABS brakes you should follow the manufacturer's instructions.
- Turn the steering wheel in the same direction as the skid and ease off the accelerator at the same time, particularly if the skid is little more than a slight slide. This should bring the wheels into line again.

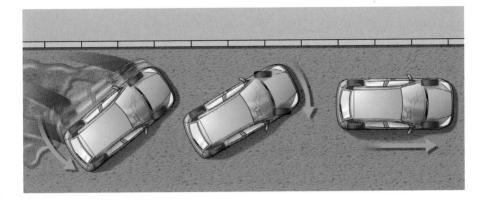

- If the skid is more than a slight slide, ease right off the accelerator and turn more definitely into the skid. That is

  - if the rear of the vehicle is going left, you should steer left to bring the front wheels into line with the back

  - if the rear of the vehicle is going right, steer to the right. Be careful not to overcorrect with too much steering. Too much movement of the front wheels will lead to another skid in the opposite direction.

If the front wheels are sliding instead of, or as well as, the back wheels, release the accelerator and don't try to steer until the wheels regain some of their grip.

Too much power on a front-wheel drive vehicle can produce the same problem. Again, ease off the accelerator.

Remember

- prevention is far better than cure
- adopt safe driving techniques which avoid the build-up to a skid
- adjust to the conditions and give yourself time to react safely.

The parking brake

You should normally apply the parking brake whenever the vehicle is stationary.

Apply the parking brake and put the gear lever into neutral when you're stopped at traffic lights or queuing behind other vehicles, unless the wait is likely to be very short.

Your foot could easily slip off the footbrake if, for example, your shoes are wet or if you're bumped from behind. You could then be pushed into another vehicle or a pedestrian.

Always leave a safe gap between your vehicle and the vehicle in front while queuing, especially on a hill. This will give you room to manoeuvre should the vehicle in front roll back.

Always keep an eye on the mirrors.

In vehicles fitted with automatic transmission, the use of the parking brake is even more important. The parking brake will help avoid

- the possibility of 'creep'
- the vehicle surging forward if the accelerator is pressed accidentally while in 'D' (Drive).

Steering

When you are learning to drive, practise steering your vehicle (at low speed at first) while keeping about 1 metre (3 feet) from the kerb.

Look well ahead, not just at the front of your vehicle. Keep your movements steady and smooth. Never make a sudden or jerky action while steering.

Steering with one hand

When you can steer a straight course with both hands on the steering wheel, try steering with only one hand.

The reason for practising steering with one hand isn't so that you can always drive like that. It's because there are times when you'll only have one hand free for steering, for example, when you're changing gear or operating a control.

Stiffen your arm slightly to help you steer a straight course without pulling the wheel down or swerving. Practise with each hand.

Changing gear

To drive safely, you must combine the skill of knowing **how** to change gear with knowing **when** to change gear as well as which gear to select. These are skills which take time – and practice – to acquire.

The gear positions

You need to know the various positions of the gear lever without having to look down.

You can practise and get to know the gear position with the clutch disengaged and the engine switched off. A light but firm touch should be all you need to move from one gear to another. Never force the gear lever.

On some gearboxes you might require slight pressure to overcome the sprung bias on the lever when you're changing gear.

First to second You might need to put a little pressure to the left on the gear lever when you change up from first to second gear. This is to prevent the lever slipping into fourth while passing through neutral.

Down to first You may need to put slight pressure to the left when you change down from third or second gear to first.

Up to fifth You will need to put pressure to the right when you change up to fifth gear.

Don't force the gear lever If you feel resistance, don't force the gear lever into any position.

Don't

- rush gear changes
- take your eyes off the road when you change gear
- coast with the clutch pedal pressed in, or the gear lever in neutral
- hold the gear lever longer than necessary.

Changing up

When to change up You need to change gear in order to match the engine speed and load to the speed of the vehicle.

This will vary with the vehicle you're driving and whether you're moving on the level, uphill or downhill. As a general rule, change up as the road speed increases.

Listening to the engine helps to determine when to change up. You'll become more familiar with this as you practise, and will soon learn to recognise the appropriate level of sound at which to change gear.

To change up you should

- place your left hand on the gear lever
- press the clutch pedal right down at the same time as you ease off the accelerator pedal. Don't take your foot off the accelerator
- move the gear lever to the next highest position required
- let the clutch pedal come up smoothly and, at the same time, press the accelerator gradually
- put your left hand back on the steering wheel.

Matching engine and road speed
Releasing the accelerator when changing up lets the engine speed drop to match the higher gear to give you a smooth gear change.

Being able to judge when it's time to change up comes with experience.

Changing down

When to change down You'll need to change down to a lower gear

- if you have slowed down and the gear you're in doesn't provide enough power for driving at the lower speed
- if you're going uphill in too high a gear and your engine labours or struggles to give enough power
- to increase the effect of the engine braking, for example, when on a long downhill gradient.

Driving in a high gear at low speed makes engine performance sluggish, and is bad driving practice.

Unless you intend to stop, you'll need to change to a lower gear once you've slowed down.

As a general rule, use the brakes to reduce speed before changing down to the most suitable gear for the lower speed.

In the early stages of learning to drive, it may help you become familiar with the gearbox if you change down through each of the gears in turn. Be guided by your instructor.

When changing down, you might need to

- raise the engine speed to get a smooth change, or
- keep a light pressure on the footbrake to stop the vehicle gathering speed on a downhill slope.

To change down

- place your left hand on the gear lever
- press the clutch pedal right down and, at the same time, either keep a little pressure on the accelerator pedal or the footbrake, whichever is appropriate to the road and traffic conditions
- move the gear lever to the most suitable lower gear for the speed
- let the clutch pedal come up smoothly. Return to the accelerator or continue braking as necessary
- put your left hand back on the steering wheel.

Remember, never rush gear changes. Smooth, even movements are best.

How much pressure is needed on the accelerator or footbrake when changing down will depend on

- the road and traffic conditions
- the speed of your vehicle at the time the clutch pedal is released.

The sound of the engine will help you judge this.

Finding the right gear

To change gear, you need to anticipate and assess the situation well in advance. Ask yourself if the gear you're in is correct for that particular situation.

Overtaking You should consider changing to a lower gear to overtake. A lower gear can give you the extra acceleration to pass safely.

Try to avoid changing gear while you're actually overtaking. It's preferable to keep both hands on the wheel during the manoeuvre.

A lower gear will give you extra engine flexibility and therefore more vehicle control.

Going downhill When descending a steep hill a lower gear gives more engine braking and control, particularly on a bend.

General rule You should change down

- to accelerate more quickly
- if your speed drops.

Smooth gear changing

Smooth, easy gear changes are essential to good driving. Take your time and think ahead. Assess the situation and act accordingly.

Selective/block gear changing

Missing out gears The flexibility of modern engines and the efficiency of braking systems and gearboxes often makes it unnecessary to change into every gear when changing up and down the gearbox.

Missing out gears at the appropriate time will give you more time to concentrate on the road ahead and allow you to keep both hands on the steering wheel for longer.

Changing down As a general rule, it is preferable and safer to brake to the desired speed and then change down into the appropriate gear. It might be necessary to maintain a light pressure on the footbrake whilst changing down.

Changing up There are many occasions when missing out gears whilst changing up is desirable; however, don't accelerate too fiercely or for too long in the lower gears. This

- uses much more fuel
- could damage your engine
- could cause wheelspin and loss of control.

How many gears to miss out It depends on the individual vehicle and the road and traffic conditions.

The most common examples when changing down are

- fifth to third
- fourth to second
- third to first.

The most common examples when changing up are

- first to third
- second to fourth
- third to fifth.

Coasting

Coasting means that although the vehicle is moving, it's not being driven by the engine. This occurs either when the clutch pedal is held down or the gear lever is in the neutral position.

Any form of coasting is wrong because

- it reduces the driver's control of the vehicle
- you might have difficulty engaging a gear if something unexpected happened
- it would almost certainly lead to the vehicle gathering speed when travelling downhill. It would mean harder braking and it removes the assistance of engine braking in a low gear.

Each time you change gear you coast a little; this is unavoidable, but it should be kept to a minimum.

Over-run

If there is only light pressure on the accelerator pedal when the vehicle is travelling at speed, the engine may not appear to be 'driving' the vehicle.

This is known as travelling on the over-run and should not be confused with coasting. There is no loss of control, because the vehicle is still in gear and either engine braking or acceleration are available immediately.

Slipping the clutch

This is holding the clutch pedal partially down so that the clutch is not fully engaged. This allows the engine to spin faster than if it was fully engaged and is often necessary when manoeuvring at slow speeds.

Slipping the clutch to compensate for being in too high a gear at a low speed is bad driving practice and should be avoided. Not only is this a bad driving technique; it can also result in excessive wear of the clutch.

Judgement

As you become more proficient, you'll be able to judge exactly the gear you need for the speed you intend and the manoeuvre you're planning.

Signalling

Signals are normally given by direction indicators and/or brake lights. There are occasions when an arm signal can be helpful.

It's important that you use the correct signal.

Use signals

- to let others know what you intend to do
- to help all other road users, including pedestrians
- in good time and for long enough to allow other road users to see the signal and act upon it.

Signal in good time, particularly before

- turning right or left
- overtaking another moving vehicle
- moving from one lane to another.

Signalling too soon can confuse rather than help – for example, when there are several side roads very close together.

Signalling too late can cause vehicles behind you to brake hard or swerve.

Watch out for situations which call for special timing in signalling. For example, when you signal to pull up on the left, make sure there isn't a junction just before the place you intend to stop. If you signal left too soon, a driver waiting at that junction might think you intend to turn left. Delay signalling until you're in a position where your signal can't be misunderstood.

Unnecessary signals

A signal might not be necessary where there is no one to benefit from it, or where the signal could confuse other road users. Consider whether a signal is necessary before

- moving off
- pulling up
- passing stationary vehicles, when you can position early and maintain a steady course.

Don't

- signal carelessly
- wave pedestrians across the road
- fail to check that the signal is cancelled after your movement is completed
- mislead other road users. Always use the correct signal.

> **Remember,** Mirror – Signal – Manoeuvre.

Arm signals

Nowadays, arm signals are seldom used. However, there are occasions when you might need to use one.

Approaching zebra crossings When yours is the leading vehicle, using an arm signal when slowing down or stopping can be helpful.

This not only tells traffic behind you that you intend to stop, but also approaching traffic and waiting pedestrians, who can't see your brake lights.

Turning right Use an arm signal when necessary

- to emphasise a difficult right turn on a road carrying fast-moving traffic
- to turn right just after moving out to pass a stationary vehicle.

Stopping Use the 'slowing down' arm signal where any confusion to other road users might be caused by a 'left turn' indicator signal.

Signalling with brake lights

Brake in good time. If necessary, lightly press the brake pedal early or more than once, to show your brake lights to traffic behind you.

Using the horn

If you're driving safely and anticipating correctly, you'll seldom need to use the horn.

Only use it if you think other road users haven't seen you or cannot see you.

On a blind bend or narrow winding road, the horn might help pedestrians and other road users who cannot see you coming.

Warning others of your presence does not relieve you of the responsibility to drive safely. Always drive with caution.

Don't sound your horn

• to reprimand other drivers

• aggressively

• in a built-up area between 11.30 pm and 7.00 am or while you're stationary at any time, unless a moving vehicle creates a danger.

Flashing your headlights

Flashing the headlights can be used in much the same way as the horn to warn other road users that you're there.

If you think a warning is necessary, flashing headlights can be particularly useful in situations where the horn might not be heard or at a time when the horn should not be used.

Avoid flashing your headlights to

• instruct other drivers

• reprimand another road user

• intimidate a driver ahead.

Other drivers flashing their headlights

Some drivers flash their headlights for a variety of reasons, including

• inviting you to pass before them

• thanking you for your courtesy

• warning you of some fault with your vehicle

• telling you your headlights are dazzling them.

When other drivers flash their headlights, don't rely on what you think they mean. Use your own judgement; the signal

• might not mean what you think

• might not be intended for you.

Make sure you know their intention before you act on the signal.

Remember, flashing of headlights might not be an invitation. The other driver might have flashed someone else or have flashed accidentally.

Moving off at an angle

Use the same drill as for moving off straight ahead covered under 'Moving off' (see page 77).

When making the routine safety checks and at the biting point ask yourself these questions:

- At what angle should I move out?
- How far will this take me into the road?

Your decision will depend on

- how close you are to the vehicle or object in front
- how wide the vehicle ahead is
- oncoming traffic.

Your window pillar can obstruct your view ahead. Make sure there's nothing in the area hidden by this obstruction.

Watch out for other vehicles behind and signal if necessary, then

- look over your right shoulder again
- release the parking brake as you ease the clutch pedal up a little more. The vehicle will begin to move. Tight clutch control is needed, so keep the clutch pedal at or just above the biting point
- give yourself time to complete the amount of steering you need to clear the vehicle in front
- release the clutch pedal smoothly when your vehicle is clear of the obstruction
- allow room for someone to open a door, if you're steering around a vehicle
- check your mirrors
- move out slowly, straighten up, and be ready to brake; a pedestrian might step out from the other side of the parked vehicle.

Moving off on hills

Moving off uphill

Your vehicle will want to roll back. To avoid this you must use the accelerator, clutch and parking brake together.

Much of the drill for moving off uphill is the same as for moving off on the level.

- With your left foot, press the clutch pedal down and hold it down.

- Move the gear lever into first.

- With your right foot, press the accelerator further than you would when starting on the level and hold it perfectly steady. The amount will depend on how steep the hill is.

- Bring the clutch pedal up to the biting point, which will be slightly higher than when you're moving off on the level.

- Make your safety checks, use your mirrors and look round over your right shoulder to check the blind spot.

- Decide whether you need to signal your intention to move off.

- Signal if necessary.

- Look round again if necessary.

- Lift the parking brake and release the button while you press the accelerator a little more. How much acceleration you need depends on the steepness of the hill.

- Let the clutch up a little more, until you feel and hear the engine trying to move the vehicle.

- Release the parking brake smoothly.

- Gradually press the accelerator as the vehicle begins to move, and bring up the clutch pedal smoothly.

Controlling the parking brake and clutch

This requires good timing. If you release the parking brake too soon, the vehicle will roll back.

The vehicle will stall if

- you hold the parking brake too long
- you bring up the clutch too quickly or too far
- you don't use enough acceleration.

Practise the steps until you've mastered the technique. Then practise moving off uphill without rolling backwards; from behind a parked vehicle and at an angle.

The more you practise this manoeuvre, the more competent you'll be at getting it right.

Remember

Allow a safe gap in any traffic because your vehicle will be slower pulling away and building up speed.

Don't cut across or block traffic coming uphill. Use the MSM routine. Avoid hasty action.

Moving off downhill

The routine is simpler than moving off uphill because the weight of the vehicle helps you to move away.

The aim is to prevent the vehicle from rolling forward down the hill whilst moving away. The most effective, and possibly simplest, method is as follows.

- Press the clutch pedal down fully.
- Engage the appropriate gear for the severity of the slope (this could be second gear).
- Apply the footbrake.
- Release the parking brake, keeping the footbrake applied.
- Check mirrors. Look round just before you move off to cover the blind spots.
- Signal if necessary.
- Only move away when you're sure it's safe to do so.
- Look round again if necessary.
- Release the footbrake and release the clutch pedal smoothly as the vehicle starts to move.

However, there may be other methods that can be employed. If they ensure that the manoeuvre is carried out under control, they are equally acceptable.

Remember

Be careful to use the right gear for the steepness of the slope to give you more control.

Don't forget that drivers coming downhill will need more time to slow down or stop. Again, leave a large enough gap before pulling away.

section **six**
TRAFFIC SIGNS

This section covers

- The purpose of traffic signs
- Signs giving warning
- Signs giving orders
- Signs giving directions and other information
- Waiting restrictions
- Road markings
- Traffic lights
- Traffic calming
- Level crossings

The purpose of traffic signs

Signs are an essential part of any traffic system. They tell you about the rules you must obey and warn you about the hazards you may meet on the road ahead.

Signs can be in the form of words or symbols on panels, road markings, beacons, bollards or traffic lights.

This section deals with the various types of traffic signs and their meaning.

To do its job, a sign must give its message clearly and early enough for you to see it, understand it and then act safely on it.

Symbols

Symbols are used as much as possible because they're

- more easily recognised and understood
- mainly standardised, particularly throughout Europe.

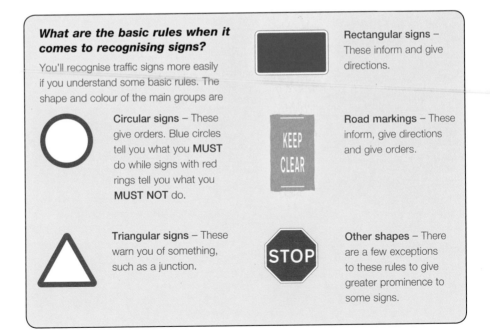

What are the basic rules when it comes to recognising signs?

You'll recognise traffic signs more easily if you understand some basic rules. The shape and colour of the main groups are

Circular signs – These give orders. Blue circles tell you what you **MUST** do while signs with red rings tell you what you **MUST NOT** do.

Triangular signs – These warn you of something, such as a junction.

Rectangular signs – These inform and give directions.

Road markings – These inform, give directions and give orders.

Other shapes – There are a few exceptions to these rules to give greater prominence to some signs.

Signs giving warning

Usually a red triangle pointing upwards, with a symbol or words on a white background. These warn you of a hazard you might not otherwise be able to recognise in time; for example, a bend, hill or hump bridge. The sign will make clear what the hazard is. You must decide what to do about it.

Narrowing roads These tell you from which side the road is narrowing (sometimes both sides), and should warn you against overtaking until you have had a chance to assess the hazard.

Children and schools The warning here is: watch out for children running out into the road, especially during school arrival and leaving times. Look out for school-crossing patrols.

Low bridge sign Even if your vehicle is low, watch out. An oncoming vehicle might have to use the centre of the road to make use of any extra headroom there.

Junctions These tell you what type of junction is ahead: T-junction, crossroads, roundabout, staggered junction and so on. The priority through the junction is indicated by the broader line.

Sharp change of direction Chevrons or roadside posts with reflectors may be used where the road changes direction sharply enough to create a hazard or to reinforce a bend warning sign where stronger emphasis is needed.

Other hazards If there's no special sign for a particular hazard, a general hazard warning sign is used: a red triangle with an exclamation mark on a white background. It will have a plate underneath telling you what the hazard is, eg hidden dip.

Signs giving orders

Signs which give orders can be

- mandatory signs; these tell you what you **MUST** do
- prohibitory signs; these tell you what you **MUST NOT** do.

Mandatory signs

Mostly circular signs with white symbols and borders on a blue background; for example

- mini-roundabout
- keep left
- turn left.

In addition

- 'Stop – children' sign (lollipop) carried by a school-crossing patrol. This is circular with black lettering on a yellow background
- 'Stop' in white on a red background, often manually controlled at roadworks
- 'Stop' and 'give way' signs appear at junctions and are very important for everyone's guidance and safety.

'Stop' signs

These are octagonal, with white lettering on a red background, usually found at a junction with a limited zone of vision. they are always accompanied by a stop line marked on the road. The line tells you how far forward you should go before stopping at the position from which you look, assess and decide if it is safe to proceed.

What you MUST do at 'stop' signs

- Stop (even if you can see the road is clear).
- Wait until you can enter the major road without causing other drivers to change speed or direction.

'Give way' signs

These consist of

- a red triangle pointing downwards
- black lettering on a white background.

They are always accompanied by road markings. However, some junctions only have the 'give way' lines. This is usually where there's relatively little traffic.

'Give way' signs and/or road markings show you that traffic on the road you want to enter has priority.

The double broken lines across the road show you where to stop, if necessary, to take your final look.

What you MUST do at 'give way' signs

- Give way to traffic already on the major road.
- Delay entering the major road until you can do so without causing any traffic already on the road to change speed or direction.

Remember
Look, assess, decide and act.

As with the 'stop' sign on the previous page, this is the only sign that is a downwards-pointing triangle. This is to ensure that it can be recognised and obeyed, even if it is obscured.

Prohibitory signs

These tell you what you **MUST NOT** do. They are easy to recognise by their circular shape and red border. The message is given by symbols, words or figures or a combination of these. The exceptions are

- 'no entry' sign (circular with white border and red background)
- 'bus lane' sign.

Speed limit signs

A red circle with a number on a white background shows the speed limit.

A white disc with a black diagonal line cancels the previous speed limit, but you must not exceed the national speed limit for the type of road you're on or the vehicle you're driving. If you're driving a light van of over 2 tonnes maximum laden weight, the national speed limit for goods vehicles of up to 7.5 tonnes maximum laden weight applies. A table showing the national speed limits for all roads and vehicles can be found on page 40 in the latest edition of The Highway Code.

Repeater signs are a smaller form of the original speed limit sign which are fitted to lampposts to remind you of the speed limit. In areas where there are regularly spaced street lights, you should assume that the 30 mph (48 km/h) speed limit normally applies, unless there are repeater signs showing a different speed limit.

Signs giving directions and other information

These help you find and follow the road you want. They can also direct you to the nearest railway station, car park, or other facility or attraction. The colours of these signs vary with the type of road. For example

- motorways – blue with white letters and border
- primary routes, except motorways – green with white letters and border, route numbers shown in yellow
- other routes – white with black letters and black or blue border.

All these roads may also display tourist signs, which are brown with white letters and border.

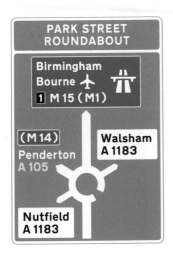

Signs giving directions on primary routes

Advance direction signs You will see these before you reach the junction. They enable you to decide which direction to take and to prepare yourself.

Direction signs at the junction These show you the way to take as you reach the junction.

Route confirmatory signs Positioned after the junction, these confirm which road you're on. These signs also tell you distances and places on your route. If the route number is in brackets, it means that the road leads to that route.

Information signs
These tell you where to find parking places, telephones, camping sites, etc, or give information about such things as no through roads.

Signs for traffic diversions

In an emergency, when it is necessary to close a section of motorway or other main road to traffic, a temporary sign may advise drivers to follow a diversion route. This route guides traffic around the closed section, bringing it back onto the same road further along its length.

To help drivers navigate the route, black symbols on yellow patches may be permanently displayed on existing direction signs, including motorway signs. A trigger sign will initially alert road users to the closure, then the symbol is shown alongside the route that drivers should follow.

A number of different symbols may be used, as in some places there may be more than one diversion operating. The range of symbols used is shown below.

Drivers and riders should follow signs bearing the appropriate symbol. These may be displayed on separate signs, or included on direction signs, giving the number of the road to follow.

Waiting restrictions

These are indicated by signs and road markings. Yellow lines along the road parallel to the kerb indicate that restrictions are in force.

Small yellow plates may be mounted on posts or lampposts nearby. These give more precise details of the restriction that applies. If there are double yellow lines painted on the road but no plates nearby, there is no waiting at any time.

Controlled parking zones In controlled parking zones, the times of operation of the zone will be shown on the entry signs. Yellow lines show where waiting is prohibited or restricted, but yellow plates are not normally provided in these zones.

White bay markings and upright signs indicate where parking is allowed.

Clearways Some areas and main roads are designated as 'no stopping' zones or clearways. This means no stopping on the main carriageway at any time, not even to pick up or set down passengers.

On urban clearways there is no stopping during the hours of operation except for as long as necessary to set down or pick up passengers.

Loading and unloading

'Loading' is defined as when a vehicle stops briefly to load or unload goods which are so heavy or bulky that it isn't easy to carry them any distance and may involve more than one trip. Picking up items that can be carried, such as shopping, doesn't constitute loading.

You may be allowed to load and unload in places where waiting is restricted. Yellow markings on the kerb show that loading and unloading is prohibited. The times when this is prohibited are shown on the nearby upright signs. There may also be special bays marked by broken white lines and the words 'Loading only' marked on the road and upright signs.

Red Routes

On many roads in London, Red Route signs and red road markings have been introduced to replace the yellow-line restrictions (see page 324). For more information on Red Routes visit **tfl.gov.uk/redroutes**

Road markings

Markings on the road give information, orders or warnings. They can be used either with signs on posts or on their own.

Their advantages are

- they can often be seen when other signs are hidden by traffic
- they can give a continuing message as you drive along the road.

As a general rule, the more paint, the more important the message.

Lines across the road

'Give way' lines Double broken white lines across your half of the road show that traffic on the road you want to enter has priority. The lines show where you should stop, if necessary, to take your final look. These may also be found on a roundabout where traffic on the roundabout is required to give way to those joining.

A single broken line is normally found at the entrance to a roundabout. This tells you that traffic coming from your immediate right has priority and you **MUST** give way.

Single 'stop' lines A single continuous line across your half of the road shows where you **MUST** stop

- at junctions with 'stop' signs
- at junctions controlled by police or traffic lights
- at level crossings
- at swing bridges or ferries.

Lines along the road

Double white lines

The most important of these are double white lines and they have rules for

- overtaking
- parking.

Overtaking When the line nearest you is continuous, you **MUST NOT** cross or straddle it except when the road is clear and you want to

- enter or leave a side road or entrance on the opposite side of the road
- pass a stationary vehicle
- pass a road maintenance vehicle, pedal cycle or horse moving at 10 mph (16 km/h) or less.

If there is not room to leave adequate space when passing, you should wait for a safe opportunity. Do not try to squeeze past.

If there's a broken white line on your side and a continuous white line on the other, you may cross both lines to overtake. Make sure you can complete the manoeuvre before reaching a solid line on your side.

Arrows on the road often warn that there's a double white line coming up. Don't begin to overtake when you see them.

Parking On a road marked with double white lines you **MUST NOT** stop or park, even if one of the lines is broken. You may, however, stop for a moment to pick up or drop off passengers or to load or unload goods.

Hatch markings

There are dangerous areas where it is necessary to separate the streams of traffic completely, such as a sharp bend or hump, or where traffic turning right needs protection. These areas are painted with white chevrons or diagonal stripes and the tarmac areas between them may also be a different colour, eg red.

In addition, remember

- where the boundary line is solid, do not enter except in an emergency
- where the boundary line is broken, you should not drive on the markings unless you can see that it is safe to do so.

Single broken lines

Watch out for places where the single broken line down the centre of the road gets longer. This shows a hazard ahead.

Lane dividers

Short broken white lines are used on wide carriageways to divide them into lanes. You should keep between them unless you are overtaking or turning right.

Lanes for specific types of vehicle

Bus and cycle lanes are shown by signs and road markings. In some one-way streets these vehicles are permitted to travel against the normal flow of traffic. These are known as contraflow lanes.

Bus lanes Only vehicles shown on the sign may use the lane during the times of operation, which are also shown on the sign. Outside those periods all vehicles can use the bus lane. Where there are no times shown, the bus lane is in operation for 24 hours a day. Don't park or drive in bus lanes when they are in operation.

Cycle lanes Don't drive or park in a cycle lane marked by a solid white line during the times of operation shown on the signs. If the cycle lane is marked by a broken line, don't drive or park in it unless it is unavoidable. If you park in a cycle lane at any time you make it very dangerous for any cyclist who is using that lane.

High-occupancy vehicle lanes You **MUST NOT** drive in these lanes during their period of operation unless your vehicle contains the minimum number of people indicated on the sign.

Reflective studs

These are

- red on the left-hand side of the road
- white on the lane or centre-of-road lines
- amber on the right-hand edge of the carriageway on dual carriageways and motorways
- green between the carriageway and lay-bys, side roads and slip roads.

At roadworks, fluorescent green/yellow studs may be used to help identify the lanes in operation.

Box junction markings

Yellow criss-cross lines mark a box junction. Their purpose is to keep the junction clear by preventing traffic from stopping in the path of crossing traffic.

You **MUST NOT** enter a box junction unless your exit road is clear. But you can enter the box when you want to turn right and you're only prevented from doing so by oncoming traffic.

If there's a vehicle already on the junction waiting to turn right, you're free to enter behind it and wait to turn right – providing that you won't block any oncoming traffic wanting to turn right.

If there are several vehicles waiting to turn, it's unlikely you'll be able to proceed before the traffic signals change.

Words on the road

Words on the road surface usually have a clear meaning, such as 'Stop', 'Slow' or 'Keep clear'.

When they show a part of the road is reserved for certain types of vehicle, for example, buses, taxis or ambulances, don't park there.

Schools

Yellow zigzags are often marked on the road outside schools, along with the words 'School – keep clear'. Do not stop (even to set down or pick up children) or park there. The markings are to make sure that drivers who are passing the area and children who are crossing the road have a clear, unrestricted view of the crossing area.

Destination markings

Near a busy junction, lanes sometimes have destination markings or road numbers on the road surface.

These enable drivers to get into the correct lane early, even if advance direction road signs are obscured by large vehicles.

Lane arrows

These tell you which lane to take for the direction you want.

Where the road is wide enough, you may find one arrow pointing in each direction

- left in the left-hand lane
- straight ahead in the centre lane
- right in the right-hand lane.

Some arrows might be combined, depending on how busy the junction is. If the road is only wide enough for two lanes, arrows might have two directions combined

- straight ahead and left in the left-hand lane
- straight ahead and right in the right-hand lane.

Left- and right-turn arrows are placed well before a junction to help you get into the correct lane in good time. They don't indicate the exact point at which you should turn. It's especially important to remember this at right turns.

Speed reduction lines

Raised yellow lines may be painted across the carriageway at the approach to

- roundabouts
- reduced speed limits when entering a village
- particular hazards.

The purpose of these lines is to make drivers aware of their speed after a period of driving at higher speeds. Reduce your speed in good time.

Traffic lights

Traffic lights have three lights which change in a set cycle

- red
- red and amber
- green
- amber
- red.

What the colours mean

- Red – stop and wait at the stop line.
- Red and amber – stop and wait. Don't go until green shows.
- Green – go if the way is clear.
- Amber – stop, unless
  - you've already crossed the line
  - you're so close to it that pulling up might cause an incident.

Approaching green traffic lights

Approach traffic lights as you would any other junction. Keep your speed down.

Don't speed up to 'beat the lights'. Be ready to stop, especially if the lights have been green for some time.

Green filter arrow

A green arrow in a traffic light means you can filter in the direction the arrow is pointing, even if the main light is not showing green. Don't enter this lane unless you want to go in the direction shown by the arrow. When turning left or right at traffic lights take special care and give way to pedestrians already crossing.

MSM routine

Use the MSM and PSL routines as you approach the lights. Pay attention to lane markings and get into the correct lane in good time. Be prepared to stop.

Advance stop lines

At some traffic lights there are advance stop lines to allow cyclists to position themselves ahead of other traffic.

When the lights are amber or red you should stop at the first white line and avoid encroaching on the marked area, which is reserved for cyclists only. However, if you have crossed the first white line at the time that the signal changes to red, you must stop at the second white line even if you are in the marked area. Allow the cyclists time and space to move off when the lights change to green.

In some areas there are bus advance areas. These should be treated in the same way as those provided for cyclists.

Special traffic lights

These are often used to control traffic where low-flying aircraft pass over the road, or at swing or lifting bridges, or other special sites such as fire stations.

They may either be

- normal traffic lights (red, amber and green) – follow the normal rules
- double red flashing lights – stop when the red lights are flashing.

If traffic lights fail

If the traffic lights fail, proceed with caution. Treat the situation as you would an unmarked junction.

School crossing warning

At some busy locations, two amber lights flashing alternately warn traffic of a school crossing point ahead.

Keep your speed down and proceed with great care.

Traffic calming

Traffic-calming measures are used to encourage people to drive at a lower speed than they might otherwise do. They are used in particularly sensitive areas where it is considered that a reduction in speed would benefit the immediate community.

Various features can be provided to slow down the speed of traffic, such as

- road humps
- road narrowings, central islands and chicanes
- mini-roundabouts.

20 mph zones

Some traffic-calmed areas are indicated only by a 20 mph (32 km/h) speed limit sign.

This speed limit sign, in addition to advising the maximum speed limit, also indicates that there may be traffic-calming features within the signed zone; these may not be individually signed.

You should drive at a steady speed within the speed limit, and avoid frequent acceleration and deceleration within these areas.

Road humps

These may be round- or flat-topped humps laid across the carriageway. They may be used on roads where there is a speed limit of 30 mph (48 km/h) or less.

In some areas the humps are in the form of 'cushions' which only cover part of the lane and are designed so that larger vehicles, especially buses, can straddle them.

If road humps or cushions are provided outside 20 mph (32 km/h) zones, there will normally be

- warning signs at the beginning of the section of road where the hump or series of humps are installed
- triangle and edge line markings at each hump.

Road narrowings

Roads may be narrowed by the use of 'build-outs' on one or both sides of the road.

If these are provided outside 20 mph (32 km/h) zones, there will normally be

- warning signs indicating on which side of the road the narrowing occurs
- 'give way' road markings on one side of the road, accompanied by signs advising priority for oncoming vehicles.

If these are on your side of the road, you **MUST** always give way to drivers approaching from the other direction.

If priority is not given in either direction, then all drivers should ensure that they can pass through the narrowing without endangering vehicles approaching from the other direction. You should not accelerate as you approach the narrowing, but be prepared to slow down or give way to approaching traffic.

Hold back and allow cyclists and motorcyclists room to pass through; don't try to squeeze through at the same time.

Mini-roundabouts

Mini-roundabouts are often used as part of traffic-calming schemes to break up a long road into shorter sections and allow traffic to join from minor roads.

Methods of dealing with mini-roundabouts are given on page 182.

Level crossings

At a level crossing, the road crosses railway lines. Approach and cross with care. Never

- drive onto the crossing unless the road is clear on the other side, or drive over it 'nose to tail'
- stop on or just after the crossing
- park close to the crossing.

Most crossings have full or half barriers, although some have no gates or barriers. If you stop at a level crossing and your wait is likely to be more than a few minutes, consider switching off your engine as this can save fuel and cut down on pollution.

Railway telephones If there is a telephone you **MUST** use it to contact the signal operator to obtain permission to cross if you're

- driving a large or slow-moving vehicle, or one with limited ground clearance
- herding animals.

Remember to telephone the signal operator again once you're clear of the crossing.

Automatic barriers

Crossings with lights A steady amber light followed by twin flashing red lights warn of an approaching train. An audible alarm to warn pedestrians will also sound once the lights show. You **MUST** obey the lights' signals.

Don't

- move onto the crossing after the lights show
- zigzag round half barriers
- stop on the crossing if the amber light or audible alarm starts to operate – keep going if you're already on the crossing.

If the train goes by and the red lights continue to flash, or the audible alarm changes tone, you **MUST** wait because another train is approaching.

Crossings without lights At crossings with no lights, stop when the gates or barriers begin to close.

Open crossings

The sign in the shape of the cross shown in the illustration below is used at all level crossings without either gates or barriers.

Crossings with lights Automatic open level crossings have flashing road traffic signals and audible warnings similar to those on crossings with barriers.

Crossings without lights At an open crossing with no gates, barriers, attendant or traffic signals, there will be a 'give way' sign.

Look both ways, listen and make sure there's no train coming before you cross.

User-operated crossings

These crossings are normally private and should be used by authorised users and invited guests only.

Crossings with signals Some crossings with gates or barriers have 'stop' signs and small red and green lights. Do not cross when the red light is on because this means that a train is approaching. Cross only when the green light is on.

If you are crossing with a vehicle

- open the gates or barriers on both sides of the crossing
- check the green light is still on and cross promptly
- close the gates or barriers when you're clear of the crossing.

Crossings without signals Some crossings have gates but no signals. At these crossings, stop, look both ways, listen and make sure that no train is approaching.

If there's a railway telephone you **MUST** contact the signal operator to make sure it's safe to cross.

Open the gates on **both** sides of the crossing and check again that no train is coming before crossing promptly.

Once you've cleared the crossing close both gates and, if there's a telephone, inform the signal operator.

Always give way to trains – they can't stop easily.

Incidents or breakdowns

If your vehicle breaks down, or you're involved in an incident on the crossing

- get everyone out of the vehicle and clear of the crossing

- if there's a railway telephone, use it **immediately** to inform the signal operator: follow any instructions you're given

- **if there's time** before a train arrives, move the vehicle clear of the crossing. You may be able to do this by putting it in first gear and then using the starter motor. Beware of the engine starting suddenly

- if the alarm sounds, or the amber light comes on, **get clear of the crossing at once – the train will not be able to stop.**

Crossings for trams

Look for traffic signs which show where trams cross the road.

Treat them in the same way as normal railway crossings.

> **Remember,** modern trams are silent. Take extra care and look both ways before crossing.

section **seven**

ON THE ROAD

This section covers

- Awareness and anticipation
- Road positioning
- Bends
- Stopping distance
- Separation distance
- Overtaking
- Obstructions
- Pedestrian crossings
- Driving on hills
- Tunnels
- Trams or light rapid transport systems

Awareness and anticipation

In any traffic situation there are some things that are obviously going to happen, as well as some things that **might** happen.

To anticipate is to take action when you expect something will or might happen.

You can anticipate what might happen by making early use of the available information on the road.

Ask yourself

- What am I likely to find?
- What are other road users trying to do?
- Should I speed up or slow down?
- Do I need to stop?

Changing conditions

Traffic conditions change constantly and you need to

- check and recheck what's going on around you
- be alert all the time to changes in conditions, and think ahead.

The degree to which you need to anticipate varies according to those conditions.

Difficult conditions

You'll find it more difficult to decide what might happen when

- the light or the weather is poor
- the traffic is heavy
- the route is unfamiliar.

Types of road

Similarly, types of road will affect how much you can anticipate.

It's easier in light traffic to anticipate what other drivers might do. It is more difficult on a busy single carriageway, dual carriageway or motorway, where their options are greater.

Driving ahead

Read the road ahead to anticipate what might happen. You need to be alert and observant at all times.

Assess the movement of all other road users, including pedestrians, along the whole stretch of road on which you're travelling.

Take in as much as possible of the road

- ahead
- behind
- to each side.

You should keep your eyes moving and

- be able to observe the middle distance and far distance, as well as the area immediately in front
- glance frequently in the mirror to see what's happening in the area you've just passed
- scan the area in your view.

Observation

If you're a new driver, you'll tend to give most of your attention to controlling the vehicle.

Practise reading the road. You don't have to be driving to do this. You can also do it as a passenger in a car or bus. Look out for

- other vehicles and pedestrians
- signals given by other drivers

- road signs and markings
- the type and condition of the road surface
- large vehicles which sometimes need extra space to manoeuvre, eg at roundabouts and other junctions
- movements of vehicles well ahead of you, as well as those immediately in front
- side roads or hills ahead. The building line may show these
- buses signalling to move out from bus stops.

Clues

Look out for clues to help you to act safely and sensibly on what you see.

Watch smaller details in built-up areas where traffic conditions change rapidly. Observe the actions and reactions of other road users.

Reflections in shop windows can often give important information where vision is restricted or when reversing into a parking space.

A pedestrian approaching a zebra crossing might step out into the road sooner than you think.

Take care approaching parked vehicles, especially if someone is in the driving seat.

Watch out for a driver stopping to set down or pick up a passenger. You may find they move off without warning or without checking in the mirrors or looking around.

When following a bus, watch for passengers standing up inside: the bus will probably stop shortly.

Remember, try to anticipate the actions of other road users.

Be aware Observing is not just seeing. How much you can see depends on how well you can see.

Your eyesight can change without you being aware of it. Have regular eyesight checks.

Your ears can also warn of what's happening around you.

At works entrances and schools you should expect an increase in pedestrians, cyclists and vehicles. Watch for vehicles picking up and setting down at school times – buses as well as cars.

School buses will also be picking up and setting down passengers where there may not be normal bus stops.

Emergency vehicles

Look and listen for emergency vehicles. As well as the normal emergency services – police, fire and ambulance – certain others, such as coastguard, bomb disposal, mountain rescue and the blood transfusion service may use blue flashing lights. The police may also use red flashing lights. Doctors on call may use green flashing lights.

You should try to keep out of the way of any emergency vehicle. Check where they are coming from: behind (mirrors), ahead or, more importantly, across your path.

Don't panic. Watch for the path of the emergency vehicle and take any reasonable – and legal – action possible to try to help it get through. They will not expect you to break the law; only to make a reasonable and safe attempt to help clear the way for them so that they can do the rest.

Look well ahead and choose a sensible place to pull into the side of the road, but do not endanger yourself or other road users or risk damage to your car.

Try to avoid stopping before the brow of a hill, a bend or a narrow section of road where the emergency vehicle may have difficulty getting through, but don't

- put yourself in a position where you would be breaking the law, for example by crossing a red traffic light or using a bus lane during its hours of operation
- break the speed limit to get out of the way
- risk damaging your tyres, wheels or steering by bumping up kerbs.

Emergency vehicles are normally travelling quickly and it is important to clear their path to allow them to do so. However, ambulances may need to travel slowly, even if they have blue lights flashing, when a patient is being treated inside. In this case it is important for them to have a smooth ride, so don't drive in a manner that would cause the ambulance to brake or swerve sharply.

Driving in busy areas

When driving in busy areas, you should be especially alert to all the possible hazards already mentioned.

You should also be particularly aware of your speed and always drive at a speed appropriate to the conditions.

The speed limit is the absolute maximum and does not mean that it is always safe for you to drive at that speed. For example, in a narrow residential street with cars parked on either side, you may need to reduce your speed considerably.

Road positioning

You should normally keep to the left when driving in Great Britain.

However, keep clear of parked vehicles, leaving room for

- doors opening
- vehicles moving off
- children running out.

Don't

- drive too close to the kerb, particularly in streets crowded with pedestrians
- weave in and out between parked vehicles. It's unnecessary and confusing to other drivers.

When necessary, ease over to the left to

- help the flow of traffic
- let a faster vehicle overtake.

The correct position You should always be in the correct position for the route you're going to take.

- Keep to the left if you're going straight ahead or turning left.
- Keep as close to the centre of the road as is safe when you're turning right.

Your position is important not only for safety, but also to allow the free flow of traffic. A badly positioned vehicle can hold up traffic in either direction.

Keep to the centre of the road if you are turning right.

One-way streets Position your vehicle according to whether you intend to go ahead, turn left, or turn right.

- To turn left, keep to the left-hand lane.
- To turn right, keep to the right-hand lane, provided there are no obstructions or parked vehicles on the right-hand side of the road you are in.
- To go ahead, be guided by the road markings. If there is no specific lane for ahead select the most appropriate lane, normally the left, in good time.

Follow the road markings and get into the correct lane as soon as possible and stay in this lane. Watch for drivers who may change lanes suddenly.

Traffic in one-way streets often flows freely. Watch out for vehicles coming past on either side of you.

Lane discipline

You should always follow lane markings, which are there for two reasons.

- They make the best possible use of road space.
- They guide the traffic.

Keeping to the lane markings is vital.

Position yourself in good time If you find you're in the wrong lane, don't try to change by cutting across other drivers at the last moment. Carry on in your lane and find another way back to your route.

Changing lanes Position your vehicle according to your route. Always check your mirrors and, if necessary, take a quick sideways glance to be sure that you won't force another road user to change course or speed. When it's safe to do so, signal in good time and when clear, move out.

- Never weave from lane to lane.
- Never straddle two lanes.
- Never change lanes at the last minute.
- Always stay in the middle of your lane until you need to change.

In heavy and slow-moving traffic Don't

- change lanes suddenly
- keep changing lanes
- straddle lanes or lane markings
- weave in and out
- obstruct 'keep clear' markings. Check for these in congested, slow-moving traffic, eg at exits, for emergency vehicles.

Allow for

- pedestrians crossing
- cyclists moving up the nearside
- large vehicles needing to straddle lanes before turning
- motorcyclists filtering
- doors opening.

Driving ahead Keep to the left-hand lane wherever possible. Don't use the right-hand lane just because you're travelling at speed.

On a carriageway with four or more lanes, don't use the lanes on the right unless signs or markings allow you to do so. Peak time 'tidal flow' systems might permit or forbid use of these lanes, depending on the time of day.

Bus and cycle lanes These are separate lanes shown by signs and road markings. Do not enter these lanes unless permitted by the signs.

You will find more information on lane discipline in section 11, which covers driving on motorways.

Approaching a road junction

Look well ahead for signs and markings.

If you have two lanes in your direction and

- you intend to turn left, stay in the left-hand lane
- you intend to go straight ahead, stay in the left-hand lane unless otherwise indicated
- you intend to turn right, move to the right-hand lane in good time.

Don't try to gain an advantage by using an incorrect lane. Trying to change back to the proper lane at or near the junction is a risky business.

If you have three lanes in your direction and you intend to

- turn left, stay in the left-hand lane
- go straight ahead, take the left-hand lane (unless there are left filter signs) or the middle lane, or be guided by road markings
- turn right, take the right-hand lane.

Slip road Some junctions also have a slip road.

Get into the left-hand lane in good time before entering the slip road. You'll be able to slow down to turn left without holding up other traffic.

Bends

Dealing effectively and safely with bends demands that you look well ahead and try to assess accurately how severe the bend is and at what speed you need to be travelling to negotiate it under control.

You should exercise sound judgement and a defensive approach. Where vision is restricted, be prepared to meet

- oncoming vehicles
- obstructions such as broken-down or slow-moving vehicles
- pedestrians walking on your side of the road.

You should

- use the footbrake to control your speed on approach
- choose the right gear for the road speed
- use the accelerator carefully
- steer to hold the correct line through the bend.

Remember, a bend can feel like a sharp corner to a driver who approaches it too fast – with disastrous results.

Positioning on bends

Left-hand bend

Keep to the centre of your lane as you approach.

Don't move to the centre of the road to improve your view round the bend. This could put you too close to oncoming traffic and a vehicle coming the other way might be taking the bend wide.

Right-hand bend

Keep to the left to improve your view of the road, but don't let a clear view tempt you to enter the bend at too great a speed.

Speed

Judging the correct road speed as you approach bends and corners takes practice and experience.

The correct speed is the one which takes your vehicle around the bend under full control with the greatest safety for you, your passengers and other road users.

That speed will depend on the

- type and condition of the road
- sharpness of the bend
- camber of the road
- visibility
- weather conditions.

Camber The camber of a road is the angle at which the road normally slopes away from the centre to help drainage.

Adverse camber Here the road slopes downwards towards the outside of the corner and the forces acting on your vehicle could cause it to leave the road more easily than on a normal corner.

Banking On a few bends, such as some motorway slip roads, the outward force may be partly counteracted by banking. This is where the road slopes upwards towards the outside of the bend.

Adjusting your speed

Don't go into a bend too fast. If necessary reduce speed before you enter the bend.

You can reduce your speed by taking your foot off the accelerator and

- allowing the road speed to fall; or by
- using the footbrake progressively and, if necessary, changing to a lower gear.

Your speed should be at its lowest before you begin to turn.

Braking on a bend Avoid braking on a bend. This can make your vehicle unstable.

The sharper the bend, the more drastic the effects of braking and the more likely the vehicle is to skid.

If any braking is necessary, brake before the bend.

Acceleration

Don't confuse 'using the accelerator' with 'accelerating', which means going faster. When dealing with bends 'using the accelerator' means using it just enough to drive the vehicle around the bend.

The correct speed at a corner or bend will depend on a number of things, including

- how sharp it is
- whether there is other traffic about.

There are no hard and fast rules, and you will have to judge

- the correct position
- the proper speed for the corner or bend
- the gear most suitable for that speed.

The secret of dealing with bends is to make sure that

- your speed is at its lowest before you start the turn
- you use the accelerator so that the engine is doing just enough work to drive the vehicle round the bend without going faster.

Too much acceleration can cause the wheels to lose their grip and skid, resulting in the vehicle swinging off course. This is particularly true on rear-wheel drive vehicles.

Only increase your speed after you have straightened as you leave the bend.

Gears Make sure you select the correct gear before you enter the bend. You need both hands on the steering wheel as you're turning.

Steering

Every vehicle 'handles' differently. It's very important that you get to know how the vehicle you are driving behaves when you're steering round a bend.

Some vehicles 'understeer'. They respond less than you would expect in relation to the amount of steering you use.

Others 'oversteer'. They respond more than you would expect in relation to the amount of steering you use.

To be able to negotiate a bend, corner or junction safely, you must be able to judge how much steering to use.

Load Any change in the centre of gravity or weight the vehicle is carrying will affect its handling on bends, compared with when it's lightly loaded.

This change may be caused by

- extra passengers
- heavy objects in the boot
- objects on the roof rack.

Tyre pressures Incorrect tyre pressures can also affect steering. Low pressure produces a heavier feel, and can cause the tyres to overheat.

Low pressure and excess pressure can affect road holding and tyre wear.

Excess pressure can affect road holding on bends and increases the risk of skidding.

Negotiating the bend

Look ahead Look well ahead for any indications, such as road signs, warnings and road markings, which will tell you

- the type of bend
- the direction the road takes
- how sharp the bend is
- whether the bend is one of a series.

Assess the situation Ask yourself

- how dangerous does it seem? Remember, the word 'slow' is usually painted on the road for a good reason
- are there likely to be obstructions on the bend? For example, slow-moving vehicles or parked cars
- are there likely to be pedestrians on your side of the road? Is there a footpath?
- what's the camber like? Remember that on a right-hand bend an adverse camber could make your vehicle veer to the left. Look well ahead – it's too late to find out in the middle of the bend when your brakes can't help you.

Always drive so you can stop safely within the limit of your vision. Take extra care where your view is restricted.

Approach with care As you approach, follow the MSM/PSL routine. Before you reach the bend

- take up the best approach position for the type of bend
- adjust your speed, if necessary, and select the most suitable gear.

Entering the bend As you enter the bend, press the accelerator just enough to keep

- the wheels gripping
- the vehicle under full control.

After you begin to turn Avoid braking, except in an emergency.

As you round the bend Keep watching for hazards as the road unfolds and your view improves.

Stopping on a bend Avoid stopping on a bend, except in an emergency.

If you have to stop, do so where following traffic can see you. This is especially important on left-hand bends, where vision can be more limited.

If you can, stop clear of a continuous centre line and give clear warning of any obstruction to other traffic. Use hazard warning lights and, if you have one, an advance warning triangle (or any other permitted warning device; see page 286).

A series of bends Double and multiple bends are almost always signed. Take note of

- road signs
- double white lines
- arrows warning you to move to the left.

For example, if the second bend followed closely after the first and you haven't taken notice of the road sign or markings, you could find yourself speeding up when you should be slowing down. This can result in hasty replanning and loss of control.

On a winding road, use your gears sensibly and select the appropriate gear for the speed. This will enable you to drive at a safe speed while keeping the right amount of load on the engine and the right amount of grip on the road.

Bends in series often swing in alternate directions. As soon as you have negotiated one, you have to prepare for the next. Look well ahead for changes in the camber of the road, which could affect your control.

At night On unfamiliar roads, the lights of oncoming traffic may help you to plan ahead. However, negotiating bends at night has its own hazards. Drive with extra care.

- Be prepared for hazards around the bend.
- Be prepared to be affected by the lights of oncoming traffic, especially on right-hand bends. Don't be taken by surprise.
- Dip your headlights in advance for oncoming traffic approaching the bend, especially on left-hand bends.

Drive defensively Always be on the lookout for other vehicles creating dangerous situations. Stay well clear of trouble, such as

- a vehicle overtaking too close to a bend
- a vehicle approaching a bend too fast
- oncoming vehicles straddling the centre lines
- oncoming vehicles skidding in bad weather
- a vehicle waiting to turn into a concealed entrance.

Stopping distance

This is the distance your vehicle travels

- from the moment you realise you must brake
- to the moment the vehicle stops.

You need to leave enough space between you and the vehicle in front so that you can pull up safely if it slows down or stops suddenly.

To do this, you must be able to judge your overall stopping distance.

Practise judging distance while you're walking. Pick out something ahead and see how far away it is. One good stride roughly equals a metre (or yard). Check your estimate and try it out with other objects.

Stopping distance depends on

- how fast you're going
- whether you're travelling on the level, uphill or downhill
- the weather and the state of the road
- the type and age of your vehicle, normally older vehicles need a longer stopping distance
- the condition of your brakes and tyres
- the size and weight of your vehicle
- your ability as a driver, especially your reaction times when applying the brakes.

Stopping distance divides into

- thinking distance
- braking distance.

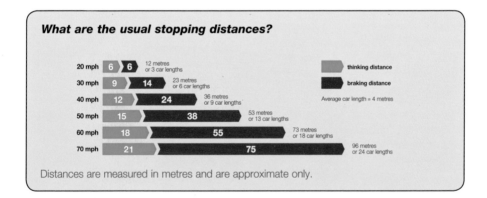

What are the usual stopping distances?

Speed	thinking	braking	Total
20 mph	6	6	12 metres or 3 car lengths
30 mph	9	14	23 metres or 6 car lengths
40 mph	12	24	36 metres or 9 car lengths
50 mph	15	38	53 metres or 13 car lengths
60 mph	18	55	73 metres or 18 car lengths
70 mph	21	75	96 metres or 24 car lengths

thinking distance
braking distance

Average car length = 4 metres

Distances are measured in metres and are approximate only.

Thinking distance

This depends how quickly you react. It takes well over half a second for most people to react.

If you're tired or unwell, it will take longer.

If you're driving at 20 mph (32 km/h), you'll travel about 6 metres (20 feet) before your brakes even begin to act.

- At 30 mph (48 km/h), you'll travel 9 metres (30 feet).
- At 40 mph (64 km/h), you'll travel 12 metres (40 feet).

The diagram opposite shows thinking distances and braking distances for speeds up to 70 mph.

Braking distance

This depends greatly on your speed and the size and weight of your vehicle.

It has even more effect on the overall stopping distance.

- At 20 mph, (32 km/h) good brakes will stop your vehicle in about 6 metres (20 feet) on a dry road.
- At 40 mph (64 km/h), twice the speed, they will take 24 metres (80 feet) to stop – that's **four** times the distance.

You need to allow much more time and room to brake in bad weather. On wet roads allow double the normal stopping distance and 10 times where the roads are icy.

Separation distance

Also your tyres won't grip the road surface so well

- on loose road surfaces
- if there is any diesel spilt on the road.

In these conditions allow much more time and room to brake.

Far too many road traffic incidents are caused by drivers getting too close to the vehicle in front.

It's essential that every driver is able to judge a safe separation distance in all road, traffic and weather conditions.

The safety of you and your passengers depends on it!

How far should you keep from the vehicle in front? Ideally, you should be no closer than the overall stopping distance that corresponds to your speed.

In heavy, slow-moving urban traffic that might not be practicable without wasting valuable road space. However, even then the gap should never be less than your thinking distance, and much more if the road is wet and slippery.

A reasonable rule to apply in good, dry conditions is a gap of one metre for each mph of your speed. For example, at 55 mph (88 km/h) a gap of 55 metres would be appropriate. In bad conditions leave at least double the distance.

A useful technique for judging one metre per mph is to use the 'two-second rule'.

Remember, your overall stopping distance is the only really safe gap and anything less is taking a risk.

The two-second rule

In good dry conditions an alert driver, who is driving a vehicle with first-class tyres and brakes, needs to be at least two seconds behind the vehicle in front.

In bad conditions, double the safety gap to four seconds or even more.

How to measure Choose an obvious stationary reference point ahead, such as a bridge, a tree or a road sign.

When the vehicle ahead passes the object say to yourself, 'Only a fool breaks the two-second rule.' If you reach the object before you finish saying it, you're too close. Multiple collisions often happen because the drivers involved were driving too close and were unable to brake in time.

You can avoid such incidents by looking well ahead and keeping your distance. Give yourself time to react.

Defensive driving

When a vehicle behind is driving too close to you, ease off very gradually and increase the gap between you and the vehicle in front. This will give you more time to react if the driver ahead should slow down or stop suddenly.

Overtaking

Because overtaking can put you on a collision course with traffic from the opposite direction, it's one of the major causes of road traffic incidents.

Overtaking at the wrong time or in the wrong place is extremely dangerous. It's vital to choose your time and place carefully.

Before overtaking you must be certain you can return to your side of the road safely without getting in the way of

- vehicles coming towards you
- vehicles you're overtaking.

Overtaking a moving vehicle

Don't overtake unless it's necessary. For example, don't rush to get past someone only to turn off that road shortly afterwards. Ask yourself if it's really necessary. If you decide it is, you need to find a suitable place.

You **MUST NOT** overtake where to do so would cause you to break the law. Details are shown in The Highway Code.

In addition, some places are never suitable. For example, **don't** overtake

- if your view ahead is blocked
- if other drivers might not be able to see you
- if there's too little room
- if the road narrows
- if you're approaching a junction
- if there's 'dead ground' – a dip in the road which might hide an oncoming vehicle.

Judging speed and distance

The speed of the vehicle you're overtaking is very important. When you're closing up behind a moving vehicle, it will cover quite a distance before you can actually pass it and probably much more than you think.

It could take you quite a long time to overtake. For example, if you're doing 30 mph (48 km/h), it could take a quarter of a mile (400 metres) just to catch up with a vehicle 200 yards (180 metres) ahead which is travelling at as little as 15 mph (24 km/h).

On the other hand, if you're travelling at 55 mph (88.5 km/h) and an oncoming vehicle is doing the same, both vehicles are actually approaching each other at 110 mph (177 km/h) or 50 metres per second.

Overtaking takes time. The smaller the difference between your speed and the speed of the vehicle you're overtaking, the longer the stretch of clear road you'll need.

Defensive driving

Never accelerate when someone is overtaking you. Be prepared to ease off, if necessary, to help them pass you.

> **Remember,** if in doubt, don't overtake. Overtaking often takes longer than you think, especially if you are overtaking a large vehicle.

Overtaking large vehicles

If you are considering overtaking, you need to keep well back to ensure that you

- get the best view of the road ahead
- allow the driver of the large vehicle to see you in their mirrors. Remember, if you can't see their mirrors, they can't see you. Be especially aware that left-hand drive lorries have different blind spots to right-hand drive vehicles.

Leave a good space while waiting to overtake. If another car fills the gap, drop back again.

If you're thinking of overtaking, note whether the vehicle you intend to overtake is loaded or unloaded. The speed of large vehicles varies greatly when they're going up and down hills. A loaded vehicle might crawl slowly uphill and then pick up speed surprisingly quickly on the downhill run. Always remember these possible changes in speed when you're thinking of overtaking. Avoid driving alongside a large vehicle; you may be in its blind spot and the driver may not be able to see you.

Overtaking slow-moving vehicles

There are several types of slow-moving vehicle which you may encounter on the roads. These include farm machinery, tractors, roadworks vehicles, refuse collection vehicles, etc. Most will have flashing amber beacons.

Tractors and farm machinery will often pull in to the left when it is safe, or if there is space to do so, to let a queue of traffic pass. However, they are not always able to do so.

It can be frustrating to be travelling behind a slow-moving vehicle, but be patient. Wait until the road ahead is completely clear of oncoming traffic and you are sure it is both safe and legal to overtake. Remember also that there may be workers in the road, for example, around roadworks vehicles or refuse collection trucks.

Don't overtake on the approach to bends, before the brow of a hill or where there are dips in the road ahead which could hide an oncoming vehicle. In rural areas, there may also be hidden entrances to farm properties from which vehicles may suddenly emerge.

Only overtake if your view of the road ahead is completely clear and unobstructed, and you are sure there's no oncoming traffic. Also check behind, to make sure no other vehicle is trying to overtake at the same time.

Leave plenty of room when overtaking and allow plenty of time for your manoeuvre. Some vehicles, especially those towing farm machinery, may be wider or longer than expected.

Overtaking on a hill

Uphill Give yourself time and room to return to your side of the road well before the brow of the hill. Your zone of vision will get shorter as you approach the brow of the hill. Don't forget that oncoming vehicles will be travelling faster and could be on top of you very quickly.

Downhill It's more difficult to slow down when going downhill. If you overtake going

downhill, you may find yourself travelling faster than you intended. Be careful not to lose control of your vehicle.

Overtaking on long hills On some long hills, double white lines divide the road so that there are two lanes for traffic going uphill, but only one downhill.

If the line is broken on the downhill side, this means you can overtake going downhill if it's safe to do so.

Overtaking on three-lane roads

Some roads are divided into three lanes, where the middle lane can be used for overtaking in either direction. These roads can be particularly dangerous. Before overtaking, you must make sure the road is clear far enough ahead. If in doubt, **wait**.

Some three-lane roads have double white lines marked on the road to allow vehicles travelling uphill to overtake.

Before overtaking

Many danger spots are marked with double white lines along the road. Look out for arrows warning you to move over to the left as you are approaching these areas.

Junction signs and hatch markings in the middle of the road are warnings not to overtake. Be ready to hold back in case traffic is waiting to turn right or slowing to turn left.

Watch the vehicle in front Before overtaking, decide what the driver in front is likely to do by watching both them and the road ahead for a while. They might

- decide to overtake
- continue to drive at the speed of the vehicle ahead of them
- intend to turn off soon
- have seen something ahead which you haven't.

Vehicles turning right Research has shown that most overtaking incidents are caused by the overtaking driver hitting a vehicle which is turning right. To avoid this type of collision you should

- consciously check the indicators of the vehicle you are about to overtake
- assume that a vehicle that is slowing down is about to turn.

Following through Never automatically follow an overtaking vehicle without being able to see for yourself that the way is clear. The vehicle in front obscures your view and hides you from the view of oncoming traffic.

Always make your own decisions about overtaking based not only on what **you** see but also on what **you** know.

Be patient. If in doubt, hold back. There might not be enough time for both of you to overtake at once.

Defensive driving

Keep well back from any vehicle which is too close to the vehicle in front and swinging in and out. Be patient, in case they do something hasty.

Steps to overtaking

To overtake, you might have to use some or all of these steps several times before the right moment arrives. For example, if someone overtakes you just as you're about to overtake you'll need to start all over again.

Use the MSM/PSL routine

M – Mirror Check your mirrors to assess the situation behind and look well ahead.

S – Signal Give a signal if it will help

- drivers behind
- the driver you are overtaking
- drivers coming towards you.

M – Manoeuvre Use the PSL routine

P – Position Be near enough to the vehicle ahead to overtake smoothly when you're ready, but not so close that you can't get a good view of the road ahead.

S – Speed Be fast enough to keep up with the vehicle in front and with enough reserve power to pass it briskly.

You might need to change down to get extra acceleration when you're ready to start overtaking.

L – Look Assess the whole situation

- the state of the road
- what the driver ahead is doing or might be about to do
- any hazards
- the speed and position of oncoming vehicles
- the speed difference between you and oncoming vehicles.

Make a final check in front and behind. Check especially for motorcyclists as they may be approaching quickly and could have been hidden from view previously. Be aware of, and check, any blind spots by taking a quick sideways glance if necessary before deciding to pull out to overtake. If it's safe, pull out on a smooth easy line, then

- overtake as quickly as you can
- move back to the left again on a smooth, easy line, but avoid cutting in.

Never begin to overtake if another vehicle is overtaking you or is about to do so. Overtake only when you are sure it's safe to do so.

Allow plenty of room When overtaking cyclists, motorcyclists or horse riders, give them plenty of room – move out as far as you would if you were overtaking a car. Never attempt to overtake them just before you turn left or if you would have to stop or slow down soon after.

If they look over their shoulder it could mean that they intend to pull out, turn right or change direction so give them time and space to do this.

Overtaking on the left

You should never overtake on the left unless

- the vehicle in front is signalling to turn right, and you can safely overtake on the left. Take care if there is a road to the left; oncoming traffic turning right into it may be hidden by the vehicle you're overtaking
- traffic is moving slowly in queues, and vehicles in the lane on your right are moving more slowly than you are.

Passing on the left

In addition, you can go past on the inside of slower traffic when

- you're in a one-way street (but **not** a dual carriageway) where vehicles are allowed to pass on either side
- you're in the correct lane to turn left at a junction.

Overtaking on dual carriageways

Overtake only if you're sure you can do so safely.

You should normally stay in the left-hand lane and only use the right-hand lane for overtaking or turning right. If you use the right-hand lane for overtaking, you should move back to the left-hand lane as soon as it is safe to do so.

Plan well ahead and use the appropriate parts of the MSM/PSL routine. For example

M – Mirrors Use your mirrors to assess the speed and position of following traffic. On a high-speed dual carriageway, start the checks in plenty of time.

S – Signal Give a signal if it will help the driver you're overtaking and other drivers further ahead. Be aware that on a dual carriageway, a vehicle in the right-hand lane signalling right may be slowing to turn right through the central reservation.

P – Position Keep well back from the vehicle you're going to overtake to give you a good view of the road ahead.

S – Speed Make sure you have enough speed in reserve to overtake briskly without breaking any speed limits.

L – Look Look ahead and assess

- the condition of the road
- what the vehicle ahead is doing
- any hazards.

Check behind again to reassess the situation; check especially for motorcyclists as they can approach very quickly. Don't begin to overtake if another vehicle is about to overtake you.

If it is safe, change lanes on a smooth easy line and overtake briskly. Make sure you're well clear of the vehicle you've overtaken before moving back to the left. Don't cut in.

Overtaking on the left You must not overtake on the left unless traffic is moving slowly in queues, and the queue on your right is moving more slowly than you.

Never move to a lane on your left to overtake.

Defensive driving

Be considerate. Don't block vehicles travelling faster than you which might want to overtake, even if they are breaking the speed limit.

Obstructions

The secret of dealing with any obstruction lies in looking and planning well ahead, combined with early and sensible use of the MSM/PSL routine.

The decision to wait or go on will depend on

- the type and width of road
- whether the obstruction is on
  - your side of the road
  - the other side of the road
  - both sides of the road
- whether there is approaching traffic
- the room available.

As a general rule, if the obstruction is on your side of the road, approaching traffic will have priority.

Don't assume that you have priority if the obstruction is on the other side of the road. Always be prepared to give way.

Procedure

Look well ahead to identify the obstruction in good time before using the routine.

M – Check your mirrors to assess the speed and position of following traffic.

S – Signal if necessary.

P – Decide on your position. Avoid keeping too far in to the left so that you have to steer past the obstruction at the last minute; a gradual change of course is required. If you have to stop and wait, keep well back from the obstruction in a position that not only keeps your zone of vision open but also doesn't impede the approaching traffic.

S – Adjust your speed as necessary. This will depend on the situation, but aim to regulate your speed to take a smooth and steady course without stopping.

L – Finally, look and assess the situation before you decide whether it's

- necessary to wait
- safe to proceed.

Obstructions on hills

These need special care. Give yourself an extra safety margin and brake earlier than normal, when necessary.

If you're travelling downhill and the obstruction is on the other side of the road, don't take your priority for granted. If it's safe, be prepared to let other traffic coming uphill, especially heavy vehicles, have a clear run. Your consideration will be appreciated.

Roadworks

These areas obviously make the usable width of road much narrower, and can either be controlled by temporary traffic lights or workers with 'stop/go' boards.

Obey all lights and signs and slow down, especially where there are workers who may be walking around on the road nearby.

More information on negotiating roadworks areas and contraflow systems can be found in section 11.

Defensive driving

Don't follow through behind the vehicle in front without being able to see for yourself that the way is clear ahead.

Keep a safe distance from the obstruction and the approaching traffic. Where space is limited, reduce speed and take extra care. The smaller the gap, the lower your speed needs to be.

Pedestrian crossings

People on foot have certain rights of way at pedestrian crossings, but are safe only if drivers follow the rules and do the right thing.

The driver and crossings

Some rules and advice apply to all types of crossing.

- You must not park
  - on a crossing; this blocks the way for pedestrians
  - within the area marked by zigzag lines; this obstructs both the pedestrian's view of approaching vehicles and an approaching driver's view of the crossing.
- You must not overtake
  - the moving vehicle nearest to a crossing
  - the leading vehicle which has stopped to give way to a pedestrian.
- Even if there are no zigzag lines, never overtake just before a crossing.
- Give yourself more time to stop if the road is wet or icy.
- Keep crossings clear when queuing in traffic, stopping before the crossing if you can see that you won't be able to clear it.

- You should take extra care where the view of either side of a crossing is blocked by queuing traffic. Pedestrians may be crossing between these vehicles, incorrectly thinking they have stopped to allow pedestrians to cross.
- Always allow pedestrians plenty of time to cross, especially if they are older or disabled, and do not harass them by revving your engine or edging forward.
- Watch out for pedestrians who try to rush across at the last minute.

Also on all signal controlled crossings you should

- give way to anyone still on the crossing even if the signal for vehicles has changed to green
- proceed with extreme caution if the signals are not working.

In addition there are extra rules for different types of crossing.

Zebra crossings

Zebra crossings are identified by flashing yellow beacons on both sides of the road and black and white stripes on the crossing. They also have white zigzag markings on both sides of the crossing and a give way line about a metre from the crossing, which marks the place for drivers to stop when necessary. Where pedestrians are waiting on the pavement at a zebra crossing and obviously want to cross, slow down and stop to let them cross.

You should stop if you can do so safely, especially

- if anyone is waiting on the pavement with a pram or pushchair
- if children or the elderly are hesitating to cross because of heavy traffic.

Be aware also of pedestrians approaching the crossing who may suddenly start to move onto the crossing, and be ready to stop for them.

You must give way to anyone who

- is already crossing
- has stepped onto the crossing.

Don't wave people across. There could be another vehicle coming in the other direction and you can't be sure what other drivers might do.

Remember, some zebra crossings are divided by a central island. Each half is a separate crossing.

Pelican crossings

These are light-controlled crossings where the pedestrian uses push-button controls to control the traffic. They have no red and amber phase before the green. Instead they have a flashing amber light, which means you must give way to pedestrians on the crossing but if it's clear you can go on.

The crossing area is shown by studs and a 'stop' line marks the place for drivers to stop when it is necessary.

Pelican crossings may be

- **straight** A pelican crossing which goes straight across the road is one crossing, even if there is a central refuge. You must wait for people coming from the other side of the refuge
- **staggered** If the crossings on each side of the central refuge are not in line, the crossings are separate.

Puffin crossings

These are user-friendly, 'intelligent' crossings where electronic devices automatically detect when pedestrians are on the crossing and delay the green light until the pedestrians have reached a position of safety.

Unnecessary delays in traffic flow are reduced because electronic devices automatically detect when pedestrians are on the crossing.

- If the pedestrians cross quickly, the pedestrian phase is shortened.
- If the pedestrians have crossed the road before the phase starts, it will automatically be cancelled.

The light sequence at these crossings is the same as at traffic lights (see page 115).

Toucan crossings

These are shared by pedestrians and cyclists. Cyclists are permitted to cycle across.

The light sequence at these crossings is the same as at traffic lights.

Equestrian crossings

These are for horse riders and may be alongside those for pedestrians and cyclists. They have wider crossing areas, pavement barriers and either one or two sets of controls, one being set at a higher position.

School-crossing patrols

Watch out for these patrols and obey their signals.

At particularly dangerous locations, two amber lights flashing alternately give advance warning of the crossing point.

Don't overtake when you're approaching a school crossing and **always** keep your speed down so you're ready to slow down or stop, if necessary.

Defensive driving

Always look well ahead to identify pedestrian crossings early. Look for the flashing yellow beacons, traffic lights, zigzag markings, etc. Use the MSM routine and keep your speed down.

Brake lights cannot be seen by the pedestrians at the crossings or oncoming traffic, so if you're the leading vehicle you should consider using an arm signal when you're slowing or stopping.

Driving on hills

You need to understand how driving uphill and downhill can affect your control of the vehicle.

- Going uphill, your engine has to use more power to pull the vehicle up the hill.

- Going downhill, your engine is helped by the weight of the vehicle.

In each case, the effect on the controls is different from driving on the level.

Going uphill

When going uphill

- you'll find it more difficult to maintain or increase speed. The engine has to work harder to make the vehicle go faster

- your brakes will slow the vehicle down quicker

- you might need to change to a lower gear to maintain your speed. If you release the accelerator or declutch (push the clutch pedal down), your speed will drop more quickly than it would on the level. Changing to a lower gear should be done without hesitation, so you don't lose too much speed

- remember to apply the parking brake before you release the footbrake when stopping, otherwise you might roll back.

Look for signs You'll see warning signs telling you how steep the upward slope is. The figures measure the gradient in percentage terms: 25% (1:4) means for every four feet along (horizontal) the road rises one foot (vertical).

The higher the percentage or the lower the second figure, the steeper the hill.

You may see another rectangular sign telling you the length of the hill and further information.

Watch out for slow-moving, heavy vehicles.

153

Assess the hill If the hill is very steep, think ahead and consider changing to a lower gear. If you do need to change gear, make sure you do so in good time.

Don't stay in high gear to try to keep your speed up. Your vehicle will climb better in a low gear.

> **Remember,** turning and climbing at the same time is hard work for the engine. If the road bends sharply, you'll find it safer and easier on the engine to change down before the bend.

Separation distance Keep well back from the vehicle ahead.

- If you don't hold back and the vehicle ahead suddenly slows or stops, you may have to brake harshly.
- Holding back may enable you to keep going gently while the vehicle ahead regains speed. This is not only safer, but it can also help to avoid congestion.

Overtaking It's sometimes more difficult to overtake uphill. You'll find oncoming traffic is travelling at a greater speed and is less able to slow down or stop quickly if necessary.

On a dual carriageway, overtaking is easier because there's no danger from oncoming traffic. Here you should keep a lookout for others following behind you who can overtake with ease. Don't block their progress.

Going downhill

When going downhill

- you'll find it more difficult to slow down and the brakes have less effect
- it's harder for the engine to hold the vehicle back. In higher gears it won't do so at all
- the vehicle runs faster if you declutch (clutch coasting)
- avoid braking on a bend
- get into a lower gear in good time, particularly if there's a bend ahead
- use the correct combination of lower gear and careful use of the footbrake to keep control of your speed.

Note
Avoid the danger of increasing speed caused by coasting, either out of gear or with the clutch pedal depressed.

Look for signs The steep hill (downwards) warning sign will give you the gradient of the downward slope.

You might also see a rectangular sign advising use of a low gear. Always obey these signs. The steeper the hill, the lower the gear.

Assess the hill Use the sign to help you think ahead. If the route is unfamiliar, or a bend limits your view of the road, change down before you begin to descend. Change smoothly and without hesitation.

Separation distance Always keep the correct separation distance from the vehicle ahead.

If you don't hold back and the vehicle ahead suddenly slows down or stops, you'll have to brake very hard. The driver behind will get very little warning.

If you hold back, you'll have time to reduce your speed more gently.

Adjust your speed On steep hills, you'll normally need to reduce speed. Change down to a lower gear to give yourself more braking power and control.

By selecting a lower gear, you should be able to avoid using your brakes too much. Excessive braking on hills can result in 'brake fade' and loss of control. Brake fade is a loss of braking power caused by the heat generated by continuous use of the brakes.

Look for 'escape lanes' which are designed to stop runaway vehicles.

Overtaking It's only safe to overtake downhill where

- there are no bends or junctions
- your view of the road ahead is clear.

You should be absolutely **certain** that you can overtake without causing oncoming traffic to slow down or change course.

Remember that the vehicle you're overtaking may build up speed, and you'll find it more difficult to slow down for oncoming traffic. They'll find it more difficult to get out of your way.

Look out for road markings, especially continuous white lines along the centre of the road.

155

Hills in towns

Take particular care in towns where older people and the very young are crossing at junctions on hills.

Traffic speeds are generally lower and vehicles closer together. As a result your zone of vision will often be that much poorer.

Pay attention to the type of vehicle ahead of you and your distance from that vehicle.

You'll find traffic lights, school-crossing patrols and pedestrian crossings are sometimes situated on a hill. Where this is the case it adds to the importance of

- using your mirrors
- recognising the sort of vehicle ahead
- leaving a suitable gap when you stop
- using your parking brake effectively
- making sure you're in the right gear for the situation.

You'll be doing these things in towns already, but on hills they have additional importance.

Tunnels

When approaching a tunnel

- switch on your dipped headlights
- do not wear sunglasses
- observe the road signs and signals
- keep an appropriate distance from the vehicle in front
- switch on your radio and tune in to the indicated frequency.

Many tunnels, particularly the longer ones in Europe, are equipped with radio transmitters so that drivers can be warned of any incidents, congestion or roadworks.

When driving through a tunnel, your visibility will be suddenly reduced. Be prepared for this change in conditions and make sure that you drive so that you can stop within the distance you can see to be clear, increasing the distance between you and the car in front if necessary.

If the tunnel is congested

- switch on your warning lights
- keep your distance, even if you are moving slowly. If you have to stop, leave at least a five-metre gap between you and the vehicle in front
- if possible, listen out for messages on the radio
- follow any instructions given by tunnel officials or variable message signs.

For action to take in the event of a breakdown or incident, see page 303.

Trams or LRT systems

Light rapid transit (LRT) systems, or 'Metros', are being introduced in many large towns and cities to provide a more efficient and environmentally friendly form of public transport.

Tram systems are common throughout Europe and there are plans to introduce them to more cities in the UK.

Trams may operate completely separately from other traffic or they may run on roads open to other traffic. As they run on rails, they are fixed in the route they follow and cannot manoeuvre around other road users. The vehicles may run singly or as multiple units, and may be up to 60 metres (about 200 feet) long. Remember that trams are silent, move quickly and can't steer to avoid you.

The area occupied by a tram is marked by paving or markings on the road surface. This 'swept path' must always be kept clear. Anticipate well ahead and never stop on or across the tracks or markings.

Take extra care when you first encounter trams until you're accustomed to dealing with the different traffic system.

Crossing points

Deal with these in exactly the same way as normal railway crossings.

Also bear in mind the speed and silent approach of trams.

Reserved areas

Drivers must not enter 'reserved areas' for the trams, which are marked with white line markings, a different type of surface, or both.

The reserved areas are usually one-way, but may sometimes be two-way.

Hazards

The steel rails can be slippery whether it's wet or dry. Try to avoid driving on the rails and take extra care when braking or turning on them, to avoid the risk of skidding.

Take care also where

- the tracks run close to the kerb to pick up or set down passengers
- the lines move from one side of the road to the other.

Tram stops

Where a tram stops at a platform, either in the middle or at the side of the road, follow the route shown by road signs and markings. If there is no passing lane signed, wait behind the tram until it moves off.

At stops without platforms, do not drive between a tram and the left-hand kerb when a tram has stopped to pick up or set down passengers.

Warning signs and signals

Obey all warning signs or signals controlling traffic. Where there are no signals, always give way to trams.

Diamond-shaped signs or white light signals give instructions to tram drivers only.

Do

- watch out for additional pedestrian crossings where passengers will be getting on and off the trams. You must stop for them
- make allowance for other road users who may not be familiar with tram systems
- be especially aware of the problems of cyclists, motorcyclists and moped riders. Their narrow tyres can put them at risk when they come into contact with the rails.

Don't

- try to race a tram where there isn't enough road space for both vehicles side by side; remember the end of the vehicle swings out on bends
- overtake at tram stops
- drive between platforms at tramway stations. Follow the direction signs
- park so that your vehicle obstructs the trams or would force other drivers to do so. Remember that a tram can't steer round an obstruction.

159

section **eight**

JUNCTIONS

This section covers

- Approaching a junction
- The junction routine
- Turning
- Emerging
- Lanes at junctions
- Types of junction
- Junctions on hills
- Junctions on dual carriageways
- Roundabouts

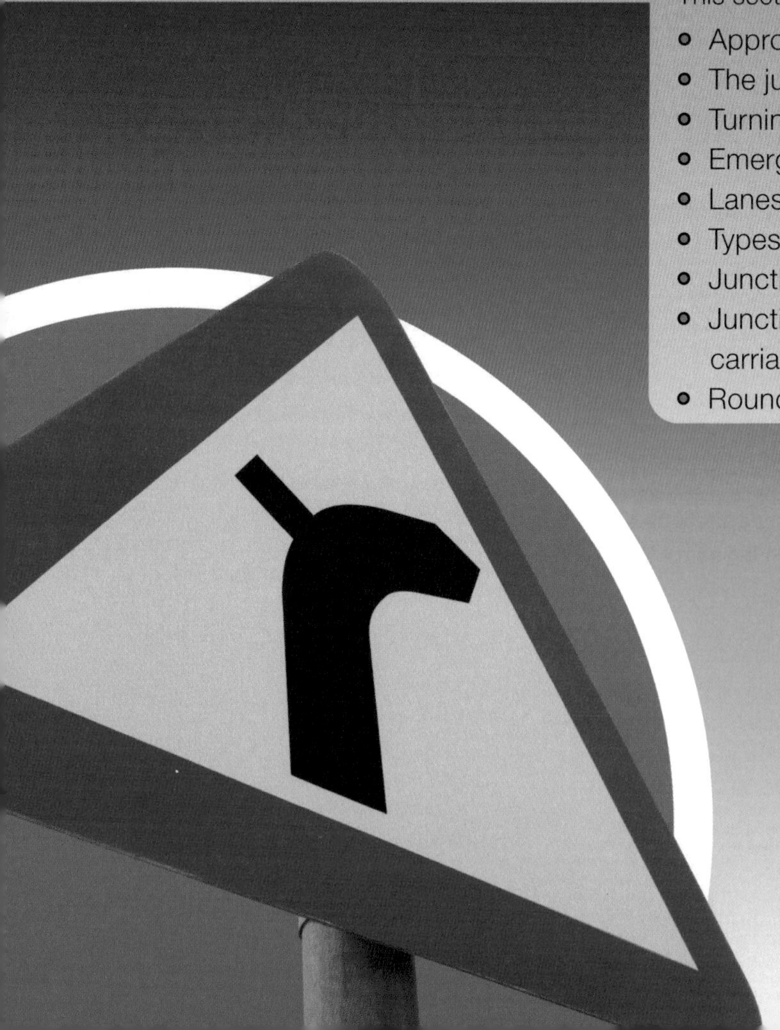

Approaching a junction

A junction is a point where two or more roads meet. Junctions are hazards where there is a greater risk of an incident occurring. Treat them with great care, no matter how easy they look.

Advance information

Look for information about the junction ahead, and the level of difficulty, such as

- the type of junction
- the amount of traffic
- warning signs
- road markings
- direction signs
- 'give way' and 'stop' signs
- traffic lights
- a break in the line of buildings
- changes in road surface.

Options at junctions

How you approach a junction depends on what you intend to do. You might want to

- cross a major road going ahead
- join a major road by turning right or left
- leave a major road by turning right or left into a minor road
- stay on a major road and pass the junction.

A major road is one with priority over another at a junction.

Priority

Usually, road signs and markings indicate priority. Where no priority is shown at a junction, take extra care.

The junction routine

At every junction use the MSM/PSL routine.

M – Check in your mirrors to assess the speed and position of vehicles behind.

S – Signal clearly and in good time.

M – Manoeuvre – use PSL.

P – Position your vehicle correctly and in good time. Early positioning lets other road users know what you are going to do.

S – Adjust your speed as necessary.

L – Look for other traffic when you reach a point from which you can see.

- Assess the situation.

- Decide to go or wait.

- Act accordingly.

If the road has lane markings

Use the correct lane for the direction you intend to take, and move into it as soon as you can.

Defensive driving

Take extra care if your path crosses or joins the path of other road users.

Check your mirrors, particularly for cyclists and motorcyclists, when turning at junctions. They can approach very quickly from behind and are less easy to see than a larger vehicle.

Turning

Turning left

Use the MSM/PSL routine on approach.

Road position Your road position should be well to the left, with the nearside of your vehicle about 1 metre (3 feet) from the kerb.

Speed on approach Left turns into minor roads are often sharper than right turns.

Make sure you

- slow down sufficiently
- select the correct gear

or you could swing wide of the corner and finish up on the wrong side of the road.

Other vehicles Watch out for vehicles

- stopping to park, or parked, just before a left-hand junction
- parked just around the corner
- approaching in the side road.

Pedestrians and cyclists

You should

- give way to pedestrians already crossing when you turn – they have priority
- keep a special lookout for cyclists coming up on your left
- take special care when crossing a cycle track, bus or cycle lane
- hold back and allow a cyclist to clear the junction before you turn, don't overtake and then cut in on them.

Avoid steering too early or too sharply; a rear wheel might mount the kerb.

After the turn

- If it's safe to do so, speed up as you leave the junction.
- Check in your mirrors so you know what's following you on the new road.
- Make sure your signal has cancelled.

Turning right

Use the MSM/PSL routine on approach.

Road position

- Move into position early when turning right. It helps other drivers.

- Position yourself as close to the centre of the road as is safe, so that vehicles can pass on your left if there's room. Take into account any parked vehicles or obstructions on the right-hand side of the road.

- In a one-way street move to the right-hand side of the road when appropriate.

Speed of approach

- Adjust your speed as necessary.

- Approach at a safe speed.

Oncoming traffic

- Watch out for oncoming traffic, especially motorcycles and bicycles which are less easily seen.

- Watch particularly for vehicles overtaking oncoming traffic.

- Stop before you turn if you have any doubt about being able to cross safely.

Emerging vehicles

- Watch for vehicles waiting to emerge from the minor road.

Pedestrians

- Give way to pedestrians already crossing the minor road. They have priority.

Obstructions

- Look carefully for anything that could prevent you entering the minor road safely and leave you exposed on the wrong side of the road, risking a serious incident.

- You **MUST NOT** cross to the other side of the centre line until you are sure you can enter the minor road safely.

Turning

Check your mirrors for overtaking traffic one final time before you turn. Don't

- cut the corner

- accelerate fiercely. Your engine should be just pulling as you turn.

Missed turn

If you miss a turning, don't cause a problem by stopping suddenly. Go past the junction and turn round at the next opportunity.

Emerging

'Emerging' is when a vehicle leaves a minor road to join, cross or turn into a major road.

You'll have to judge the speed and distance of any traffic on the road you intend to join or cross, and only emerge when it's safe to do so. This needs care and sometimes patience as well.

Assess the junction. Check road signs and markings and use the MSM/PSL routine.

'Give way' sign or lines A 'give way' sign and lines across the road means that you must give way to traffic which is already on the road you intend to enter.

If you can emerge without causing drivers or riders on that road to alter speed or course, you can do so without stopping. Otherwise, you must stop.

'Stop' sign You must always stop at a 'stop' sign, no matter what traffic is like on the road you intend to enter.

Move off only when

- you have a clear view
- you're sure it's safe.

Junctions without signs or road markings

Treat these with great care.

Don't assume you have priority at an unmarked junction.

MSM/PSL routine

M – Look in your mirrors to assess what's behind.

S – Signal left or right, as appropriate, in good time.

M – Manoeuvre – use PSL.

P – When turning left, keep well to the left, about 1 metre (3 feet) from the kerb. When turning right, position yourself in good time as close to the centre of the road as is safe. In a one-way street move to the right-hand side of the road.

S – Reduce speed. Be prepared to stop; you must give way to traffic on a major road.

L – Look in all directions at the earliest point from which you can see clearly. Keep looking as you slow down or stop, if necessary, until you're sure it's safe to enter the major road.

Other traffic

Bends and hills could make it more difficult to see traffic coming towards you.

If the vehicle approaching from your right is signalling to turn left into your road, wait until you're sure the vehicle is turning and not just pulling up on the left beyond your road.

Motorcyclists are especially vulnerable at junctions. Look out for them

- coming from behind as you approach the junction
- travelling along the road you are joining, as they can be very difficult to see.

When to go

You have to decide when to wait and when it's safe to go. That decision depends largely on your zone of vision.

Your zone of vision is what you can see from your vehicle. It is determined by

- buildings and hedges
- bends in the road or contours in the land
- moving and parked vehicles
- available light and the weather.

As you approach a junction, your zone of vision on to the other road usually improves. The last few feet are critical.

You can only decide whether to wait or go on when you have put yourself in a position where you can see clearly.

Watch out for cyclists, motorcyclists, powered wheelchairs/mobility scooters and pedestrians as they are not always easy to see.

Sometimes parked vehicles interfere with your zone of vision so that you have to inch carefully forward to see more. If another vehicle or a pedestrian is not in your zone of vision, you're not usually in theirs.

Looking means that you need to assess the situation, decide whether it's safe and act accordingly.

An approaching vehicle, particularly a bus or a lorry, can easily mask another moving vehicle which may be overtaking.

Watch out particularly for motorcyclists when emerging. They can be especially difficult to see, being smaller than other vehicles but approaching just as fast. They can very easily be masked by another vehicle, especially if they are overtaking.

After emerging

- Speed up to a safe speed for the road and conditions as soon as possible.
- Use your mirrors to check the speed and position of traffic behind.
- Make sure your indicator is cancelled.
- Keep a safe distance from the vehicle in front.
- Don't attempt to overtake until you've had time to assess the new road.

When turning right, even though there might be little traffic approaching from the right, don't be tempted to move out and drive down the centre of the road hoping to fit into a gap in the traffic. If the road narrows, or if there are junctions or bollards, you will have nowhere to go.

Defensive driving

When turning left or right into a major road, it takes time to complete the steering manoeuvre safely.

You need to accurately assess the speed of approaching traffic.

If in doubt, wait!

Lanes at junctions

When you approach a junction

- do so in the correct lane for the direction you intend to take; don't switch lanes to gain advantage
- look well ahead and watch for traffic and direction signs
- look out for signals from vehicles about to change lanes
- look out for vehicles suddenly changing lanes without signalling.

Articulated or long vehicles Stay clear of large vehicles at junctions. They need much more room than smaller vehicles and may take up a position that seems incorrect to you.

They often swing out to the right before turning left, and to the left before turning right.

Be ready for them to stop if their way is blocked.

Passing minor roads

Look out for road signs indicating minor roads, even if you're not turning off.

Watch out for emerging vehicles. Their view is often obscured at junctions. A vehicle might pull out in front of you.

If this happens, and you're not sure that the driver has seen you, slow down. Be prepared to stop.

Be tolerant and don't harass the other driver by sounding your horn aggressively or driving too close.

Overtaking

Don't overtake at, or when approaching, a junction. A left-hand signal from the vehicle in front is not an indication for you to pull out and pass.

The road surface

Always watch out for slippery surfaces or loose chippings. Avoid braking while you're turning. Plan ahead and brake before the junction.

Defensive driving

Adjust your overall speed when passing a series of minor roads so you can stop within the distance you can see to be clear.

Types of junction

There are five main types of junction

- T-junctions
- Y-junctions
- staggered junctions
- crossroads
- roundabouts.

Each type of junction can have many variations.

What you intend to do at the junction determines how you approach each type.

T-junctions

This is where a minor road joins a major road.

Normally the road going straight ahead, along the top of the 'T', has priority.

The minor road will either have

- a 'stop' sign and road markings
- a 'give way' sign and road markings
- 'give way' lines only
- no road sign or markings.

If you're emerging from the minor road, follow the procedure on pages 165–167.

Driving on the major road If you want to go straight ahead

- take note of any road signs and markings
- watch out for vehicles emerging to turn left or right
- avoid overtaking any vehicle on the approach to a junction.

Defensive driving

Adjust your overall speed when passing a series of side roads on the left. Watch out for vehicles emerging onto the major road.

Hatch markings On busier roads the major road is often split before and after the junction, with a turn-right filter lane protected by white diagonal hatch markings (or chevrons) surrounded by a broken or unbroken white line.

Join and leave the major road at these junctions exactly as you would a dual carriageway.

Areas of hatch markings painted on the road

- separate streams of traffic
- protect traffic waiting to turn right.

Where the boundary line is solid, do not enter except in an emergency.

Where the boundary line is broken, you should not drive on these markings unless you can see it's safe to do so.

Junctions on bends Look well ahead for traffic signs and road markings which indicate priority.

These junctions need extra care, especially when turning right from a major road which bends to the left, because

- your field of vision might be limited
- traffic might be approaching at speed from your left
- you'll need time to manoeuvre safely.

Your position before you turn must not endanger either oncoming traffic or yourself.

Wait until there's a gap in the traffic and act positively.

Unmarked junctions Never assume priority over another road if there are no road signs or markings. What's obvious to you might not be obvious to drivers on the other road.

Watch carefully for vehicles

- approaching the junction on the other road
- waiting at the junction
- emerging from the junction to join or cross your path.

Any vehicle crossing

- might assume priority and expect you to give way
- might not assume priority, but might have misjudged your speed or not seen you.

Such a vehicle creates a hazard. You should respond in a safe and sensible manner. Anticipate and adjust your speed accordingly to avoid a collision.

Y-junctions

Y-junctions can be deceptive because they often call for little change in direction.

Normally the road going straight ahead has priority and joining roads have either 'give way' or 'stop' signs. However, there are many exceptions. Watch out for oncoming vehicles positioned incorrectly. The drivers might have misjudged the junction.

Going straight ahead on the major road

- Look well ahead for road signs and markings.
- Watch out for vehicles emerging to turn left or right.
- You must not overtake when approaching any junction.

Emerging from a minor road If the angle of approach to the major road is very sharp and from the right, the view to your left might be restricted.

If you position your vehicle towards the major road at a right angle as you approach the 'stop' or 'give way' lines, you will improve your view.

This is especially important if your vehicle has no rear side windows – a van, for example.

Staggered junctions

These are junctions where roads join from both the right and the left so that the path from one side road to the other will be staggered.

Driving on the major road Look well ahead for road signs and markings. Use the MSM/PSL routine.

Adjust your speed as necessary and prepare to stop, especially if your view is limited or if another driver's view of you might be limited.

Watch for vehicles

- emerging from either minor road to turn left or right
- on the major road turning into a minor road on the left or right
- driving across the main road from one minor road into the other.

Emerging When emerging from a minor road to cross the major road and enter the other minor road, watch out for traffic approaching from both directions.

Turning left then right When it's safe to emerge, drive to the centre of the major road opposite the minor road you intend to enter and check the traffic again before entering the minor road.

If you're travelling only a short distance from one minor road to another one almost opposite, take extra care and make sure the gap in traffic is wide enough in both directions.

Look, assess, then decide. Either go if it's safe, or wait.

Crossroads

Crossroads are often road traffic incident black spots, so take extra care, especially on roads carrying fast-moving traffic. Incidents often involve vehicles turning right.

The procedure when turning at crossroads is much the same as at any other junction.

You'll need to assess the crossroads on approach, so look well ahead and check for road signs and markings which might indicate priority.

Driving on the major road

- Watch for road signs and markings.

- Watch for emerging traffic. Be especially careful of vehicles trying to cut across, using gaps in the traffic. They may misjudge your speed.

- Adjust your speed approaching crossroads.

Turning right Getting your position and speed correct is vital. Look out for traffic on the road you're joining, as well as on the road you're leaving.

Check your mirrors before starting to turn, especially if you've had to wait.

Turning right when an oncoming vehicle is also turning right

When two vehicles approaching from opposite directions both want to turn right, there are two methods that can be used. Either method is acceptable, but it will usually be determined by

- the layout of the crossroads
- what course the other driver decides to take
- road markings.

Turning offside to offside

The advantage of this method is that both can see oncoming traffic.

In congested traffic conditions, leave a space for approaching traffic to turn right.

Turning nearside to nearside

This method is less safe because the view of oncoming vehicles is not clear. Watch out for oncoming traffic hidden by larger vehicles. Motorcyclists and cyclists are particularly vulnerable as they would be hidden by any type of vehicle.

Be ready to stop for oncoming vehicles.

Police control or road markings sometimes make this method compulsory.

Defensive driving

Try to get eye contact with the driver of the approaching vehicle to determine which course is best. Your speed should allow you to stop if the other driver cuts across your path.

Approaching on a minor road If you approach the crossroads on one of the minor roads and want to turn onto the major road, as long as the minor road opposite is clear, you should treat it as if you are emerging from a T-junction.

If you want to turn onto the major road, and another vehicle is approaching the crossroads from the minor road opposite, then

- if you are turning left or going straight on, you should proceed with extra caution and make sure no vehicle from the opposite direction is going to cross your path

- if you are turning right and the other vehicle is going ahead or turning left, you should normally wait for the other vehicle to clear the junction before you make your turn, because you would otherwise be cutting across their path

- if you are turning right and the other vehicle is turning right, you should try to make eye contact with the other driver to establish who should proceed as neither of you have priority.

Unmarked crossroads

Treat unmarked crossroads with extreme caution since neither road has priority. Never assume you have priority if there are no signs or markings.

Drivers approaching on other roads might also assume they have priority, and an incident could result.

Proceed only when you're sure it's safe to do so.

Remember **LADA** – you must **L**ook, **A**ssess and **D**ecide, before you **A**ct.

Take extra care when your view is restricted (by vehicles, walls, hedges, etc).

Junctions on hills

You may need to take extra care when negotiating junctions on hills.

Downhill junctions

- Getting into the correct position at a safe speed is essential when you're approaching a downhill junction.

- Make early use of mirrors, signals, brakes, gears and steering to get into position.

- Use the junction routine MSM/PSL. Choose a point with a good all-round view before you look, assess, and decide to go or wait if necessary.

- Oncoming traffic will be climbing more slowly. If you need to cross its path, don't move from your 'look' position until your way is clear.

- Don't block oncoming traffic and cause a hold-up.

Uphill junctions

Judge your position and speed accurately when climbing towards a junction. Your position is particularly important to drivers following you.

- If you intend to turn right, keep as close to the centre as is safe.

- If you stop in the wrong position you could force drivers behind to stop unnecessarily.

Joining a hill at a junction

It is relatively easy to judge the speed of vehicles coming uphill.

Turning left at a T-junction into a road where you'll be driving uphill is reasonably easy. You don't have to cross traffic and it's easier to judge the flow of traffic coming uphill.

Turning right at a T-junction into a road where you'll be driving uphill is more difficult. You have to cross fast-moving traffic coming downhill. At the same time, you have to fit into the flow of traffic coming up from the left without blocking them.

Junctions on dual carriageways

On a dual carriageway, lanes in one direction are separated from lanes in the other direction by a central reservation. There may be a safety barrier along this central reservation.

Some dual carriageways are very similar to motorways, with slip roads to join and leave. However, motorway regulations do not apply and you may come across slow-moving traffic such as cyclists or farm tractors.

Emerging from a side road

To turn left If there's no slip road, emerge as you would to turn left into a major road (see page 163). If there is a slip road, emerge as you would to join a motorway (see section 11).

- Adjust your speed to that of traffic on the main carriageway.

- Look for a gap in traffic and move into the left-hand lane.

- A quick sideways glance might be necessary to check the position of other vehicles (but see page 66).

- Stay in the left-hand lane until you get used to the speed of the traffic in the other lanes.

- Don't emerge unless you are sure you won't cause traffic to alter speed or course.

To turn right You need to cross the first carriageway before you can join the carriageway you want.

- Assess whether the central reservation is deep enough to protect the full length of your vehicle.

- If the central reservation is deep enough, cross the first carriageway when it is safe and then wait for a gap in the traffic on the second carriageway.

- If the central reservation can't contain the length of your vehicle, you must not begin to cross until the dual carriageway is clear in both directions.

- Don't emerge unless you're sure you won't cause traffic on the major road to alter speed or course. This is particularly important if you're driving a longer vehicle, or towing a caravan or trailer.

Defensive driving

Watch out particularly for motorcyclists at these junctions. They can be difficult to see due to their narrow profile and they may be travelling fast on the dual carriageway. They may also be hidden behind slower-moving traffic which they are overtaking.

After you join the carriageway

- Check your mirrors.
- Cancel any indicator signal.
- Drive in the left-hand lane.
- Accelerate as soon as you can to a suitable and safe speed for the new road.
- Don't overtake until you are used to the conditions on the new road.

Always look for signs which might indicate a higher speed limit on the dual carriageway. Allow for this when you assess the speed of oncoming traffic.

Turning left from a dual carriageway

If there is no slip road, use the same procedure you would for turning left into a side road.

- Use the MSM/PSL routine and get into the left-hand lane in plenty of time.
- Signal left much earlier than you would on ordinary roads because of the higher speeds involved.
- Reduce speed in good time.

If there is a slip road on the left, use the same procedure as you would for leaving a motorway (see page 236).

Turning right from a dual carriageway

The central reservation sometimes has gaps for turning right. Watch out for special approach lanes.

- Use the MSM/PSL routine.
- Signal right and move into the right-hand lane much earlier than you would on normal roads because of the higher speeds often involved.
- Observe any lane markings.
- Reduce speed in good time.

Take particular care when turning. You might have to cross the path of fast oncoming traffic in two or more lanes. If in doubt, wait.

Roundabouts

Roundabouts allow traffic from different roads to merge or cross without necessarily stopping.

Priority Before you enter a roundabout, you normally give way to any traffic approaching from your immediate right. However, you should keep moving if the way is clear.

In a few cases, traffic on the roundabout has to give way to traffic entering. Look out for 'give way' signs and road markings on the roundabout.

Some roundabouts have traffic lights (sometimes part-time) which determine priority.

Always use the MSM/PSL routine on approach.

Approaching a roundabout

Always look well ahead for the advance warning sign. Especially at large or complex roundabouts this will give you a clear picture of the layout of the roundabout, together with route directions.

The sign will enable you to select the most suitable lane in which to approach the roundabout.

Watch out also for advance warnings of appropriate traffic lanes at the roundabout. These are often backed up by road markings, which usually include route numbers.

- Get into the correct lane in good time.
- Don't straddle lanes.
- Never change lanes at the last moment.

Where possible, it's a good idea to look across the roundabout and identify the exit you're aiming to take. This will help you to plan the safest course on the roundabout itself.

Procedure

Adopt the following procedures unless road signs or markings indicate otherwise.

Going left

- Indicate left as you approach.
- Approach in the left-hand lane.
- Keep to that lane on the roundabout.
- Maintain a left turn signal through the roundabout.

Going ahead

- No signal is necessary on approach.
- Approach in the left-hand lane. If you can't use the left-hand lane because, for example, it's blocked, use the next lane to it.

- Keep to the selected lane on the roundabout.
- Check your mirrors, especially the nearside exterior mirror, if one is fitted.
- Indicate left after you have passed the exit just before the one you intend to take.

Going right or full-circle

- Indicate right as you approach.
- Approach in the right-hand lane.
- Keep to that lane and maintain the signal on the roundabout.
- Check your mirrors, especially the nearside exterior mirror, if one is fitted.
- Indicate left after you have passed the exit just before the one you intend to take.

More than three lanes Where there are more than three lanes at the approach to the roundabout, use the most appropriate lane on approach and through the roundabout, unless road signs or markings tell you otherwise.

> **Remember,** when using the right-hand lane to go ahead or turn right, be aware of traffic in the lane to your left.

Defensive driving

Always keep an eye on the vehicle in front as you're about to enter the roundabout.

Don't assume that the driver will keep going, as they may stop while you're still looking to the right. Many rear-end collisions happen this way. Make sure the vehicle has actually moved away.

Always check the vehicle in front before moving off.

Hazards Roundabouts can be particularly hazardous areas. While negotiating the roundabout you should be especially aware of

- pedestrians: in many areas, zebra crossings are located near the entrances and exits to roundabouts. Even if there are no formal crossings, pedestrians may attempt to cross the road at these junctions. Always be aware of pedestrians who may be trying to cross the road

- cyclists and horse riders: they often keep to the outside of the roundabout even when intending to turn right. Take extra care and allow them plenty of room

- motorcyclists and cyclists: it is often difficult to see them on a roundabout

- long vehicles: because of their length, they might take a different course or straddle lanes as they approach the roundabout and as they go round it. Watch out for their signals and allow for the rear of their vehicle cutting in

- all vehicles: be prepared for vehicles to cross your path to leave at the next exit. Always be on the lookout for their signals

- the road surface: this can become polished and slippery when wet. Avoid braking and severe acceleration when on the roundabout

Mini-roundabouts

Approach these in the same way as a roundabout: slow down and be prepared to give way to traffic from the right. Remember, however, there's less space to manoeuvre and less time to signal. For example, there's often insufficient time to signal left when leaving. Also

- vehicles coming towards you might want to turn right. Give way to them
- be sure any vehicle on the roundabout is going to leave it before you join it
- beware of drivers who are using the roundabout for a U-turn
- you must pass round the central markings unless you are driving a large vehicle or towing a trailer which is physically incapable of doing so.

Try to avoid using a mini-roundabout to make a U-turn, but be aware that other drivers may do this.

Double mini-roundabouts

- Treat each roundabout separately and give way to traffic from your right.
- Take careful all-round observation before you enter.

Multiple roundabouts

At some complex junctions, a large roundabout can incorporate a series of mini-roundabouts at the intersections.

You need to take extra care because traffic can be travelling in both directions around the large roundabout.

Look and assess Keep a good lookout and assess the situation at each mini-roundabout. Look for direction signs well in advance.

How close does a
biker have to be
before you see them?

THINK!
Take longer to
look for bikes.

section **nine**

MANOEUVRING

This section covers

- Before manoeuvring
- Reversing
- Turning around
- Parking

Before manoeuvring

You need to make choices based on legality, safety and convenience before manoeuvring. Your knowledge of The Highway Code, road signs, road markings and common sense will help you decide.

Ask yourself

- Is this a safe place?
- Is the manoeuvre within the law here?
- Is it a convenient place?

You must also ask yourself

- Will I be able to control my vehicle here?

You alone can answer that question. For example, an experienced driver might have no difficulty reversing downhill but, if you've not attempted it before, you might feel unsure of yourself. Only when you can say 'Yes' to all four questions can you be sure the place is suitable.

Other road users

Avoid inconveniencing other road users. Another driver or road user should not have to slow down or change course.

Decide if it's safe or whether it would be better to wait. Watch for other road users approaching, but avoid being too hesitant.

When other vehicles stop for you

Other drivers or riders may stop out of courtesy. However, you must satisfy yourself that they are actually stopping for you and not for some other reason. Check it's clear in all directions before you act upon any signal.

Use of the accelerator

Whichever manoeuvre you carry out, use the accelerator smoothly as this saves fuel and cuts down on noise.

Reversing

Reversing is not difficult to master, it just needs practice until you become confident. Start by reversing in a straight line, then go on to reversing round corners and more complicated manoeuvres.

Your vehicle will respond differently in reverse gear. You can't feel the car turning with the steering as you would in forward gears, and you have to wait for the steering to take effect.

The secret is to ensure the vehicle moves slowly enough. This way the steering movements will have the greatest effect.

Avoid turning the steering wheel while the vehicle is stationary ('dry' steering). It could cause damage to the tyres and increased wear in steering linkages.

- Remember which way the wheels are facing.
- Turn the steering wheel the way you want the rear of the vehicle to turn.

How to sit

Turn slightly in your seat. If you're reversing straight back or to the left, hold the steering wheel near the top – at 12 o'clock – with your right hand, and low on the wheel with your left hand.

If this position is too difficult because of your build, hold the wheel at 12 o'clock with your right hand. Your left arm can rest on the back of your seat or the back of the front passenger seat.

Seat belts

You may remove your seat belt while carrying out a manoeuvre which involves reversing. Don't forget to refasten it before driving off.

How to steer

When to begin steering?

In reverse, it's often helpful to begin turning or straightening up sooner than seems necessary.

Remember, reverse slowly and you'll have time for

* unhurried control of the vehicle
* checks to the front, side and rear.

What to check

All-round observation is just as important when you're reversing as it is when you're going forward.

* Check for other road users before you reverse; motorcycles, cyclists and pedestrians are more difficult to see.
* Check to the rear, particularly for children playing behind the vehicle.
* Check all round – forwards, behind, over both shoulders and in all mirrors. Do this before you reverse.
* If in doubt, get out and check.
* Keep checking all the time you're moving backwards, particularly behind you and to the sides, and especially at the point of turn.

Always be ready to stop.

Turning around

There are three methods of turning around.

- Using a side road.
- Turning in the road.
- Making a U-turn.

It's usually safest to use a side road. Alternatively you could drive round a block of side streets.

On narrow or busy roads It's normally safer to

- find a side road on the left or right, and use a turning off that road into which you can reverse
- go into the side road and use forward and reverse gears to turn round.

Remember also

- never to reverse into a main road from a side road
- not to reverse without making sure it's safe, even if that means getting help
- not to reverse for a long distance. It's an offence to reverse further than necessary for the safety of yourself and others
- to always be ready to give way and stop.

Driveways Another place you may need to reverse is when you are using your driveway.

You should reverse into your driveway, so you can drive out forwards onto the road.

If you need to turn around, don't use other people's driveways. You should drive on until you find a suitable side street.

Reversing into a side road on the left

After selecting a safe side road, use the MSM routine as you approach the corner.

If a signal is necessary, don't indicate too early that you intend pulling up on the left after the corner. You could mislead the traffic behind or anyone waiting to emerge. Your brake lights will tell the traffic behind that you are slowing down.

Stop your vehicle reasonably close to the kerb and parallel to it. The sharper the corner, the further out you need to be. Apply the parking brake and select neutral.

Taking observation and starting the manoeuvre Turn slightly in your seat. You'll find control easier.

Assess the position of your vehicle in relation to the kerb through the rear window. This is the relative position in which you need to end up when you finish reversing.

Select reverse gear. Set the engine revs to a steady hum. Bring the clutch pedal to the biting point and check all round.

When you're sure it's safe, start reversing.

As a general rule Keep the clutch pedal at, or near, the biting point. Keep the vehicle moving slowly enough by making proper use of the accelerator, clutch and brakes. The combination of the controls will depend on the slope of the road.

You should relate the position of the rear nearside wheel, just behind the back seat in most cars, to the edge of the kerb. Try to keep that wheel parallel to the kerb.

Start to turn left as the rear wheels reach the beginning of the corner. As a general guide, you should be able to follow the kerb as it disappears from view in the back window and reappears in the side window.

The amount of steering needed depends on how sharp the corner is. Remember to keep the vehicle moving slowly.

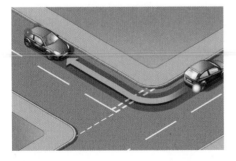

Continuous observation Keep a good lookout throughout, but particularly before you start to turn. The front of your vehicle will swing out and present the greatest hazard to any passing traffic.

Remember to check all blind spots before you start to turn. If any other road users are likely to be affected by your actions, pause until it's safe to continue.

Completing the manoeuvre When you begin to see into the side road, be ready to straighten up the steering.

Where there's a kerb in the new road, you can use the kerb to help you determine when to take off the left lock.

> **Remember,** keep on the lookout for other road users, particularly
> - pedestrians about to cross behind you
> - vehicles approaching from any direction.

Try and keep the vehicle about the same distance from the kerb as when you started, and parallel to it.

Reversing into a side road on the right

A useful manoeuvre where

- there isn't a side road on the left
- you can't see through the rear window
- your view to the sides is restricted, for example, in a van or a loaded estate car.

It actually involves two manoeuvres.

Moving to the other side of the road after passing the junction For this part of the manoeuvre you'll need to make

- full use of your mirrors
- a proper judgement of position and speed
- a proper assessment of the side road as you pass it.

Reversing into the side road itself

When doing this you'll need to

- stop your vehicle reasonably close to and parallel with the kerb – the sharper the turn, the further out you'll need to be
- sit so that you can have a good view over your right shoulder and still be able to see forward and to the left.

All-round observation is even more important on a right-hand reverse because you're on the wrong side of the road in the path of oncoming traffic.

- When you're sure it's safe, start reversing. Don't rush, but keep the vehicle moving by using the controls as for a left-hand reverse.
- It's easier to judge your distance from the kerb because you can look directly at it.

Throughout the manoeuvre keep a good lookout for other road users, particularly

- pedestrians about the cross behind you
- vehicles approaching from any direction.

Making a U-turn

A U-turn means turning the car right round without any reversing.

You might find you can do a U-turn in a wide, quiet road or at a large roundabout.

It's a potentially dangerous manoeuvre, when carried out at places other than large roundabouts, because you may have to cross lines of opposing traffic.

Never make a U-turn

- on a motorway
- in a one-way street
- wherever a road sign forbids it.

Before making a U-turn Always ask yourself

- Is it safe?
- Is it legal?
- Is it convenient?
- Is the road wide enough?

If in doubt, don't attempt it.

Observation Good all-round observation is particularly important before a U-turn.

Be aware that other drivers won't be expecting you to make a U-turn.

Avoid mounting the kerb.

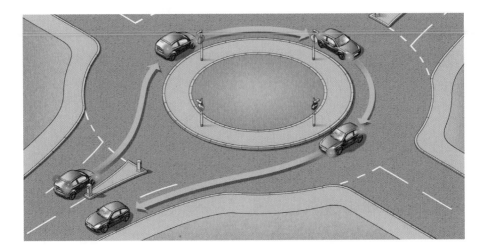

Turning in the road

You'll find this manoeuvre useful for turning when you can't find a side road or an opening.

The secret of this manoeuvre is to keep the vehicle moving slowly while steering briskly. Close control of the clutch is essential.

Before you turn Choose a place where

- you have plenty of room
- there's no obstruction in the road or on the pavement.

Stop on the left. Avoid lampposts or trees near the kerb.

Select first gear and prepare to move.

Check all round, especially your blind spots. Give way to passing vehicles.

Turning across the road Slowly move forward in first gear, turning your steering wheel briskly to full right lock. Your aim is to get the vehicle at a right angle across the road.

Just before you reach the opposite kerb, still moving slowly, begin to steer briskly to the left. Your wheels will then be ready to reverse left.

As you near the kerb, declutch and use the footbrake to stop. It may be necessary to use the parking brake to hold the vehicle if there is a camber or slope in the road.

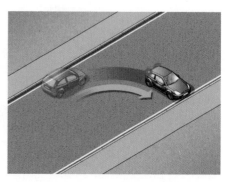

To reverse Select reverse gear.

Check the way is clear all round. Look through the rear window over your left shoulder to start with. Reverse slowly across the road, turning the steering wheel as far to the left as possible (full left lock).

Look round over your right shoulder as the vehicle nears the rear kerb. At the same time, turn your steering wheel briskly to the right.

Press the clutch pedal, and use the footbrake to stop.

Your wheels should be pointing to the right, ready to drive forward again.

To drive forward again Apply the parking brake if necessary, and select first gear.

Check that the road is clear and drive forward when it's safe to do so.

You might have to reverse again if the road is narrow or your vehicle is difficult to steer.

Straighten up on the left-hand side of the carriageway.

If your vehicle overhangs the kerb at any point, make sure there are no pedestrians nearby or any street furniture (lamp-posts, bins, signs) or trees that you might hit.

Remember, all-round observation is essential throughout the manoeuvre.

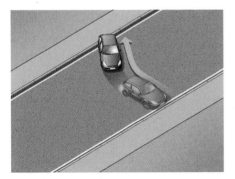
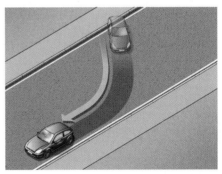

Parking

Whenever possible, park off the road or in a car park. If you have to park on the road, choose a safe place.

Ask yourself

- Is it safe?
- Is it convenient?
- Is it legal?

Road signs and markings

These will help you decide places where you should avoid parking your car, such as

- the approach to pedestrian crossings
- school entrances
- near junctions
- other restricted places.

Road signs and markings will also tell you if there are restrictions

- at certain times of the day
- on particular days of the week.

In general, The Highway Code lists places where you should not or must not park. Make sure you know these, and use common sense.

Never use your hazard warning lights as an excuse for stopping where you should not.

Never copy another driver's bad example. It won't excuse you from any penalties.

Parking on the road

Always use the MSM routine and signal, if necessary, before you park.

Try not to touch the kerb when you park. Scraping your tyres can weaken them with possibly serious results.

Don't park so near to other vehicles that it will be difficult for you and them to get out. This is especially important if the other vehicle is displaying a Blue Badge. Allow room for a wheelchair to be manoeuvred or loaded in these cases. As a general rule park parallel with, and close to, the kerb.

Always switch off the engine and headlights (and fog lights) when you park. Make sure that the parking brake is applied firmly before you leave the vehicle.

Remember that unless your vehicle is parked in an authorised parking place, it could cause an obstruction. Never leave your vehicle where it could prevent emergency vehicles passing, particularly in narrow residential roads where vehicles often park on both sides of the road.

You'll acquire better parking skills with practice.

When parking you should

- take care to plan your parking
- always manoeuvre your vehicle slowly
- never park in a space reserved for Blue Badge holder unless either you, or the passenger you are carrying, are the holder of a Blue Badge.

You should also make sure that you won't hit another road user, or cause another driver or rider to swerve, when you open your car door. Look out particularly for bicycles and motorcycles. Make sure any passengers do the same and also that they don't hit pedestrians on the pavement when opening their door.

Parking on hills

If you park your vehicle on a slope, remember the following:

Parking facing uphill

- Stop your vehicle as close as you can to the nearside kerb, if there is one.
- Leave your steering wheel turned to the right. If the vehicle rolls backwards, the front wheels will be stopped by the kerb.
- If there is no kerb, leave your steering wheel turned to the left. If the vehicle rolls back it won't roll across the road.
- Leave the vehicle in first gear with the parking brake firmly applied.

Parking facing downhill

- Leave your steering wheel turned to the left. The kerb should stop any forward movement.
- Leave your vehicle in reverse gear with the parking brake firmly applied.

Leaving a gap

Parking on a slope is more difficult than on the flat and can take more room. You should leave a bigger gap to allow extra space for manoeuvring. A larger gap will help both you and others.

Vehicles with automatic transmission

When you park facing either uphill or downhill in a vehicle with automatic transmission, make sure your vehicle is stationary and the parking brake is firmly applied before using the selector setting 'P' (Park).

If your vehicle has no 'P' setting

- turn your front wheels to the kerb
- make sure your parking brake is firmly applied.

Reverse parking

This makes use of the vehicle's manoeuvrability in reverse gear to park in a restricted space.

Remember, while you're carrying out this manoeuvre, you could be a hazard to other road users.

Position and observation

Good all-round observation is essential throughout this manoeuvre.

Don't start to manoeuvre if you're likely to endanger other road users.

Other drivers might not be aware of your intentions, so before you pull up at the place you've chosen to park, remember to carry out the MSM routine.

Positioning your vehicle

Stop your vehicle reasonably close to, and parallel with, the parked vehicle ahead of the gap.

Your vehicle should be about level with, or slightly ahead of, the parked vehicle. This will depend on the size of the gap and the length of your vehicle.

You can start practising using only one parked car. When you have mastered the technique, you should be able to park between two vehicles.

The gap should be at least one-and-a-half times the length of your own vehicle.

Manoeuvring into the gap

Apply the parking brake, if necessary. Show your brake lights by pressing the footbrake. Select reverse gear to show the reversing light(s). This warns other road users of your intentions. Check all round.

Bring the clutch up to biting point and, if it's still safe, release the parking brake if you applied it. Ease the clutch pedal up just enough to start to move.

Hold the clutch pedal steady at, or just above, the biting point. Reverse slowly using left lock, but watch the corner of the parked vehicle.

Remember, keep a good lookout for other road users throughout this manoeuvre, particularly

- pedestrians
- oncoming vehicles
- passing traffic.

Don't forget to look round as you begin to reverse into the space. The front of your vehicle could swing out into the path of passing traffic.

Try lining up the rear offside (right-hand side) of your vehicle with the nearside headlight of the vehicle behind the space you're entering.

Straightening up in the gap

Straighten up by taking off the left lock.
Keep a careful eye on the position of your
vehicle. There's a danger of 'clipping' the
vehicle in front at this point.

When you're sure the front of your vehicle
is clear of the parked vehicle use sufficient
right lock to gradually bring your vehicle
parallel with, and reasonably close to, the
nearside kerb. Straighten up by taking the
right lock off and adjust the position of
your vehicle as necessary.

Defensive driving

Other road users may not understand your
intention. Showing your reversing lights
should help. If another vehicle pulls up close
behind, move on and park somewhere else.

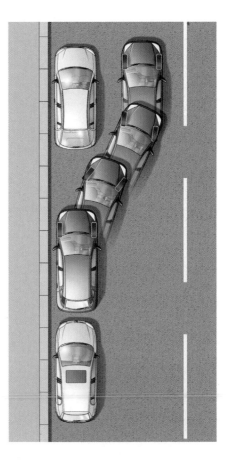

Car parks

Arrow markings and signs show you which lanes to take inside the car park. Follow these. Don't drive against the traffic flow.

Indoor car parks

Use dipped headlights in multi-storey, underground or other indoor car parks. This helps other drivers and pedestrians to see you.

Parking

Unless there's space at the end of the row, you'll have to fit in between two other vehicles.

Check that there's

- enough space for you to centre your vehicle
- enough room to open the doors safely.

Whether you're reversing in or going forward, move slowly so the steering has the maximum effect and gives you time to make corrections.

Reverse parking

Unless other cars are badly parked, you'll nearly always find it best to reverse into a parking space. You'll have a better view when you drive away, especially with back-seat passengers or at night.

You can line up

- driving forward past the space and then turn as you reverse into the parking space, or
- turning as you approach the space, so that you are in a position from which you can reverse into the space.

Choose whichever method suits the configuration of the car park or a combination of both.

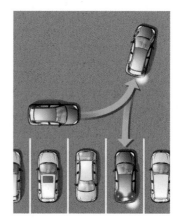

Park squarely in the marked spaces

Always try to park squarely in the marked spaces otherwise the car next to you might have to squeeze in, or there might not be enough room for its doors to be opened.

Parking forwards

Some car parks are designed for you to park forwards to make it easier to load shopping. In these cases take extra care as you reverse out of the parking space because pedestrians and vehicles may be passing behind.

You might also find it more difficult to drive out because your wheels may be at the wrong angle when you reverse to leave.

If you haven't enough room to go forward all the way into a tight space, you might need to nose in then back out and straighten up to move into the space.

Remember the following when parking.

- Before entering the car park, use your mirrors and signal.
- Look at the layout, markings and signs to guide you. Choose a space.
- Use your mirrors and signal again if necessary.
- Check your position and keep your speed down. Look out for pedestrians.
- Make sure your vehicle is squarely parked between the white lines in one space.

Take great care when reversing out of a parking space. Check for pedestrians and vehicles behind you.

section **ten**

DEFENSIVE DRIVING

This section covers
- Defensive driving
- Observation
- Signalling
- Hazards
- Lighting and weather conditions
- Other road users

Defensive driving

The roads today are busier than they've ever been, and they're getting busier all the time.

As well as heavy traffic, the driver often has to cope with unpredictable, irrational, offensive and sometimes dangerous driving behaviour.

Such behaviour makes today's road conditions hostile in a very real sense, with a higher risk of incident. In such conditions, drivers need to learn and practise a suitable strategy.

That strategy is called 'defensive driving', sometimes known as 'planned driving'.

Defensive driving is based on effective observation, good anticipation and control. It's about always questioning the actions of other road users and being prepared for the unexpected, so as not to be taken by surprise.

Defensive driving involves

- awareness
- planning
- anticipating
- staying in control

and driving with

- responsibility
- care
- consideration and courtesy.

Safety

You should put safety above all else. This means having real concern not only for your own safety, but also for that of other road users, including the most vulnerable – those walking or riding.

Expect other people to make mistakes, and be ready to slow down or stop – even if you think you have priority.

Never assume that other road users will do the correct thing. Your safety lies mainly in your own hands. The better your control of your vehicle and road space, the safer you'll be.

A good example

Your driving should always set a good example to other road users.

Your good example could make a deep impression on another driver, especially a learner or inexperienced road user, and perhaps save lives in the future.

Reducing hostility

With defensive driving, you'll show more patience and anticipation. This will help to reduce the number of incidents which result in

- open hostility
- abusive language
- threats
- physical violence.

Avoid the kind of driving that

- gives offence to other road users
- provokes reaction
- creates dangerous situations.

Never drive in a spirit of competition. Competitive driving is, inherently, the opposite of defensive driving. It increases the risks to everyone.

Defensive driving

Make allowances if someone cuts in front of you, hold back and increase the distance between you and them. That way, if they brake suddenly, you have given yourself a greater safety margin.

When you check in the mirrors, just looking is not enough. You must act sensibly on what you see.

Make allowances even if someone else is driving recklessly; keep calm and don't be tempted to retaliate.

Observation

Look at other road users and assess their

- speed
- behaviour
- possible intentions.

If you're not observing effectively, you can't assess a traffic situation correctly.

At junctions, there's no point in just looking if your view is obstructed by, for example, parked vehicles. You must also move carefully into a position where you can see without moving out into the path of oncoming traffic. Remember LADA

- **L**ook
- **A**ssess and
- **D**ecide before you
- **A**ct.

That's what effective observation is all about.

Observing what's ahead

A skilful driver constantly watches and interprets what's happening ahead.

Always drive at such a speed that you can stop safely within the distance you can see to be clear.

A good driver will constantly scan the road ahead and to the side and, by frequent use of the mirrors, be aware of the situation behind.

Approaching a bend Ask yourself

- Can I see the full picture?
- How sharp is the bend?
- Am I in the right position?
- Is my speed right?
- What might I meet?
- Could I stop if I had to?

Approaching a junction Ask yourself

- Have I seen the whole junction?
- Can other drivers see me?
- Am I sure they have seen me?
- Have I got an escape route if they haven't?

Left-hand drive vehicles

If you are driving a left-hand drive vehicle, take special care and make full use of your mirrors.

Zone of vision at a junction

Your zone of vision is what you can see as you look forward and to the side from your vehicle. As you approach a junction, your zone of vision onto the other road usually improves.

You may need to get very close before you can look far enough into another road to see if it's safe to proceed. The last few feet are often crucial.

Sometimes parked vehicles restrict your view so much that you need to stop and inch forward for a proper view before you emerge.

- Look in every direction before you emerge.
- Keep looking as you join the other road.
- Be ready to stop.
- Use all the information available to you – look through the windows of parked vehicles.
- Use the reflections in shop windows to observe oncoming traffic.

Screen pillar obstruction The windscreen pillars can cause obstructions to your view of the road. You should be aware of this effect, particularly when

- approaching junctions and bends
- emerging from junctions.

Road users such as motorcyclists, cyclists and pedestrians may be completely obscured by the pillar.

You should be aware that some 4x4s have very large blind spots – they can obscure groups of pedestrians, a motorcyclist or a small car.

If you can't see the driver's face, they won't be able to see you.

Other road users It can be difficult to see some other road users, especially when you are emerging from a junction. Those who are particularly at risk are

- pedestrians; they frequently cross at a junction and often find it difficult to judge the speed and course of approaching traffic
- cyclists; they can be difficult to see, because they can easily be obscured by trees and other objects, especially if they are riding close to the side of the road. They might be approaching at a higher speed than you expect
- motorcyclists; like cyclists they are often less easy to see than other traffic, but they are likely to be moving much faster than cyclists.

Think once

Think twice

Think bike!

Always make sure it's safe to proceed.

Never rely solely on a quick glance – give yourself time to take in the whole scene.

If another vehicle or a pedestrian is not in your zone of vision, you're not usually in theirs.

Making eye contact with other road users helps you to know whether they have seen you.

Observing traffic behind you

You should always know as much as you can about the traffic behind you.

Before you move off, change direction or change speed, you need to know how your action will affect other road users.

You must also be aware of traffic likely to overtake.

Using your mirrors Using your mirrors regularly and sensibly enables you to keep up to date with what's happening behind, **without** losing touch with what's going on in front. They must be clean and properly adjusted to give a clear view.

When should you use your mirrors?

Before you signal or make any manoeuvre. For example, before

- moving off
- changing direction
- turning right or left
- overtaking
- changing lanes
- slowing or stopping
- opening a car door.

Looking around You should look around to check your blind spot before moving off.

A quick sideways glance This is sometimes helpful, for example, to check your blind spot

- before you change lanes, especially on a motorway or dual carriageway
- where traffic is merging from the left or right.

However, looking around on the move can be dangerous, particularly when driving at high speeds. In the time you take to look around, you lose touch with what's happening in front.

Remember that a vehicle travelling at 70 mph (112 km/h) covers around 30 metres (about 100 feet) per second. Even if it only takes half a second to look round, you will still have travelled 15 metres (about 50 feet).

Just looking is not enough! You must act sensibly on what you see. Take note of the speed, behaviour and possible intentions of traffic behind you.

Another driver's blind spot Avoid driving in another driver's blind spot for any longer than necessary.

Approaching green traffic lights

Ask yourself

- How long have they been on green?
- Are there many vehicles already waiting at either side of the junction? (If there's a queue, the lights are probably about to change)
- Do I have time to stop?
- Can the vehicle behind me stop? If it's a large goods vehicle, it might need a greater distance in which to pull up.

Don't

- try to beat the traffic signals by accelerating
- leave it until the last moment to brake. Harsh braking causes skids and could cause loss of control.

Another driver might anticipate the change of signals by accelerating away while the lights are still showing red and amber. A combination of these actions by drivers often results in a collision that could be avoided.

Traffic signals not working

Where traffic signals are not working, treat the situation as you would an unmarked junction and proceed with great care.

Signalling

Signal to warn others of your intention and to help other road users, which could be anyone using the road in a variety of ways.

Road users include

- drivers of other motor vehicles
- drivers of large or slow-moving vehicles
- motorcyclists
- users of powered mobility vehicles
- cyclists
- pedestrians
- horse riders
- crossing supervisors
- road workers
- persons directing traffic.

Signal clearly and in good time.

Give only the signals illustrated in The Highway Code.

Direction indicator signals

Help other road users to understand your intention by

- signalling in good time so that they have time to see and react to your signal

- positioning yourself correctly and in good time for the manoeuvre you intend to make.

Conflicting signals A signal with the left indicator means 'I am going to turn left' **or** 'I am going to stop on the left'.

Avoid using your left indicator before a left-hand junction if you intend to stop on the left just after the junction. A driver waiting at that junction might think you're turning left and drive out into your path.

- Wait until you've passed the junction, then indicate that you intend to stop.

- Reduce speed by braking gently, so that your brake lights warn drivers behind you.

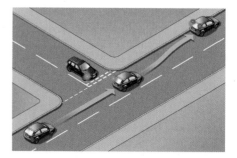

If you're waiting to emerge and a vehicle seems to be indicating its intention to turn left, wait until you can see that it is actually going to turn before you pull out. Otherwise you might drive into its path.

> **Remember,** roundabouts often have several lanes of traffic with vehicles changing speed and direction. It's important that you give any signals correctly and at the right time.

Warning signals

The horn There are few situations when you'll need to use the horn.

Using the horn doesn't

- give you priority
- relieve you of your responsibility to drive safely.

Sound it only if

- you think someone may not have seen you
- you want to warn other road users of your presence; for example, at blind bends or junctions.

Avoid using a long blast on the horn as this can alarm pedestrians. If a pedestrian doesn't react to a short signal on the horn, it could mean they're deaf. Take care around horses as they could be startled by the sound of a horn.

Never use your horn as a rebuke. Don't use it to attract the attention of someone at the side of the road or to signal your arrival to someone to whom you are giving a lift.

Unless a moving vehicle poses a danger, it is illegal to use your horn

- when stationary
- when driving at night (11.30 pm to 7.00 am) in a built-up area.

Flashing your headlights Do this as an alternative to the horn to remind others that you're there.

Don't flash your headlights at anyone to indicate that they should go ahead or turn.

If someone flashes their headlights at you Before you act on the signal, make sure

- you understand what they mean
- the signal is meant for you.

Never assume it's a signal to proceed.

Ask yourself

- What's the other driver trying to tell me: 'Stop', 'Go', 'Turn', 'Thank you'?
- If I move, will it be safe?
- Is the signal intended for me or for another road user?
- Am I causing a hold-up by staying where I am?
- Is the other driver really signalling, or were those headlights flashed accidentally?

The consequences rest with you.

On motorways and dual carriageways If you think a warning is necessary, flashing your headlights is usually better than using your horn. Be alert for such warnings from other drivers.

If a driver behind starts flashing their headlights and driving dangerously close

- stay calm
- don't be intimidated.

Move back to the left as soon as there's a safe gap and you have checked you can do so without cutting in on vehicles that you have overtaken.

Changing course is your responsibility.

Act sensibly.

> **Remember,** the only official meaning for the flashing of headlights is to let other road users know you're there – the same as using the horn.

Hazards

A hazard is any situation which could involve adjusting speed or changing course. Hazards can be either static or moving.

To identify a static hazard, you must look well ahead for clues such as

- road signs
- changes in road conditions
- parked vehicles
- junctions.

Moving hazards include all road users, such as

- other vehicles
- motorcyclists
- cyclists
- users of powered mobility vehicles
- pedestrians
- horse riders
- road workers
- persons directing traffic
- animals, particularly dogs off the lead.

Remember, as soon as you've recognised a hazard, you must use the mirrors to assess

- how other road users will affect your planning
- how your actions will affect traffic behind.

Allowing time and space

Always leave yourself enough time and space to cope with what's ahead.

- Keep your eyes moving.
- Look well ahead, in the far and near distance, especially in town where things change quickly.
- Check regularly on what's behind you.
- Watch for clues about what's going to happen next.

For example; a parked car could spell danger if the driver is sitting in it, or you see vapour from the exhaust in cold weather. This could indicate that

- a door might open suddenly
- the car might pull out without warning.

If you can see underneath a parked vehicle, and you can see feet at the other side, a pedestrian might appear suddenly.

Effective observation and anticipation are your main defence.

Always keep a good separation distance between you and the vehicle in front. Leave a gap of at least one metre or yard for each mph of your speed, or use the two-second rule (see page 140).

In bad conditions, leave at least double the distance or a four-second time gap.

Tailgating When a vehicle behind is too close to you, ease off the accelerator very gradually and increase the gap between you and the vehicle in front.

Large vehicles Take extra care when following large vehicles, especially at roundabouts, junctions, entrances, etc.

The driver might have to take a course that seems incorrect to you; for example, moving out to the right before turning left.

Keep well back from any large vehicles that are in the process of manoeuvring to the left or right.

Don't get caught out by trying to pass on the left.

Large vehicles can also block your view. Your ability to see and plan ahead will be improved if you keep back.

Remember, if you are following a large vehicle too closely, the driver might not be able to see you in their mirrors. If you can't see their mirrors, the driver can't see you.

Recognising hazards

Events can happen at the same time, or in quick succession. In the illustration below, the driver of the blue car must pull out to pass the stationary coach, but

- is the green car really going to turn left? (The driver might have forgotten to cancel the indicator from a previous turn)

- if the green car does turn, will the pedestrian with the briefcase decide to cross?

- when will the driver of the blue car notice the red car, which may want to turn left?

If you're travelling too fast, you're not likely to be able to cope with all the events at once. This is how other road users, who might not be doing anything wrong, can turn a straightforward piece of driving into a hazardous situation.

> **Remember,** the defensive driver is always
>
> - **in the correct position**
> - **travelling at the correct speed for the road, traffic and weather conditions**
> - **in the right gear**
> - **anticipating and prepared for the next change in the traffic situation.**

The action you need to take will vary from one hazard to another. Any action which involves a change of speed or course is called a manoeuvre.

A manoeuvre can vary from slowing slightly to turning on a very busy road.

Approaching any hazard

Follow the MSM/PSL routine every time you recognise a hazard (see page 70).

Mirror(s) Check the position of traffic following you.

Signal If necessary, signal your intention to change course or slow down. Signal clearly and in good time.

Manoeuvre Carry out the manoeuvre if it's still safe to do so. Manoeuvre has three phases – Position, Speed, Look.

Position Get into the correct position in good time to negotiate the hazard. This helps other road users to anticipate what you intend to do.

Positioning yourself too late can be dangerous. Ask yourself

- can I see and be seen?
- are other vehicles restricting my course of action?
- have I enough room to get out of any difficulties?

Avoid cutting in front of other drivers or riders.

If lanes are closed or narrow because of roadworks, move into the correct lane in good time.

- Don't wait until the last minute.
- Don't overtake and squeeze in later on – you'll only increase the frustration of drivers already waiting.

Speed Ask yourself

- Could I stop in time if the vehicle in front braked suddenly?
- Am I going too fast for the road conditions?
- Am I in the right gear needed to keep control?

Be prepared to slow down as you approach a hazard. Always be ready to stop.

Look Keep looking ahead to assess all possible dangers. This is particularly important at a junction. Look in all directions, even if you're not turning.

If you're joining a road, keep looking as you turn from one road to the other. Watch out for

- traffic turning across your path
- motorcyclists, as they are more difficult to see and can easily be hidden by other vehicles
- pedestrians.

Country roads

These roads present their own hazards. Take extra care and reduce your speed as you approach bends and junctions.

Bends and junctions Bends can often be sharper than you think they are going to be. They may also obscure other more vulnerable road users, such as pedestrians, horse riders and cyclists or larger slow-moving farm vehicles which may take up the whole width of the road.

Junctions, especially minor junctions or entrances to farm premises, are not always signed and may be partially hidden.

Other road users Many roads in country areas have no pavements or footpaths. Where this is the case, pedestrians are advised to walk on the right-hand side of the road so they can see oncoming traffic. However, you should always be prepared to find people walking or jogging on your side of the road.

Horse riders and cyclists are also often found on country roads. Give them plenty of space, always be patient and wait until it is safe before overtaking, especially on narrow or winding roads.

Narrow roads with passing places On single track roads, look well ahead and be prepared to stop. If you see an oncoming vehicle

- pull into the passing place if it's on the left
- be prepared to reverse into a passing place if necessary
- wait opposite if it the passing place is on the right.

Avoid driving onto the verge; it may be soft, with hidden gulleys, which could damage your vehicle's suspension.

If your view ahead is restricted by hedges or bends, reduce speed and take extra care.

If another driver wishes to overtake, pull into or stop opposite a passing place to allow them to do so.

Lighting and weather conditions

Driving at night or in certain weather conditions can present its own hazards.

At night

You can't see so far ahead at night, but try to get help from

- illuminated signs
- reflective signs
- reflectors between white lines
- the glow of vehicle headlights on trees and buildings, indicating a corner or junction.

Be aware of the hazards of driving at night. In particular

- it can be difficult to judge distance and speed from the headlights of approaching vehicles
- bright lights on some vehicles make it difficult to see less bright lights, such as those of cyclists or low-powered motorcycles
- keep a good lookout for pedestrian crossings, traffic lights, and other road users, and don't let shop and advertising signs distract you.

More information about driving at night can be found in section 13.

Weather conditions

Many different weather conditions can make driving more difficult. More information about these can be found in section 12.

Rain and wet roads can create hazards at any time of year.

Rain Rain makes headlights less effective at night. On dark and poorly lit roads, slow down and watch for unlit objects such as roadworks, builders' skips or parked cars. Drive more slowly and carefully in rain. Match your speed to the conditions.

Wet roads Stay alert to the road surface ahead because you might have to brake. Ask yourself

- is the road wet or slippery?
- is it a good surface on which to brake?

If the surface is wet, allow more time in which to stop.

A wet road means

- less efficient braking
- a longer distance needed to stop
- a greater risk of skidding.

Drive more slowly on wet roads and take extra care.

At night, wet roads can

- increase distracting reflected light
- make unlit objects even less visible.

Other road users

You, as a driver, are not the only person using the road. Most other road user types are more vulnerable than you are because they are less well protected in the event of a collision.

Cyclists

Make allowances for cyclists. They have every right to be on the road. The younger the cyclist, the more you must watch them.

Allow cyclists plenty of room; they might

- glance round, showing they might be about to move out or turn
- make sudden sideways movements into your path
- be carrying light but bulky objects which may affect their control and balance
- weave about, slow down, or stop and get off on a hill
- swerve round potholes or inspection covers or to avoid being hit by a car door being opened
- have problems in bad weather, particularly strong crosswinds
- have difficulty on poor road surfaces or where tramlines are set in the road.

Look out for them particularly when you are

- in slow-moving traffic
- emerging from a junction
- negotiating a roundabout.

Do not assume that cyclists will stay within cycle lanes; it is sometimes safer for them to use the road. Do not drive aggressively or try to intimidate them.

When travelling at low speeds, such as at junctions, cyclists are likely to be more unstable and therefore more vulnerable. Give them plenty of room.

Motorcyclists

Make allowances for motorcyclists.

Much of what has been said about cyclists also applies to motorcyclists. They are very vulnerable because, like cyclists, they are much smaller than other vehicles, with a narrow profile which makes them difficult to see. However, they also travel much faster than cyclists, so situations develop much more quickly than those involving cyclists.

Many road traffic incidents happen because drivers fail to notice motorcyclists, so look out for them when

- emerging from junctions. The motorcyclist may be travelling along the major road and may be hidden behind other traffic. They may also be hidden by signs, trees, street furniture, etc

- turning into a road on your right. The motorcyclist may be following, overtaking or meeting you. Oncoming motorcyclists may be particularly difficult to see if they are being followed by a larger vehicle

- changing lanes or moving out to overtake slower-moving or parked vehicles.

> **Remember,** motorcyclists and cyclists are harder to see than other vehicles and are exposed to bad weather, slippery roads and uneven surfaces. Look out for them, especially at junctions.

Think once

Think twice

Think bike!

Pay special attention to motorcycles and scooters displaying L plates. The riders of these machines may be riding on the road with very little experience, so they are particularly vulnerable.

Powered vehicles used by disabled people

These small vehicles can be used on the pavement and on the road. They are extremely vulnerable when they are on the road because of

- their small size, especially their low height

- their low speed (they have a maximum speed of 8 mph (12 km/h)).

They are often not easy to see. On a dual carriageway where the speed limit exceeds 50 mph (80 km/h) they should be displaying an amber flashing light, but on other roads you may not have that advance warning.

Buses and coaches

Look well ahead when you see buses and coaches at a bus stop. Be aware of

- people getting off the bus or coach and not looking properly before they cross the road (even if they look, their view is often restricted)

- buses and coaches pulling away from the bus stop. If they are signalling to move out, always give way to them if you can do so safely.

Remember, always think of the other road user, not just of yourself.

Pedestrians

Always drive carefully and slowly in areas where there are likely to be pedestrians, such as residential areas and crowded shopping streets.

Be particularly careful in Home Zones and Quiet Lanes where people could be using the whole road for a range of activities.

Always look out for pedestrians when

- turning from one road into another – give way to any who are crossing the road into which you're turning

- approaching pedestrian crossings. Never overtake on the approach to a crossing

- driving past a bus or tram stop as pedestrians may emerge suddenly into the road.

Keep your speed down when driving in an area where there are pedestrians, especially children. If a pedestrian is in collision with a car, the survival rate of the pedestrian reduces drastically the faster the car is travelling.

Older people Several factors make older people more vulnerable.

Poor eyesight or hearing might mean they are not aware of approaching traffic. They might not be able to judge the speed of approaching traffic when crossing the road. Even when they do realise the danger, they may be unable to move quickly, or they may become flustered.

They may also take longer to cross the road. Be patient and do not hurry them by revving your engine or edging forwards.

People with disabilities Take special care around people with disabilities.

Visually impaired people may not be able to see you approaching. They may carry a white cane or use a guide dog. The guide dog has a distinctive loop-type of harness. Remember the dog is trained to wait if there is a vehicle nearby.

A person with hearing difficulties is not easy to identify, so take extra care if a pedestrian fails to look your way as you approach. Remember they may not be aware of your presence. They may have a guide dog wearing a distinctive yellow or burgundy coat.

Those who are deaf and blind may carry a white cane with a red band or may be using a guide dog with a red and white harness. They may not see or hear instructions or signals.

Children Take extra care where children might be around, particularly in residential areas and near schools and parks.

Drive carefully and slowly past schools, especially during school start and finish times. Be aware that

- a school-crossing patrol may stop you to escort children across the road
- children may be getting on or off a bus showing a 'school bus' sign.

Children are impulsive and unpredictable. Therefore, drive slowly in narrow roads where parked cars obscure your view.

Look out for parked ice-cream vans. Children are more interested in ice cream than they are in traffic, and they may run into the road unexpectedly.

Animals

Animals are easily frightened by noise and vehicles coming close to them. You should

- drive slowly and quietly; don't sound the horn

- keep your engine speed low; don't rev your engine or accelerate rapidly once you have passed them

- always watch out for animals on unfenced roads, as they may step out in front of you. You should always be able to stop safely within the distance you can see to be clear, especially at night when your lights are dipped.

Give animals as much room as possible.

People in charge of animals If someone in charge of animals signals to you to stop, do so and switch off your engine.

Horses Be particularly careful when approaching horses, especially those being ridden by children.

As a driver you should

- look out for horses being led or ridden on the road

- take extra care and keep your speed down at left-hand bends especially on narrow country roads

- slow down when you see a horse rider on the road.

Be aware that at roundabouts and at junctions where a horse rider is turning right, they may signal right but keep to the left-hand side of the road (and the outside lane round the roundabout) for safety.

As you approach a horse rider from behind

- slow down, give them plenty of room and be prepared to stop

- don't sound your horn or rev your engine. Horses can be easily scared by noise and may panic around fast-moving vehicles

- look out for signals given by the riders and heed a request to slow down or stop.

Always pass horses slowly, giving plenty of room.

Take special care when meeting what appears to be a riding school group. Many of the riders might be inexperienced. Horses are potential hazards and you should always take great care when meeting or passing them.

Also look out for horse-drawn vehicles and treat them in a similar way to horses being ridden.

section **eleven**

DRIVING ON MOTORWAYS

This section covers

- Driving on motorways
- Motorway signs and signals
- Joining a motorway
- On the motorway
- Lane discipline
- Overtaking
- Leaving a motorway
- Weather conditions
- Stopping on motorways
- Motorways at night
- Roadworks
- The novice driver

Driving on motorways

Motorways differ from ordinary roads in that they're designed to help traffic travel faster and in greater safety. This puts greater demands on both driver and vehicle.

Motorways are statistically safer than other roads in relation to the number of incidents occurring. However, when they do happen, motorway incidents usually occur at higher speed and involve more vehicles. As a result, injuries are usually more serious – often with greater loss of life.

Because traffic travels faster, conditions change more rapidly. You need to be alert and have total concentration.

Before you drive on a motorway

- Car drivers must hold a full driving licence.
- You should have a thorough knowledge of all rules within The Highway Code but particularly those dealing with motorways.
- You need to know and understand motorway warning signs and signals.

Concentration

You need to be fit and alert to drive anywhere, but particularly on motorways. Never use the motorway if you feel tired or unwell.

General guidelines on dealing with fatigue are given on page 19 but the problems when driving on motorways tend to be greater because of the long distances and the monotony of the journey.

Research has found that fatigue accounts for 15–20% of incidents on monotonous roads (especially motorways). These tend to result in more serious injury than the average collision because of the high speed of the impact (there is often no braking beforehand).

If your journey seems monotonous and you feel drowsy, keep a window open until you reach a service area. Plan plenty of rest stops, especially at night.

Parking is forbidden except at service areas. If you need rest, you'll sometimes have to travel a long distance before an exit or a service area. Remember it's an offence to stop on the hard shoulder, an exit or a slip road, except in an emergency.

Stop at a service area if you need a rest.

Your vehicle

You must only drive a vehicle which is allowed on a motorway and make sure your vehicle is safe and in good working order.

The following types of vehicle must not be used on the motorway

- motorcycles under 50 cc
- certain slow-moving vehicles with oversized loads – except with special permission
- invalid carriages less than 254 kg unladen weight
- agricultural vehicles.

Also, motorways **MUST NOT** be used by pedestrians, cyclists, horse riders or holders of provisional car and motorcycle licences.

Before you use the motorway High speeds and long distances increase the risk of mechanical failure.

You should carry out the following checks on your vehicle.

- **Tyres** They must be in good condition and inflated to the correct pressure. Follow the guidance given in the vehicle handbook which may give different pressures to be used when the vehicle is loaded.
- **Brakes** Check they can stop you safely.
- **Steering** Check it is in good order.

- **Instruments and warning lights** Make sure they are all working correctly.
- **Mirrors** Make sure they are clean and correctly positioned.
- **Windscreen and windows** Make sure they are clean. Top up the reservoir for the windscreen washers, and the rear window washer, if your vehicle has one.
- **Lights and indicators** Make sure they are all working correctly.

For safety, convenience and good vehicle care you should also check the following items.

- **Fuel** Make sure you have enough fuel to avoid running out between service areas.
- **Oil** High speeds may mean your engine uses oil faster. Running out can be dangerous and costly.
- **Water** Higher speeds can mean a warmer engine, especially in traffic tailbacks in hot weather.

Make sure your load is secure Check that everything carried on your vehicle or trailer is safe and secure. If anything should fall from your vehicle or from another, stop on the hard shoulder and use the emergency telephone to inform the authorities. **Never** try to retrieve it yourself.

Motorway signs and signals

Signs

Leading to the motorway Direction signs from ordinary roads to the motorway have white lettering and figures on a blue panel, often bordered in white.

These signs may stand alone or be included in other larger signs of various colours.

On the motorway You may find the following types of sign on the motorway

- advance direction signs
- countdown markers
- signs giving information about service areas
- signs with a brown background. These indicate tourist attractions which can be reached by leaving at the next exit.

All these signs are very much larger than those on ordinary roads because you need to be able to see them from a distance. This is a good reminder that you must leave more room for all manoeuvres on motorways.

Each junction has an identifying number which corresponds with current road maps. This is to help you plan your route and know where you need to leave the motorway.

Speed limit signs

- Signs which display a speed limit within a red ring indicate mandatory maximum speed limits. You **MUST** obey these signs. If you don't, you risk prosecution.

- Black and white rectangular signs recommend maximum speed limits which you **MUST** observe.

Signals

Signals warn of dangers ahead, such as

- incidents
- fog
- icy roads
- delays
- standing traffic.

Flashing amber lights Look out for flashing amber lights and signs, either on the central reservation or overhead. These warn you of

- lane closures
- roadworks
- other hazards.

They might also show a temporary maximum advisory speed limit. You should

- slow down to the speed limit

- be ready to slow down even further to pass the obstacle or danger
- look out for signs giving further advice
- don't speed up until you see the sign ending the temporary restriction (or there are no more flashing amber lights).

Red lights Some signs have flashing red lights as well.

A red light (it may be a red 'X') warns you that you **MUST NOT** go beyond the red light in that lane. You should

- start to slow down in good time
- be ready to change lanes.

If the red light flashes on a slip road, you **MUST NOT** enter it.

If a red light flashes on the central reservation or at the side of the road, you **MUST NOT** go beyond the signal in any lane.

Joining a motorway

You can get onto a motorway

- where a main road becomes a motorway. This is indicated by a specially worded sign
- by joining at any entry point. A slip road leads onto the motorway.

At an entry point where a slip road leads to the motorway, adjust your speed to that of the traffic already on the motorway before joining it. Give priority to traffic already on the motorway.

Join where there's a suitable gap in the left-hand lane. Use the MSM/PSL routine.

A quick sideways glance might be necessary to verify the position of other vehicles. Try to avoid stopping at the end of the slip road unless queuing to join other slow-moving traffic.

At some slip roads there is no need to join by merging because the joining lane may continue as a dedicated lane. Signs and road markings normally indicate this arrangement.

Do

- indicate your intention to join the motorway
- make sure you can be seen
- assess the speed of the traffic on the motorway before you try to join.

Don't

- force your way into the traffic stream
- drive along the hard shoulder.

Once you've joined the motorway, keep in the left-hand lane* until you've had time to judge and adjust to the speed of the traffic already on the motorway.

*In a very few cases, the lane merges from the right. Take extra care when joining or meeting traffic at these locations.

On the motorway

Seeing and being seen

Make sure you start out with clean mirrors, windscreen, windows and lights. Use your washers, wipers and demisters whenever necessary to ensure you can see clearly.

You need to use your mirrors frequently and much earlier than on normal roads. Because of the higher speeds on motorways, they are even more important.

Always try to avoid staying where you might be in another vehicle's blind spot. This is especially important when the other vehicle is a large vehicle. A good indication is if you can't see the driver's mirror, the driver probably won't be able to see you.

Effective observation

Keep your eyes moving between the road ahead and your mirrors, so that you always know what's happening all around you.

Continually reassess the movement of the vehicles

- directly ahead (in the near and far distance)
- alongside you
- behind you.

At high speeds, situations change rapidly. Effective observation helps you prepare for any sudden developments.

For example, an increase in the number of vehicles ahead could mean that traffic is slowing down and 'bunching'. A flashing breakdown light will warn you to slow down until you're sure of what's happening.

If you see serious congestion ahead, you can use your hazard warning lights briefly to alert drivers behind you. This can reduce the risk of rear-end collisions, especially in bad weather.

Being seen on a motorway

Because of the higher speeds, your vehicle must be seen much earlier on a motorway than on an ordinary road.

Poor daylight In poor daylight, you should use your headlights.

Fog In fog, where visibility drops below 100 metres (328 feet), you may find it helpful to use fog lights in addition to your headlights.

You **MUST** switch your fog lights off when visibility improves. This is the law. They're misleading and can dazzle other drivers if left on. They may also make your brake lights less conspicuous.

Headlight flashing The level of noise is higher on a motorway, particularly in wet weather, and other road users may not be able to hear your horn.

If you think a warning is necessary, flash your headlights instead.

Watch out for any such warnings intended for you.

Driving and braking

At motorway speeds, braking should normally be

- unhurried
- progressive.

If you slow down gradually without putting your foot on the brake, it allows traffic to move more freely. If you are constantly touching the brake pedal and causing your brake lights to show, it encourages those

behind to do the same, causing braking and accelerating, so hindering smooth flow of traffic.

Following traffic at the correct distance will enable you to adjust your speed without having to constantly brake and accelerate heavily. This will aid the smooth flow of traffic.

It is when you are driving on a motorway that you may find it most useful to use cruise control if it is fitted (see page 60). This will help you to maintain a constant speed and may help you save fuel.

Defensive driving

- Anticipate problems; take avoiding action before they develop.
- Slow down in good time.
- Keep your distance from the vehicle ahead.
- Take particular care when overtaking lorries, as some have poor visibility to their right.

Never brake suddenly Defensive driving will reduce the likelihood of having to do so.

Remember, leave plenty of space between yourself and the vehicle ahead for controlled braking. Always check in your mirrors before you brake.

Keeping your distance

The faster the traffic, the more time and space you need for every driving action.

You should always

- give yourself greater margins than on ordinary roads
- make sure there's enough space between you and the vehicle ahead.

Traffic normally travels faster because there are usually no

- ordinary junctions
- sharp bends*
- roundabouts*
- steep hills (see page 232)
- traffic lights.

Slow-moving vehicles are generally forbidden.

*Some motorway links, where motorway regulations also apply, have roundabouts and sharp bends.

How big a gap? Leave a gap of at least one metre or yard for each mph of your speed. A useful method of judging this is to use the two-second rule described on page 140.

This rule is reinforced on some motorways where there are chevrons painted on the carriageway. Keep at least two chevrons between you and the vehicle in front.

Bad weather Leave at least double the space if the road is wet.

In icy conditions, you'll need up to 10 times the stopping distance that you do for dry conditions.

Tailgating This is a very dangerous practice, especially on motorways, where it is often the cause of serious incidents.

Lane discipline

Lane discipline is vitally important on motorways. You should normally drive in the left-hand lane.

Two-lane motorways

On a two-lane motorway, the correct position for normal driving is in the left-hand lane.

The right-hand (offside) lane is for overtaking only. Once you have overtaken you should return to the left-hand lane as soon as it is safe to do so. It's not the 'fast lane'.

Large goods vehicles are permitted to use either lane.

Motorways with three or more lanes

Because of the volume of traffic on three-lane motorways, many are being widened to four or more lanes in each direction.

Keep to the left-hand lane unless there are a great many slower vehicles ahead – it's possible to stay in the centre or outer lanes while you are overtaking a number of slower moving vehicles, but don't stay in these lanes

- longer than you have to
- if you are delaying traffic behind you.

Drivers of large goods vehicles, buses, coaches or any vehicle towing a trailer are not allowed to use the extreme right-hand lane of a motorway with more than two lanes, unless one or more lanes are temporarily closed.

Don't stay in an overtaking lane longer than it takes you to move out, overtake and move in again safely. Make sure you don't block traffic that is not allowed to use the outer lane.

Changing lanes

Don't change lanes unnecessarily. You should

- keep your vehicle steady in the centre of the lane
- not wander into another lane.

MSM routine Always use the MSM routine well before you intend to change lanes.

At higher speeds, you must start the routine much earlier.

Look and, if necessary, signal in good time. Remember vehicles might come up behind you very quickly.

The sooner you indicate, the sooner other drivers are warned of your intended movement. They'll expect a change in the traffic pattern and have time to prepare for it.

Be particularly aware of motorcyclists; they can be difficult to see due to their narrow profile but they may be travelling at high speeds. In congested situations they may filter between lanes of slower-moving traffic.

Crawler and climbing lanes

A steep hill on a motorway might have a crawler or climbing lane to avoid heavy vehicles slowing down the flow of traffic.

Controlled motorways

These motorways generally have signs advising drivers not to change lanes.

When other vehicles join

After you pass an exit, there's usually an entrance where other vehicles can join.

- Don't try to race them while they're on the slip road.
- Look well ahead; if there are several vehicles joining the motorway be prepared to adjust your speed.
- Show consideration for traffic joining the motorway and if it's safe, move to another lane to make it easier for joining traffic to merge.
- Take extra care if the motorway curves as drivers on the slip road may have difficulty seeing vehicles on the motorway.

Motorway interchanges

Where motorways merge or separate you might be required to change lanes, sometimes more than once.

Pay attention to the overhead direction signs and move into the correct lane in good time.

Where the hatch markings indicate splitter islands, stay in your lane.

Assess conditions well ahead and watch for other drivers changing lane.

Changes in traffic conditions

Traffic conditions can vary as much on a motorway as on an ordinary road.

There can be rush hour traffic near cities, heavy traffic near roadworks and constantly busy sections in other places.

These differences will be more noticeable on two-lane motorways.

Defensive driving

React to changes well in advance. Don't wait until you're forced to react.

Further information on lane discipline for other road types can be found in section 7.

Overtaking

Leave a safe distance between you and the vehicle you intend to overtake.

Use the appropriate parts of the MSM/PSL routine. For example

Mirror Check behind to verify the speed, course and position of traffic behind you.

Position You should be able to move out smoothly to the right without making any sudden movements.

Speed Make sure you're going fast enough or can accelerate quickly enough to overtake without blocking any vehicle coming up behind.

Look Look ahead and use your mirror to check if there's anything preventing you from overtaking safely; for example, a lane closure ahead or traffic coming up much faster from behind in the right-hand lane.

Try to anticipate whether the vehicle ahead will move out to overtake.

A quick sideways glance into the blind area might sometimes be necessary before you change lanes.

Remember LADA

- **L**ook
- **A**ssess well ahead
- **D**ecide – don't rush
- **A**ct – only when you're sure it's safe.

Mirrors You must use your mirrors regularly and sensibly.

Remember that vehicles coming up in the right hand lane are likely to be moving faster than you are. Watch out particularly for motorcyclists as they are more difficult to see. Watch for vehicles returning to the lane you intend to use.

Signal You must signal well before you start to move out. This gives drivers behind you plenty of time to anticipate what you intend to do and could influence any manoeuvres they're planning.

Pulling out

Check your mirrors again, and take a quick sideways glance into the blind spot, before pulling out smoothly into an overtaking lane. Overtake as quickly and safely as possible.

Moving back into the left

Pass the vehicle and signal, if necessary, before moving back into the left as soon as you're sure it's safe to do so. Don't cut in too soon in front of the vehicle you've just passed.

Look well ahead for any vehicles about to move out into the lane into which you intend to move. Allow plenty of room. Finally, make sure your indicator signal cancels properly.

Overtaking on the left

Never overtake on the left, unless the traffic is moving in queues and the queue on your right is moving more slowly than the queue you are in.

On busy motorways

If you come up behind traffic moving more slowly than you are when you are overtaking, be patient and

- don't intimidate the driver ahead by repeatedly flashing your headlights and driving dangerously close behind
- wait until the vehicle ahead can move safely to the left, then proceed.

Defensive driving

Let faster traffic pass you. If other drivers are breaking the speed limit, don't add to the danger by trying to enforce the legal speed limit. Don't move to a lane on the left to overtake.

Never use the hard shoulder to overtake – unless directed to do so by traffic signs at roadworks, by police officers or Highways Agency traffic officers in uniform.

Leaving a motorway

Unless you're going to the end of the motorway, you'll leave by moving left from the left-hand lane into the slip road. Position yourself in the left-hand lane in plenty of time.

Plan well ahead, particularly on motorways with three or four lanes.

Road signs

Use the road signs and markers to help you time your exit and use your mirrors and indicators appropriately.

You'll have plenty of time to observe the signs and markers so there's no need to rush.

One mile before the exit A junction sign with road numbers, unless there are exits very close together.

Half a mile before the exit A sign with the names of places accessible from that exit.

Countdown markers These are positioned at 270 metres (300 yards), 180 metres (200 yards) and 90 metres (100 yards) before the start of the slip road.

Where a lane splits off from the motorway as a dedicated lane, countdown markers are not provided.

To leave the motorway

Use your mirrors and signal in good time. Remember to use the MSM/PSL routine.

Get into the left-hand lane early, unless you're already in it.

On a motorway with three or four lanes, this could mean changing lanes more than once. You must follow the MSM/PSL routine for each change of lane.

> **Remember,** use your mirrors and signal left in good time to move into the left-hand lane.

Don't

- cut straight across into the slip road
- move to the left more than one lane at a time
- cut across at the last moment, especially from the second lane of a three- or four-lane motorway.

The hard shoulder is **not** an exit road, and you must avoid queuing on it.

Occasionally, where motorways merge, there may be an exit just before the one you intend to take. In these cases, or where there are service areas near to exits, look well ahead for the advance warning signs.

If you miss your exit, carry on to the next one.

End of motorway

There will be 'end of motorway' signs at all exits. These mean that the road you're joining may have different rules.

Remember to watch for any signs telling you what these are, particularly

- speed limits
- a dual carriageway
- two-way traffic
- a clearway
- a motorway link road
- part-time traffic lights.

Remember, because of the change in traffic conditions you need to watch for pedestrians, cyclists and other road users who are prohibited on motorways.

Speed when leaving a motorway

After driving at motorway speeds for some time, your judgement of speed will almost certainly be affected; 40 or 45 mph (60 or 72 km/h) will seem more like 20 mph (32 km/h). Stay aware of your speed.

- Adjust your driving to suit the new conditions.
- Check your speedometer. It will give you the accurate speed.

Remember, even if you do not have to reduce your speed because the road you are joining is a dual carriageway, drivers of some other vehicles have to conform to a lower speed limit. Be aware, therefore, that they may reduce their speed.

Reduce speed at first

For the sake of safety, reduce your speed until you're accustomed to the change of conditions. It could take you time to adjust.

Motorway slip roads and link roads often have sharp curves which should be taken at much lower speeds.

Look ahead for traffic queuing at a roundabout or traffic signals.

Weather conditions

The advice given in section 12 (all-weather driving) is even more important on a motorway.

Wet weather

Visibility can be made worse because at higher speeds vehicles, especially large ones, throw up more spray. So

- use your headlights to help other drivers see you. Don't use rear fog lights unless visibility is less than 100 metres (328 feet)
- always reduce your speed when conditions are poor. Driving is safer at lower speeds
- adjust your speed to suit the conditions and leave larger separation distances, at least double the normal gap.

Ice or frost

The presence of ice or frost can seriously affect your handling of the vehicle.

Try to anticipate the road surface conditions. If your steering feels light, it is an indication that there may be frost or ice. A very gentle touch on your brakes to see their response could help you judge the road surface conditions.

Allow up to 10 times the distance for braking.

Crosswinds

Wind is another motorway hazard.

Wind can affect your steering. If it's coming from the left on an exposed stretch of motorway, be especially careful. A sudden gust as you pass a large vehicle, or come out from under the shelter of a bridge or embankment, can send you swerving to the right.

In strong wind, drivers of high-sided vehicles or those towing caravans are likely to experience difficulties. Motorcyclists are also often seriously affected by strong crosswinds. Allow for this when overtaking these vehicles.

Fog

Driving on the motorway when the weather is foggy can be particularly hazardous.

If there's fog on the motorway, you must be able to stop well within the distance you can see to be clear.

- Use dipped headlights.
- Check your mirrors and slow down; fog affects both visibility and judgement of speed and distance.
- Check your speedometer and leave plenty of space between your vehicle and the vehicle ahead.

Fog can drift quickly and is often patchy.

If a motorway warning sign shows 'FOG'

- be prepared
- reduce speed in good time.

Unfortunately, multiple pile-ups are all too common in foggy conditions. They don't just happen. They are caused by drivers who are

- travelling too fast
- driving too close to the vehicle in front
- assuming there's nothing in the fog ahead
- ignoring the obvious!

If there is fog

- switch on your fog lamps if visibility drops below 100 metres (328 feet)
- be prepared to leave the motorway
- be on the alert for incidents ahead
- watch out for emergency vehicles coming up behind, possibly on the hard shoulder.

Remember, don't 'hang on' to the lights of the vehicle ahead. You'll be too close to brake if it stops suddenly.

Stopping on motorways

You must only stop on a motorway if

- red lights or other signs or signals tell you to do so
- you are asked to stop by the police, Highways Agency traffic officers or Vehicle and Operator Services Agency officers
- it's an emergency
- it will prevent an incident.

You must not stop to pick up or set down anyone on any part of a motorway, including a slip road.

The hard shoulder Use the hard shoulder only in an emergency.

Slowing down and stopping

If you have to slow down or stop on the carriageway as a result of traffic congestion, switch on your hazard warning lights to warn traffic behind you of the obstruction ahead. Once you are sure they have been seen, switch them off.

Breakdowns and incidents

Information about how to deal with breakdowns and incidents on a motorway can be found in section 15, page 289 and section 16, page 295 respectively.

Parking

Service areas are the only parking places provided on motorway routes. To reach the services, follow the same procedure as for a motorway exit.

Once you are off the motorway, slow down and be aware that a low speed will feel very different after motorway driving. Watch out for sharp turns into car parking areas. Other drivers could fail to reduce their speed sufficiently. Once you have stopped in the car park, keep children and animals under control.

When you leave your vehicle, remember to lock it. Don't leave valuables (cameras, etc) on view. Be a careful pedestrian.

To rejoin the motorway, follow the same procedure as when joining the motorway at any entrance.

Motorways at night

Section 13 deals in general with driving at night and much of it applies to motorway driving.

Take special note of 'Your eyes in the dark' on page 267.

> **Remember,** if you've just left a well-lit service area, give your eyes time to adjust to the darkness.

Use your headlights

Always use your headlights, even on motorways which are lit. Use dipped beam if you're likely to dazzle drivers ahead or oncoming drivers, particularly on a left-hand curve.

If you're dazzled You may have to slow down, but don't brake too hard; there might be a vehicle behind you.

Judging speed

It's harder to judge speed and distance both on a motorway and at night.

If you change lanes to overtake, or to leave the motorway, use your indicators earlier and give yourself even more time.

Reflective studs

These can help you determine the road layout. Their positions are as follows.

- **Red** Between hard shoulder and carriageway.

- **White** Between lanes.

- **Amber** Between edge of carriageway and central reservation.

- **Green** Between carriageway and slip road exits and entrances.

- **Fluorescent green/yellow** At contraflow systems and roadworks.

Roadworks

Incidents can often happen at roadworks when drivers fail to observe simple rules of safety. Obey all signs, including speed limit signs.

Approaching roadworks

- Reduce speed in good time when warned by advance warning signs, gantry signs or flashing signals – don't leave everything to the last minute as this can greatly increase the chance of mistakes and incidents.

- Get into the lane indicated for use by your vehicle in good time.

- Where lanes are restricted, merge in turn.

- When you drop your speed it may seem as if you are travelling more slowly than you really are – it is important to observe the speed limit and not just slow down to the speed that feels safe to you.

- Look out for road workers who are placing or removing signs. They might need to cross the carriageway, especially when temporary barriers and cones are being erected or dismantled.

Travelling through roadworks

- Obey all speed limits, they have been imposed for a reason. Roadworks are complicated areas and you will need more time to spot hazards, for your own safety and the safety of road workers.

- If all drivers observe the speed limits, it helps to keep traffic moving and not 'bunching up' – this is good for journey times and the environment.

- Keep the correct separation distance from the vehicle ahead; you will need time to brake if the vehicle in front stops suddenly.

- Avoid sharp braking and sudden steering movements.

- Don't change lanes when signs tell you to stay in your lane.
- Don't let your attention wander; road workers can appear in unexpected places and can be difficult to spot in cluttered areas.

Exiting roadworks

Stay within the speed limits even when you are leaving the coned areas. There may be road workers' vehicles leaving the roadworks at this point. Even if you see the road worker, remember that they may not have seen you. Don't speed up until you're clear of the roadworks.

> **Remember,** people may be working at roadworks sites and their safety is at risk if you do not follow the advice above.

Contraflow systems

These are temporary systems where traffic travelling in opposite directions shares the same carriageway. They allow traffic to keep moving during repairs or alterations on the other carriageway.

The lanes are often narrower than normal lanes. Red and white marker posts separate traffic travelling in opposite directions and fluorescent or reflective bright green/yellow studs often replace normal ones.

Contraflow systems may also be found on other roads carrying fast-moving traffic.

Watch out for
- lane change signs
- vehicles broken down ahead – there's often no hard shoulder
- vehicles braking ahead – keep your distance.

Mobile roadworks

Minor maintenance work may sometimes be carried out without the need for major lane closures. Slow-moving or stationary works vehicles, with a large arrow on the back of the vehicle, are used to divert traffic to the right or left as appropriate.

There are no cones or other delineators when these vehicles are being used.

The novice driver

Driving on motorways places greater demands on the driver's skill, observation, anticipation, planning and concentration. It's important that you get proper guidance before you attempt to drive on your own on a motorway.

If you've recently passed your test, you should take further professional instruction before driving on a motorway. The Pass Plus training scheme aims to improve your driving skills and make you a safer driver, and it includes a section on motorway driving. You can get details of the Pass Plus scheme by calling **0115 936 6504** or visiting **direct.gov.uk/passplus**

If you've recently passed your test, haven't driven for a while, or your driving hasn't included heavy, fast-moving traffic, your decision-making skills might not be up to the standard needed.

You should

- ask advice from a professional instructor who can give you valid, safe instruction
- use every chance to observe and learn as a passenger
- select fairly quiet sections of motorway to practise on
- get used to driving at 60–70 mph (96–112 km/h) and keeping up with the flow of the traffic.

> **Remember,** don't drive on a motorway until you're fully prepared. The next move you make always has to be the right one.

Bear in mind that the vehicles on either side and behind you could weigh over 30 tonnes and be travelling at 50–60 mph (80–96 km/h) or even faster.

section **twelve**

ALL-WEATHER DRIVING

This section covers

- Your vehicle
- Ensuring a clear view
- Wet roads
- Crosswinds
- Fog
- Snow and ice
- Bright sunshine
  and hot weather

Your vehicle

Whatever the weather, make sure your vehicle and equipment are in good condition and regularly checked and serviced.

In bad weather the condition of your vehicle is even more important, especially your tyres and brakes.

Different weather conditions can lead to a variety of different hazards, both from season to season and from region to region.

Tyres

Check tyre condition and pressures frequently. Make sure that the tyres have a good tread, that the walls are undamaged and that they are inflated to the correct pressure.

Also check your tyres for uneven wear of the tread, either across or around the tyre, which could be due to a mechanical defect. Have your vehicle checked, any fault put right and a new tyre fitted if necessary.

Good tyres are especially important in snow, on icy roads and in heavy rain. Be prepared; don't wait until the bad weather shows up the deficiency – it might be too late, and your life could depend on a few millimetres of rubber which should have been there.

Brakes

Keep your brakes in top condition. Stopping takes much longer on wet, slippery roads, even with perfect brakes.

Ensuring a clear view

The biggest single danger to any driver is being unable to see properly. You won't be able to make the right decisions if you can't see the road clearly.

Always keep your windscreen, mirrors and windows clean and clear.

Wipers and washers

Make sure your wiper blades are effective.

Make sure washers are working and keep the reservoir filled. Use an additive, as it helps

- to prevent freezing in winter
- to clear dead insects and smears off the windscreen in summer.

Misting up

Misting up of the mirror and glass inside the car affects your ability to see. Even on a summer's day a sudden shower can make the glass mist up inside.

- Keep a dry cloth handy and clean all inside glass.
- Wipe the windows dry before you set out.
- Use your demisters. If your car has a heated windscreen, use it early. Also, use your heated rear window to maintain your rear vision.
- Open your windows to clear mist, if necessary.
- If your car is fitted with air conditioning, this can assist with clearing windows.

Read your vehicle handbook and follow the maker's suggestions for effective heating and ventilation.

Many anti-mist and anti-frost accessories are available, including

- liquid for keeping glass clear
- de-icers
- prepared cloths
- electrically heated glass.

Warm, dry air works best, is by far the cheapest and is usually in plentiful supply once the engine has warmed up.

Wait until the windscreen has cleared completely before pulling away.

However, when you start from cold, you won't be able to create warm air so use a dry cloth or a chamois leather. If you have a passenger, ask them to help keep side windows clear – this is essential when manoeuvring.

Icy weather

If the weather is particularly icy, your windows and windscreen can be frozen over.

Give yourself plenty of time to clear the windscreen. Before setting out, wait until your demister and heater are working well enough to keep the whole of the windscreen and rear window clear.

Take care not to damage wiper blades, which may have frozen onto the windscreen or rear window. Never use boiling water to clear the windscreen; you could break the glass. Use water that is barely lukewarm or even cold – this is still warmer than ice and will start the defrosting process.

Rain

Use dipped headlights in poor visibility (such as rain, drizzle, mist, or very poor light) so that other drivers can see you.

Rain can drastically reduce your view through the windscreen and windows and in the outside driving mirrors.

The cleaner the glass, the sooner the wipers can clear the outside of the screen. Always keep the washer bottle topped up.

Keep your speed down in very wet weather. Some windscreen wipers are not efficient enough to deal with very heavy rain.

In dirty weather conditions, clean your windscreen, windows, indicators and lights as often as necessary.

Remember, whatever the weather, don't drive unless you can see properly all around.

Wet roads

Stopping distance

Wet roads reduce tyre grip, so slow down. Give yourself plenty of time and room for slowing down and stopping. Keep well back from other vehicles. On a wet road, you should allow at least double the braking distance for a dry road.

After a spell of dry weather, rain on the road can make the surface even more slippery. Take extra care, especially when cornering. Be aware that different road surfaces might affect the grip of your tyres.

Remember, the less tread on your tyres, the greater the increase in braking distance.

Consider others Pedestrians and cyclists can easily get drenched by passing vehicles. Look well ahead and show consideration by slowing down or giving them more room when it's safe to do so. Also give cyclists room to pull out to avoid large puddles.

Aquaplaning

A great danger when driving at speed in very wet weather is the build-up of water between the tyre and the road surface. As a result your vehicle actually slides forwards on a thin film of water as your tyres lose contact with the road surface. This is called aquaplaning. Even good tyres cannot grip in this situation.

A clear indication that you are aquaplaning can be that the steering suddenly feels very light. When this happens, slow down by easing off the accelerator. Never brake or try to change direction, because when you're aquaplaning, you've no control at all over steering or braking.

The higher your speed on a wet road, the more likely you are to aquaplane. You must keep your speed down and watch for water pooling on the road surface.

Even at lower speeds, if the front and rear tyres on one side of the vehicle hit a patch of deeper water, the vehicle may swerve because of the additional resistance on that side.

Spray

Another reason for keeping your speed down on wet roads is the amount of water thrown up by other vehicles.

Overtaking or being overtaken by heavy vehicles on a motorway can be an unnerving experience.

If necessary, slow down to increase the distance between you and the large vehicle, remembering to look in your mirrors before you do so.

Sometimes wipers can't keep the windscreen clear even when working at full speed. This results in the driver being temporarily blinded to conditions ahead; you may need to slow down.

If water sprays up under the bonnet, it can stop the engine or affect the electronic controls.

Dealing with floods

When you have to pass through a flood, take your time. Stop and assess how deep the water is. Don't just drive into it. Some roads that are likely to flood have depth gauges. Check the depth on these.

Deep water If the water seems too deep for your vehicle, turn back and go around the flood by another road. It might take a little longer, but that's better than finding yourself stranded.

If the water is too deep it could

- flood the exhaust, causing the engine to stop
- find its way into the air intake on some vehicles, causing serious engine damage.

Shallow water If the water is not too deep, drive on slowly but be sure to keep to the shallowest part. Remember, because of the camber of the road, the water is probably deepest near the kerb and shallowest at the crown.

Driving through floodwater Drive in first gear as slowly as possible but keep the engine speed high and steady by slipping the clutch.

- If the engine speed is too low, you might stall.
- If you go too fast, you could create a bow wave. Water will flood the engine and it could cut out.

Try to strike a balance.

Engines and water Some types of diesel engine will tolerate a certain amount of water, but many modern fuel systems are electronically controlled and are, therefore, affected by water.

All petrol engines can be seriously affected by even small amounts of water being splashed onto the electrical components; these can include engine management systems, coil, distributor, leads and so on.

Crossing a ford

The depth of water at a ford varies with the weather and is usually greater in winter. There may be a depth gauge in the area. If the water is not too deep for your vehicle, cross using the same technique as you would for a flood.

Remember to test your brakes after you cross. There might be a notice reminding you to do so.

Don't try to displace the water by 'charging' at the flood or ford.

- You could lose control.
- Your vehicle will probably stall.
- You could end up blocking the road.

Test your brakes

Water can reduce the effectiveness of your brakes, so test your brakes whenever you have passed through water on the road. When you've driven safely through, check your mirrors first and then test your brakes.

If they do not work properly, it will help to dry them out if you apply light pressure to the brake pedal while driving along slowly. Do not drive at normal speed until you are sure they are working properly.

Crosswinds

Some vehicles can become unstable in strong crosswinds (or side winds), because of their large surface area and comparatively low weight.

This can happen particularly on exposed stretches of road such as motorways, viaducts and bridges.

The effect can vary from a slight pull on the steering wheel to a distinct wander, possibly into the path of another vehicle.

In very bad cases, the whole vehicle can be lifted bodily off the road with very serious results.

Cyclists and motorcyclists

In gusty conditions, watch for cyclists or motorcyclists being blown sideways and veering into your path. Allow extra room when overtaking.

High-sided vehicles

Drivers of high-sided vehicles, or those towing caravans, trailers or horseboxes (particularly empty ones) should

- pay special attention to forecasts of strong winds
- avoid well-known trouble spots and high bridges.

Drivers of these vehicles should be constantly alert for the effects of wind near bridges and embankments, even on normal journeys in reasonable conditions. If there is a severe weather warning, consider if your journey is really necessary.

Other drivers should bear this in mind when about to overtake, or when being overtaken by, these particular types of vehicle.

Fog

Fog is one of the most dangerous weather conditions. An incident involving one vehicle can quickly involve many others, especially if they're driving too close to one another.

Motorway pile-ups in fog have sometimes involved dozens of vehicles. All too often there's a loss of life or serious injury, which could easily have been prevented.

Observe the obvious It doesn't need a sign to tell you it's foggy if you can only see a short distance ahead!

Avoid driving in fog

Take alternative transport or postpone your journey, if at all possible. If you must drive, give yourself time to prepare.

> **Remember,** if the fog is thick and you can see the rear lights of the vehicle ahead, then you may be too close to stop in an emergency.

Check all lights, clean your windscreen, and so on. Allow more time for the journey.

Use of lights

Correctly adjusted fog lights can be a valuable aid when driving in fog.

In daylight You **MUST** use your dipped headlights and/or front fog lights when visibility is seriously reduced.

- They'll be seen from a much greater distance than sidelights.
- They won't dazzle other drivers or pedestrians in the daytime.

You could also consider using dipped headlights, or at least sidelights, in relatively light fog. Remember that, even if you think **you** can see far enough ahead, your own vehicle might not be clearly visible to others until you're too close. If in any doubt, always try to maximise your visibility in the interests of safety.

Use fog lights if your vehicle is fitted with them.

At dusk Use dipped beams at dusk and other times when visibility is poor.

At night In darkness you might need to depend entirely on fog lights, or alternate between fog lights and dipped beams through stretches of thick and thin fog.

High-intensity rear fog lights If your vehicle has high-intensity rear fog lights, use them in fog only when visibility is seriously reduced. Normally this means when you cannot see for more than 100 metres (328 feet).

Remember, you MUST switch fog lights off when visibility improves – it is the law. Using them at other times, such as in the rain, can dazzle drivers behind you.

Adjust your lights Change your lighting with the conditions. For example, when you're queuing in traffic and the driver behind has already seen you, it can be helpful to switch off your rear fog lights temporarily to avoid dazzling them.

Driving in fog

Poor visibility is frustrating and a strain on the eyes. Your ability to anticipate is dangerously restricted. It's also much more difficult to judge distances and speed in fog when outlines become confusing. You can easily become disoriented – especially on an unfamiliar road.

In the interests of safety, you **MUST**

- slow down – check the speedometer from time to time
- be able to stop well within the distance you can see to be clear
- use your windscreen wipers to keep the outside of the screen clear
- use your demister to keep the inside of the screen clear. Use your heated windscreen if your vehicle has one.

Fog itself doesn't claim lives, but the standard of driving in fog results in death and destruction which could have been avoided.

Do

- give yourself plenty of time and space to deal with whatever is ahead. Decide what's a safe speed for the conditions and stick to it. Don't let other drivers push you into driving faster
- watch out for emergency vehicles. There could well be an incident ahead.

Don't

- follow the vehicle in front too closely
- try to keep up with the vehicle ahead. You'll get a false impression that the fog isn't too bad if you 'hang on' to the lights of the vehicle ahead because it will displace some of the fog
- use main beam when you're in fog as the fog reflects the light and can dazzle you, reducing your visibility even further. It can also dazzle other drivers.

Fog patches The density of fog varies. Sometimes the fog is patchy. One moment it can be fairly clear, the next extremely dense. Avoid the temptation to speed up between the patches.

Following another vehicle Slow down and leave plenty of room for stopping. There may be something ahead which you cannot possibly see until you're too close to it.

If the vehicle ahead has to stop suddenly, you must leave enough time to react and brake.

You may not see or recognise that the vehicle ahead is braking or has stopped as soon as you would in clear weather.

You need to be able to brake safely, so remember the road surface is often slippery in fog.

Overtaking Overtaking in fog can be particularly dangerous. You could well find that visibility ahead is much worse than you thought, and you won't be able to see oncoming traffic soon enough.

Junctions

Dealing with junctions in fog needs particular care, especially when turning right. You should

- open your window(s) and switch off your radio/CD player so you can hear any approaching traffic
- start indicating as early as you can
- make the greatest possible use of your lights. If you keep your foot on the brake pedal while you're stopped, your brake lights will give drivers behind an extra warning
- use the horn if you feel it will help, and listen for other vehicles.

Don't turn or emerge until you're absolutely sure it's safe.

Road markings Dipped headlights will pick out reflective studs, but it's not so easy to recognise other road markings when driving in fog. Explanations of the different coloured studs are given on page 112.

Remember, motorcyclists can be much more difficult to see in fog as they have only one headlight and tail light.

Try to keep a central position between lane lines or studs. Don't mix up lane lines and centre lines. Driving too close to the centre could mean you're dangerously near someone coming the other way who might be doing the same thing. Driving on the centre line as a means of finding your way is extremely dangerous.

Stopping

Parking Never park on a road in the fog if you can avoid it. Find an off-street parking place. However, if it is unavoidable, always leave your parking or side lights on.

Don't leave dipped headlights or the main beam on. In foggy conditions, these can lead other road users to wrongly think they have drifted over to the extreme right-hand side of the road. If they quickly try to correct this positioning in order to keep to what they think is the left-hand side, they would mount the pavement.

This would be very dangerous for any pedestrians and other road users nearby. There might also be damage to walls, properties, street furniture and other vehicles. In rural areas there might be a ditch instead of a path, or even an embankment leading down to water.

Breaking down If you break down, get your vehicle off the road if you possibly can. Inform the police, and make arrangements to remove it as soon as possible if it creates an obstruction. Never leave it without warning lights of some kind, or on the wrong side of the road.

Snow and ice

Is your journey really necessary?

In winter, especially if the weather doesn't look good, check the local weather forecast before setting out. If snow or ice is forecast, don't drive unless your journey is essential.

Before setting off

If you consider it necessary to travel, it is useful to carry the following in case you get stuck or your vehicle breaks down

- warm drink and emergency food
- warm clothing and boots
- de-icer/ice scraper
- torch
- first aid kit
- spade or shovel
- jump leads
- blanket
- old sacks.

You should also

- clear all snow and ice from all of your windows so that you can see clearly all round
- ensure all lights are clean and free from snow so they can be seen by other road users
- make sure the mirrors are clear and the windows are demisted thoroughly so that you have the best visibility possible
- clear snow from the bonnet and roof so that it doesn't fly off and cause a danger to other road users such as motorcyclists or cyclists.

Starting off on snow

If you experience wheelspin when you're starting off in deep snow, don't race the engine because the wheels will dig in further.

Try to move the car slightly backwards and then forwards out of the rut. Use the highest gear you can.

In these conditions, it's worthwhile carrying a spade and some old sacks. These can be useful to help get you going when you've become stuck in snow.

Snow chains are available which can be fitted over existing wheels and tyres to help avoid getting stuck and to reduce the danger of skidding.

Driving in snow

When falling snow reduces visibility, use your dipped headlights as you would in heavy rain or fog. Falling or freshly fallen snow need not cause too much difficulty, providing you remember to

- increase the gap between you and the vehicle in front, remembering to look in your mirror before slowing down

- test your brakes, very gently, from time to time, but be sure to look in your mirrors before braking. Snow can pack behind the front wheels or around brake linkages under the car and so affect steering and braking

- be prepared to clear the windscreen by hand. Your wipers, even with the aid of the heater, may not be able to sweep the snow clear. Snow might collect and pack around your lamps and indicators

- drive with care, even if the roads have been treated. Conditions can change over very short distances

- try to find out about weather and traffic conditions ahead by listening to travel bulletins on the radio and noting any information on the variable message signs.

In areas which are subject to prolonged periods of snow, it may be an advantage to fit

- snow chains (attachments which fit over existing wheels and tyres)

- mud and snow (M and S) tyres with a tread pattern designed for these conditions.

Snow will cover up road markings – take care when you cannot see which road has priority.

Driving in icy conditions

Overnight freezing usually results in an icy surface, especially on less-used roads. Look for signs of frost on verges, etc.

It's even more dangerous when the roads are just beginning to freeze or thaw. The combination of water and ice adds up to an extremely slippery surface.

Rain freezing on roads as it falls (black ice) is an invisible danger. As with aquaplaning, your steering will feel especially light.

When driving on ice

- you need to keep your speed down
- treat every control – brakes, accelerator, steering, clutch and gears – very delicately.

If it's very cold, treat all wet-looking surfaces as though they are frozen because they probably are. If the road looks wet but there is no sound from the tyres, expect ice.

Braking on snow and ice

All but the most gentle braking will lock your wheels on packed snow and ice.

If your front wheels lock, you can't steer. If you can't steer, you can't keep out of trouble.

For vehicles without ABS brakes, in slippery conditions, repeatedly applying and releasing the brakes will slow the vehicle down and enable you to keep control.

Using this method will allow some degree of steering control.

Get into a lower gear earlier than normal. Allow your speed to fall and use the brake pedal gently and early to keep your speed well under control.

Braking distances Braking distances on ice can easily be 10 times normal distances.

Downhill braking Downhill braking calls for careful speed control well before reaching the actual hill, as well as while you're on it.

By selecting a low gear, the engine compression will help to hold the vehicle back and reduce the overall speed.

Anti-lock brakes ABS may reduce the risk of vehicle instability when braking on snow and ice. However, they cannot compensate for poor judgement or excessive speed. They will not help your tyres stay in contact with the road surface in ice or snow.

Cornering on ice and snow

Time your driving and adjust your speed so that you don't have to use your brakes at all on a bend.

Approach a corner at a steady speed, using as high a gear as you reasonably can.

- Be gentle with the accelerator.
- Don't use the clutch unless you absolutely have to.
- Steer smoothly – sudden movements must be avoided.
- Take just as much care coming out of a turn.

Braking on an icy or snow-covered bend is extremely dangerous. The centrifugal force will continue to pull you outwards and the wheels will not grip very well. This could cause your vehicle to spin.

Climbing hills on ice and snow

Speed must be kept down on icy and slippery roads. But this can bring with it other problems.

For example, when going uphill you might lose momentum. Trying to regain speed and keep going could cause severe wheel-spin and loss of control.

If you have to stop, it could be difficult to start again.

Leave a good gap between you and the vehicle in front. If it stops you'll at least have a chance to keep going while it restarts, or even pass it altogether.

To reduce the chances of wheelspin, use the highest gear you reasonably can.

Don't rush a hill thinking you'll change down on the way up. Before reaching the hill, get into a gear which will take you all the way up.

Changing gear is not easy on an icy slope. It takes very delicate footwork to avoid wheelspin and loss of speed.

Other vehicles on snow and ice

If you find a vehicle heading toward you that is obviously out of control, try to make maximum use of engine braking if there's time. If you must use the brake pedal, be as gentle as possible.

Avoid braking and steering at the same time to get out of the way. Both are dangerous in icy conditions.

Constantly assess what's ahead. Be prepared, and look for escape routes.

Bright sunshine and hot weather

Be prepared

Before you begin a long journey, make sure you're prepared for the weather.

Tyres Tyre pressures should be checked and adjusted when they're cold.

Don't check the pressure when you've been driving for a while because tyres will be warm and the reading will be inaccurate.

Coolant Before you start your journey, check the level of coolant in the system.

Clear windscreen There are generally more flies and insects about in hot weather, and your windscreen needs to be kept clean.

Keep the windscreen as clear as possible of water and grease marks. This helps to cut down glare.

Check the level in the washer reservoir and top up if necessary. Using an additive may help to keep the windscreen clean.

Driving

Glare One of the main problems when driving in sunny conditions is glare. This can seriously reduce your ability to see.

Reduce speed and take extra care. If the roads are wet, reflected glare can increase the problem.

Drive slowly and carefully if you are being dazzled by bright sunshine. Watch out particularly for pedestrians and cyclists, and make sure you can stop quickly if necessary.

Constant sun in your eyes can be exhausting on a long journey and may well affect your concentration.

Even if you don't feel the need for them, the correct sunglasses can reduce the glare and keep your eyesight effective for longer. This is especially important if you're driving abroad, where conditions are hotter and the sunlight brighter than you may be used to.

Low-angle sun Glare can be worse in the winter when the sun is low in the sky. Wear sunglasses and/or use your visor to cut out as much glare as possible. Avoid looking directly into the sun.

Coping with heat

Make sure you use adequate ventilation inside the car. Air conditioning helps, if you have it. Take plenty of breaks and refreshment on a long trip.

If you feel sleepy, stop and rest where it's safe. Never stop on the hard shoulder of a motorway when you feel tired. Use the service areas or get off the motorway.

Listen to travel information and try to avoid known traffic hold-ups.

Overheated engines in long traffic queues are the most frequent causes of breakdowns in these conditions.

Road surfaces

Soft tarmac During long periods of hot weather, many tarmac road surfaces become extremely soft. Take care when braking and cornering.

Oil Oil and water can make the hot surface of the road slippery and dangerous, particularly if there's a sudden rain shower after a long dry spell.

Take extra care; watch your speed and keep your distance.

Loose chippings Many highway authorities replace the granite chipping road surfaces during the summer. Always observe the special warning speed limits and keep well back from the vehicle in front.

Flying stone chips can cause not only expensive damage to your vehicle, but also serious injury to pedestrians and other road users.

section **thirteen**

DRIVING AT NIGHT

This section covers
- Your vehicle lights
- Driving in the dark
- Built-up areas
- Overtaking or following at night
- Parking at night
- Meeting other vehicles

Your vehicle lights

In the dark, your vehicle lights are the most important source of information both for you and for other road users. They also tell other drivers your movements. Use them with care and consideration.

Always

- keep your headlights clean
- use your headlights at night, dipped or full beam, as appropriate
- use dipped headlights at any time when the light is poor, even during the day, as this will make you more visible to others.

You should

- check all your lights before and during a long journey
- fix any lighting fault immediately, for your own safety and the safety of others. Carry spare bulbs where applicable
- remember that extra weight at the rear of your vehicle could cause your headlights to dazzle other road users. Some models have headlamp adjusters to deal with this.

Auxiliary driving lights

Auxiliary driving lights are main beam headlights and may be used to improve the view of the road ahead. However, they must only be used in conjunction with the obligatory main beam headlights and they must all switch off at the same time.

Only one pair of dipped beam headlights may be fitted to a vehicle. Front fog lights **MUST NOT** be used to improve the view of the road ahead, except in seriously reduced visibility.

Junctions at night

Brake lights can dazzle. Don't keep your foot on the brake pedal if you're waiting at a junction or queuing in traffic, except in fog – use the parking brake.

However, switch off your indicator light only if it's dazzling the driver behind and, if you do switch it off, make sure you switch it on again before you move off.

Driving in the dark

You'll find you're very much more limited in dark conditions. You can't see as far as you can in daylight, so less information is available.

Problems vary widely with the type of road and amount of traffic.

Speed at night

You need to be more alert and aware that you can't safely drive as fast in the dark as you can in the daylight. This includes driving at dusk or dawn, even in good weather.

Never drive so fast that you can't stop well within the distance you can see to be clear. That is, within the range of your lights.

To enable you to see the greatest distance, you should normally use main beam headlights on unlit roads unless

- you're following another vehicle
- you're meeting oncoming traffic.

On lit roads you should normally use dipped headlights.

If you can't stop safely within the range of your lights, you're going too fast.

Note
Fluorescent material shows up well in daylight or at dusk, but is of little use in the dark. Only reflective material shows up well in headlights.

Avoid dazzling others

If you meet any other road user, including cyclists and pedestrians, dip your headlights in good time to avoid dazzling them.

At dusk

You may find it best to put your headlights on at dusk, just before lighting-up time. At this time in the evening many shades of vehicle paintwork such as black, blues and greys and surprisingly white and silver as well, seem to blend in with the failing light.

Colours, particularly the more neutral ones, become less easy to distinguish than you would expect in the half-light of dusk. The situation is often made worse by the fact that some vehicles will already be using lights and some will not.

Ultimately, it can mean that some unlit vehicles can be almost invisible until you are very close to them. Don't be afraid to be the first driver to switch on – it's better to see and be seen.

At dawn

The opposite applies. Don't switch off your headlights until you're sure it's safe. Make sure you can see and be seen. If you are driving a dark-coloured car you should

- switch on earlier
- switch off later.

When you drive with your headlights on, other drivers can

- see you earlier
- tell which way you're heading. This is often difficult in the half-light without lights.

Your eyes in the dark

You should have your eyesight checked regularly. Ask yourself, 'Can I really see as well as I would like?'

If you can't see so well in the dark, it might be your eyes that are to blame; driving in the dark may be highlighting the need for an eyesight check.

How far can you see? Test yourself in a suitable place.

Pick an object within the range of your lights and see if you can stop by the time you reach it. You'll be surprised how difficult this is with dipped lights on an unlit road, and shows that you should take a good look before you dip your lights.

Lighter-coloured objects are easier to see at night.

Adjusting to darkness Give your eyes a minute or two to adjust to the darkness, particularly when you're coming out of a brightly lit area or building.

You can always use the time to clean your lights, mirrors, windscreen, etc. Remember this when you leave a motorway service area after a rest or refuelling stop.

A clean windscreen cuts down dazzle.

Don't

- wear tinted glasses or sunglasses
- spray the windscreen or windows with tints.

Built-up areas

The phrase 'built-up area' refers to areas such as town centres and residential streets. They also have regularly spaced street lighting. Unless signs show otherwise, this would normally mean that there is a 30 mph (48 km/h) speed limit in force (see rules 113 and 124, as well as the speed limits table on page 40 of The Highway Code).

Always use dipped headlights, or dim-dip if fitted, in built-up areas at night. It helps others to see you. In areas where street lights cause patches of shadow watch out for pedestrians, especially those in dark clothes, who can be difficult to see.

Remember to

- be on the alert for pedestrians
- approach pedestrian crossings at a speed at which you can stop safely if necessary
- watch for cyclists and joggers.

Noise at night

Keep all noise to a minimum.

- Don't rev your engine.
- Close your car doors quietly.

Remember that neighbours and children may be asleep. Take extra care setting and disarming the anti-theft alarm on your vehicle.

Using the horn at night You must not use your horn between 11.30 pm and 7.00 am in a built-up area (except to avoid danger from a moving vehicle).

If you need to warn other road users of your presence at night, flash your headlights.

Overtaking or following at night

You'll need to take extra care before attempting to overtake at night. It's more difficult because you can see less. Only overtake if you can see that the road ahead will remain clear until after you have finished the manoeuvre. Don't overtake if there's a chance you are approaching

- a road junction
- a bend or hidden dip in the road
- the brow of a bridge or hill, except on a dual carriageway
- a pedestrian crossing
- road markings indicating double white lines ahead

or if there's likely to be

- a vehicle overtaking or turning right
- any other potential hazard.

Stay clear and dip

Make sure you don't get too close to the vehicle ahead, and always dip your lights so you don't dazzle the driver. Your light beam should fall short of the rear of the vehicle in front. Remember your separation distance.

On a dual carriageway or motorway where it's possible to overtake, don't use full beam in the face of oncoming drivers.

If you're being overtaken

Dip your lights as soon as the vehicle passes you, to avoid causing glare in the mirrors of the overtaking vehicle.

Parking at night

Cars and light goods vehicles (1525 kg or less, unladen), invalid carriages and motorcycles can park without lights on roads with a speed limit of 30 mph (48 km/h) or less. They must comply with any parking restrictions, and not park within 10 metres (32 feet) of a junction.

They must also be parked parallel to, and close to, the side of the road or in a designated parking place and facing in the direction of the traffic flow.

If you have to park on any other road, you should never

* leave your vehicle without side or parking lights unless a sign indicates that lights are not required. It would be better to get it off the road altogether

* leave your vehicle standing on the right-hand side of the road, except in a one-way street.

Always switch your headlights off when you stop, even for a short while. It's an offence to leave them on when the vehicle is parked. The fixed glare can be very dazzling especially if, for any reason, the vehicle is on the offside of the road facing oncoming traffic. Leaving lights on can also use up the battery.

Meeting other vehicles

Another vehicle's lights can tell you in which direction they're heading and can give you an idea of their speed. Oncoming lights should raise a number of questions in your mind, such as

- how far away is the vehicle and how fast is it moving?
- should I slow down while we pass each other?
- how soon should I dip my lights?
- how far ahead can I see before I dip?
- before I dip, is there anything on my side of the road
  - that I might endanger?
  - that might endanger me?

Examples include a stationary vehicle, a cyclist, a pedestrian, or an unlit builder's skip.

When your headlights are on full beam

- dip early enough to avoid dazzling oncoming drivers, but not too early
- check the left-hand verge before you dip.

If you're dazzled

If the headlights of oncoming vehicles dazzle you, slow down and, if necessary, stop. Don't look directly at oncoming headlights.

Don't retaliate by leaving your lights on full beam and dazzling the oncoming driver.

On a left-hand bend

Dip earlier. Your headlights will cut straight across the eyes of anyone coming toward you. On a right-hand bend this might not happen, or it won't happen so soon.

section **fourteen**

BASIC MAINTENANCE

This section covers
- Fuel
- Oils and coolant
- Steering and suspension
- Brakes
- Tyres
- Electrical systems
- Basic fault-finding

Fuel

Don't let the fuel in your tank run too low. This can cause running problems and even damage the engine. Fill up before you reach that stage. Some vehicles have a warning light which shows when the fuel is getting low.

Fuel cans If you carry reserve fuel in a can, make sure it is of an approved type for carrying fuel. It's illegal and dangerous to carry petrol in a container not intended for that purpose.

Motorway driving Make sure you have plenty of fuel before driving on a motorway.

Driving at higher speeds tends to use more fuel and there can sometimes be quite a distance between service areas.

Petrol engines

Choose the right grade of petrol. Using the wrong grade could damage your engine.

Leaded fuel must not be used in vehicles fitted with a catalytic converter. Even one tankful can permanently damage the system.

Diesel engines

Diesel fuel is environmentally friendly, provided the engine is tuned correctly. Take care to avoid spilling diesel fuel when refuelling, since it will cause an extremely slippery surface.

Warning Take care never to put petrol into a diesel vehicle, or diesel fuel into a petrol-engined vehicle. Look carefully at the pump you're going to use!

Oils and coolant

Engine oil

Oil is necessary to lubricate your engine. You need to keep the oil at the level recommended by the vehicle manufacturer. Check regularly and top up the oil when necessary, especially before a long journey.

Ideally you should check the oil level every time you fill up with fuel.

How to check the oil level The dipstick will tell you the amount of oil in the engine. See the vehicle handbook.

You should check the oil while the engine is cold for a more accurate result. You'll need a clean, dry cloth to wipe the dipstick.

- Ensure the vehicle is on a level area and not on a slope.
- Look for the dipstick on the engine block of your vehicle.

Take particular care if your vehicle is fitted with automatic transmission. There may be an additional dipstick for transmission oil level checks. Consult the vehicle handbook.

Oil changes Observe the manufacturer's recommendations. If you make a lot of short journeys, change the oil at more frequent intervals, especially in dusty conditions. Remember to have the oil filter changed at the same time.

Warning Oil is toxic and can cause skin problems. Use protective gloves or a barrier cream and always wash oil off your hands immediately.

Keep containers storing oil out of reach of children.

Oil use The amount of oil an engine will use depends on

- the type of engine
- the amount of wear
- how you drive.

Don't

- run the engine when the oil level is below the minimum mark
- add so much oil that the level rises above the maximum mark. You'll create excess pressure that could damage the engine seals and gaskets, and cause oil leaks. Moving internal parts can hit the oil surface in an overfull engine and may do serious or even terminal damage.

Warning light If the oil pressure warning light on your instrument panel comes on when you're driving, stop as soon as you can and check the oil level.

The oil in your engine has to perform several tasks at high pressures and temperatures up to 300 °C. It helps to

- resist wear on the moving surfaces
- combat the corrosive acids formed as the hydrocarbons in the fuels are burnt in the engine
- keep the engine cool.

It also has to withstand gradual contamination from both fuel and dirt.

Make sure you always use the lubricants recommended in the vehicle handbook.

Lubricating oils – gearbox

Most vehicles have a separate lubricating oil supply for the gearbox.

This oil is especially formulated for use in the gearbox and you should always follow the instructions in the vehicle handbook.

It's not necessary to drain the gearbox in most cases, but the level should be checked at service intervals.

Lubricating oils – final drive/rear axle

Front-wheel drive vehicles may not have a separate supply for the final drive and gearbox, but most have a common filler/level plug. The specified gear oil should be used to top up.

With rear-wheel drive vehicles there's a filler/level hole at the rear of the differential (on the rear axle) which can be more easily reached when the vehicle is raised, but remember to keep the vehicle level.

It's important that the correct hypoid-type extreme pressure (EP) oil specified in the vehicle handbook is used.

You may have to squeeze the top-up oil in via a plastic bottle and tube.

Coolant

Vehicles today use a mixture of water and anti-freeze to make up the coolant. This helps to keep most engines comparatively cool and it is kept in the radiator all the year round.

The anti-freeze contains a corrosion inhibitor which reduces rust and oxidation in alloy engines and prolongs the life of the system. In cold weather, maintain the recommended strength of anti-freeze. Have it checked at least annually – late summer or early autumn is best.

You should check the coolant level frequently, particularly before a long trip, topping up with coolant as necessary. Look for the high/low level markings on the header tank, where one is fitted. The need to top up often might indicate a leak or other fault in the cooling system. Have it checked by your garage or dealer.

It's a good idea always to carry a supply of coolant with you.

Warning

- Never remove a radiator or header tank cap when the engine is hot.
- Never add cold water to an overheated engine, let it cool for a while first.
- Don't overfill or the system will blow the excess out as soon as it warms up.

Steering and suspension

Steering

If you feel or hear any knocking or rattling noises from the steering or suspension you should seek advice.

Excessive movement or play in the steering wheel may indicate wear in the steering mechanism. You should seek qualified advice without delay.

Power-assisted steering

When the ignition is on and/or the engine is running, movement of the steering wheel will cause hydraulic pressure or electrical energy to assist the driver and make the steering easier. If the steering needs a lot of effort (becomes heavy) the power assistance system may not be working properly.

Before starting a journey, two simple checks can be made. Gentle pressure on the steering wheel, maintained while the ignition switch is moved to 'on' or the engine is started, should result in a slight but noticeable movement as the system begins to operate.

Alternatively, turning the steering wheel just after moving off will give an immediate indication that the power assistance is functioning.

Check the level of fluid in the pump reservoir regularly when the engine is switched off. The level should be between the 'min' and 'max' marks.

Never run the engine without oil in the pump reservoir. You could severely damage the pump or cause it to seize up completely.

Suspension

Check the condition of shock absorbers by examining them for signs of fluid leaks and by bouncing the vehicle. It should not continue to bounce unduly when tested. If in doubt, seek qualified assistance.

Worn shock absorbers make a vehicle difficult to control and can increase your stopping distance.

Brakes

Brakes are one of the most important elements in driving safety.

Footbrake

Note any variations in braking efficiency. If the brakes feel spongy or slack, get them checked by a qualified mechanic. They are too important to be ignored.

Testing your brakes Test the brakes every day as you set out. Choose a safe spot on the road.

If you hear any strange noises, or if the vehicle pulls to one side, consult your garage immediately.

Check the brake fluid level regularly, but don't overfill. Look for the high/low markings on the reservoir. Make sure the brake fluid reservoir is kept topped up. Consult the vehicle handbook.

Parking brake

Check for excessive wear on the parking brake in the following way. When applying the brake, ensure that there's no excessive travel of the brake lever and that the lever locks securely. The parking brake must prevent the vehicle from moving.

Adjust the parking brake setting if

- the amount of travel is above the limit specified in the vehicle handbook
- the vehicle can roll on a gradient when the parking brake is fully set.

Regular servicing

Regular servicing will help to make sure your brakes are safe. Follow the manufacturer's recommendation on service intervals. Unless you're a skilled amateur mechanic, leave brake checking, adjustment and replacement of brake pads and shoes to your garage.

If you're in any doubt about your vehicle's ability to brake safely, don't use it. Have it checked immediately.

Warning lights

Most vehicles are equipped with a warning signal to indicate certain faults within the braking system. If the red warning signal shows, consult your vehicle handbook or obtain guidance from a competent mechanic. Driving the vehicle with a brake defect could be dangerous and may constitute an offence.

Anti-lock braking systems If your vehicle has anti-lock brakes, there will also be a warning light for that system to indicate a fault. If this light comes on, have the brakes checked immediately. Consult your vehicle handbook or your garage before driving the vehicle. Only if it's safe, drive carefully to the nearest garage.

On a motorway If you have any reason to suspect that your brakes are defective when you're driving on a motorway, leave at the next exit and drive carefully to a garage.

Tyres

Your tyres are your only contact with the road. The area of contact is as small as the sole of a shoe for each tyre. Tyres won't grip properly and safely unless they're in good condition and correctly inflated; they can easily become damaged. Make sure you check wear and tear and replace them when necessary.

The penalties for using faulty tyres or tyres worn beyond the minimum legal tread depth are very severe. They may include a fixed fine of up to £2500, discretionary disqualification and driving licence endorsement for every faulty tyre.

The condition of your tyres

- Check that the walls of the tyres are free from cuts and bulges.
- Check that all your tyres have a good depth of tread right across and all around them. The legal requirement for cars, vans, trailers and caravans is not less than 1.6 mm tread depth across the central three-quarters of the breadth of the tyre and around the entire outer circumference. However, it is recommended that you replace your tyres before this legal limit is reached.

- Have the wheel alignment and wheel balance, suspension and braking system checked regularly. If there's a fault, get it put right as soon as you can, otherwise the wear on the tyres will be excessive or uneven.
- If you see that parts of the tread are wearing before others, seek advice. This can indicate a tyre, brake, steering or suspension fault.

Don't let grease and oil stay on your tyres. Remove anything (stones, glass, etc) caught in the treads. These can work their way in and cause damage.

Tyre pressure

You can't guess pressures just by looking at a tyre, except when it's obviously flat.

Check your tyres regularly – at least once a week. Use a reliable gauge and follow the vehicle handbook for the correct tyre pressure.

Check your tyres and adjust the pressure when they're cold. Don't forget the spare tyre and remember to refit the valve caps.

The handbook will also tell you if you need different pressures for different conditions.

Generally, the pressure should be higher for a heavily loaded vehicle or if you're intending to drive at high speed for a long distance, eg motorway journeys.

Tubeless tyres When you're replacing a tubeless tyre, fit a new valve to the wheel.

> **Remember,** it's so dangerous to use a car with a tyre not properly inflated that it's an offence.

Punctures should only be repaired if the damaged tyre can be vulcanised (a specialist hot-weld process) to meet legal requirements.

You should run in new tyres at reasonable speeds for the first 100 miles (160 km) because they don't grip the road surface quite so well when they are new and shiny.

How to save wear and tear on tyres

- Check tyre pressures frequently.
- Avoid driving over potholes and broken road surfaces. If you can't avoid them, slow down.
- Don't drive over kerbs or scrape the wheels along them when manoeuvring. You'll damage the wall of the tyre and this could cause a blow-out later.
- Hitting the kerb can also affect the tracking of the front wheels. If there are any signs of uneven front tyre wear, have the steering checked.
- Think and plan ahead. Avoid high speeds, fast cornering and heavy braking, all of which increase tyre wear.

Electrical systems

Battery

Most modern batteries are maintenance-free and sealed for life. The terminals should be secure, clean and greased.

If the battery is fitted with a filler cap or caps, check the level of the fluid. The plates in each cell should be covered. Top up with distilled water if necessary, but avoid overfilling.

Lights

Check the operation of the front and rear lights, brake lights and indicators, including hazard lights, each time you use the vehicle.

Make use of reflections in windows and garage doors, or ask someone to help you.

It's a good idea to carry a selection of spare bulbs, if applicable. Your vehicle handbook should give the bulb replacement procedure, if relevant.

Headlights **MUST** be properly adjusted to

- avoid dazzling other road users
- enable the driver to see the road ahead adequately.

All lights **MUST**

- be clean and in good working order
- show a steady light.

Indicators

- must be clearly visible and in good working order
- must flash between once and twice per second.

Windscreen washers and wipers

Check the windscreen washer mechanism and the washer reservoirs. Make sure there's enough liquid.

The washer can be very important in wet, muddy conditions. If you carry a supply of water, you can use a sponge to wash away any heavy dirt wherever you happen to be.

Check the wipers. Replace worn or damaged blades. If your vehicle is fitted with headlight washers, the same attention should be paid to these.

The horn

Check the horn is working properly and sounding clearly. Take care not to alarm or annoy others when doing so.

Basic fault-finding

For detailed advice consult either the vehicle handbook, a workshop maintenance manual or a qualified mechanic.

The tables on pages 368–369 give only a brief guide to simple fault-finding and remedies.

If you have any doubts about the roadworthiness of the vehicle, obtain specialised assistance without delay. Don't ignore the warning signs.

Remember, prevention is better (and cheaper) than cure. Having your vehicle serviced according to the maintenance schedule helps the engine work more efficiently. This will save fuel and reduce the effect on the environment by cutting emissions. If you notice any fault, consult your garage.

Some minor faults can be easily identified and corrected, but with the more complex engine management and electronic systems in modern motor vehicles, anything beyond a simple repair is better left to qualified mechanics; especially when the vehicle's warranty might be affected.

Maintenance

Check all levels and systems as recommended.

Changing filters and spark plugs at the recommended intervals will help keep your vehicle reliable and prolong its life.

Air filter Replace the air filter at the intervals recommended by the manufacturer, or sooner if the vehicle is used in exceptionally dusty conditions.

Overhead camshaft engines On this design of engine it's vital to replace the camshaft drive belt at the recommended intervals. Serious damage can be caused to the engine if the belt breaks.

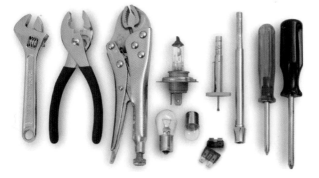

BREAKDOWNS

This section covers

- o Breakdowns
- o Breakdowns on motorways
- o On dual carriageways
- o Punctures and blow-outs

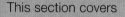

Breakdowns

You can reduce the chances of breaking down with preventive maintenance and regular vehicle checks. However, no matter how careful you are, your vehicle can still break down – a puncture or engine problem is always possible.

Knowing how to deal with such a situation efficiently and safely is essential for every driver.

Many breakdowns are the result of

- neglect
- failing to make routine checks
- inadequate preventive maintenance
- abuse of the vehicle.

Don't drive on ignoring unusual noises or symptoms or if you're concerned that the problem might be serious.

Be prepared

Carry a tool kit in your vehicle. The following items are useful to keep for emergency use

- a warning triangle (or other permitted warning device; see overleaf)
- spare bulbs and fuses
- a torch
- vinyl tape
- wire
- jump leads
- a tow rope
- pliers
- a plastic container of water.

If you do break down it is useful to wear high-visibility clothing so you can be seen by other road users. Consider carrying a fluorescent and reflective waistcoat (fluorescent so it can be seen in daylight and reflective so it can be seen at night).

National breakdown/motoring organisations By joining a national organisation or taking out breakdown insurance, you'll save a great deal of time and money if you break down.

Most services include an option to take your vehicle and passengers either to your destination or to your home.

The annual fee is usually less than the cost of a single motorway breakdown call-out.

Warning devices

Permitted warning devices There are various warning devices that you can buy to place on the road to warn other drivers when you have broken down. Don't use any of these warning devices

- on a motorway
- as an excuse to leave your car in a dangerous position.

Advance warning triangles Advance warning triangles fold flat and don't take up much space in the car. You should carry one and use it to warn other road users if your car is obstructing the highway or is in a dangerous position as a result of a breakdown or a road traffic incident.

Where to position the triangle You should place the triangle on the road, well back from the car.

- On a straight, level road, put the triangle 45 metres (147 feet) from your vehicle.
- On a winding or hilly road, put the triangle where drivers will see it before they have to deal with any bend or hump in the road.
- On a very narrow road, put the triangle on the nearside verge or footpath.

Always use your hazard warning lights as well as a warning triangle, especially at night.

Other warning devices These include traffic cones, flat traffic delineators (which resemble a flattened cone) and traffic pyramids. At least four of any of these should be placed in a line behind your vehicle to guide traffic past. A flashing amber light may be used with any of these warning devices, but may not be used on its own.

Alternatively a flexible yellow sheet displaying a red triangle can be placed on the vehicle as long as it does not obscure the number plate, lights or reflectors.

When you break down

As a general rule, brake as gently as possible and pull over as far to the left as possible to keep your vehicle away from approaching traffic.

If the breakdown affects your control of the car

- try to keep in a straight line by holding the steering wheel firmly
- avoid braking severely
- steer gently on to the side of the road as you lose speed.

If possible, get your car off the road and

- use your hazard warning lights to warn others
- keep your sidelights on if it is dark or visibility is poor

- wear high-visibility clothing to help other road users see you if you need to get out of your car
- do not stand behind your vehicle where you might obscure the lights
- use a warning device, particularly if you've broken down near a bend or over the brow of a hill. Do not use one if you have broken down on a motorway.

Keep children and animals under control, and away from the road.

Always take great care when you are placing or retrieving a warning device.

Contact the police if your vehicle is causing an obstruction, and a breakdown service if you're unable to rectify the fault yourself.

Don't

- ask for help from passing strangers
- accept help from strangers
- leave your vehicle for any longer than you really have to.

Drivers travelling alone You might feel vulnerable if you're travelling alone and you break down – especially on an isolated stretch of road, a dual carriageway or a motorway.

You should spend as little time as possible away from your vehicle.

When you telephone for assistance, make it clear to the operator that you're travelling alone. Priority will often be given in these cases.

Moving your vehicle

If your vehicle cannot be repaired where it has broken down, it will need to be moved.

There are three options

- being recovered by a breakdown organisation to which you belong (the best option)
- calling out a local garage (probably the most costly)
- being towed by a friend (the most dangerous – in no circumstances should an inexperienced driver consider this).

If you are being towed, remember that the braking will not be as effective and the steering will feel heavier if the engine is not running.

Tunnels

For breakdowns and incidents in tunnels see page 303.

Breakdowns on motorways

If you cannot reach the next exit or service area, steer your vehicle onto the hard shoulder as safely as possible, and as far to the left as you can, away from traffic.

When you stop it is a good idea to have your wheels turned to the left so that if you are hit from behind, your vehicle is not pushed on to the main carriageway.

When you stop

Once you have stopped

- switch on your hazard lights to warn other drivers that you've broken down
- make sure your sidelights are on in poor visibility or at night
- don't open the offside doors
- warn your passengers of the dangers of passing vehicles
- keep animals inside
- with your passengers, leave the vehicle by the nearside door away from the traffic. Lock all doors, except the front passenger door
- ask your passengers to wait near the vehicle, but on the embankment away from the hard shoulder
- telephone the emergency services (let them know if you are a vulnerable motorist such as disabled, older, travelling alone or with young children). If possible use a roadside emergency telephone which will pinpoint your position, rather than a mobile phone (see page 290).

Never

- attempt even simple repairs on the motorway
- place any kind of warning device on the carriageway or hard shoulder.

Disabled drivers If you have any kind of mobility difficulty you should stay in your vehicle and

- keep your seat belt fastened
- switch on your hazard warning lights
- display a 'help' pennant or use a mobile phone, if you have one in your vehicle, and be prepared to advise the emergency services of your location.

Calling for help

Emergency telephones These telephones are connected to control centres and are on most stretches of motorway at one-mile intervals.

Look for a telephone symbol and arrow on marker posts 100 metres (328 feet) apart along the hard shoulder.

The arrow directs you to the nearest phone on your side of the carriageway. Walk to the telephone, keeping on the inside of the hard shoulder.

Never cross the carriageway or an exit or entry slip road to reach a telephone or for any other purpose.

Using the emergency telephone The telephone connects you to a control centre, who will put you through to a breakdown service. Always face the traffic when you speak on the telephone.

You'll be asked for

- the number on the telephone, which gives your precise location
- details of your vehicle and your membership details, if you belong to one of the motoring organisations
- details of the fault.

If you're a vulnerable motorist such as a woman travelling alone, make this clear to the operator. You'll also be told approximately how long you'll have to wait.

Mobile phones If you are unable to use an emergency telephone, use a mobile phone if you have one in your vehicle.

However, before you call, make sure that you can provide precise details of your location. Marker posts on the side of the hard shoulder identify your location and you should provide these details when you call.

Waiting for the emergency services

Wait on the bank near your vehicle, so you can see the emergency services arriving.

Don't wait in your vehicle unless another vehicle pulls up near you, and you feel at risk.

Many motorway deaths are caused by vehicles driving into people on the hard shoulder. When you're on the hard shoulder you're much more likely to be injured by motorway traffic than suffer a personal attack.

If anyone approaches

• get into the vehicle

• lock all the doors

• lower the window slightly

• speak through a small gap.

Then ask for identity and tell them that the police or control centre have been told and the emergency services are coming.

A Highways Agency traffic officer or a person claiming to be from the emergency services should have

• an identity card

• your details: your name and information about the breakdown.

Leave your vehicle again as soon as you feel the danger has passed.

If you can't get your vehicle onto the hard shoulder, switch on your hazard warning lights and leave your vehicle only when you can safely get clear of the carriageway.

To rejoin the motorway

Use the hard shoulder to build up speed before joining the other traffic when it's safe to do so. Don't try to move out from behind another vehicle or force your way into the stream of traffic.

Remember to switch off your hazard warning lights before moving off.

On dual carriageways

Some dual carriageways are similar to motorways; they have

- a hard shoulder
- emergency telephones at regular intervals.

Most dual carriageways do not have a wide hard shoulder. If you break down on one of these get your car safely away from the road if you can – onto the grass verge or lay-by if there is one.

Do not stop on unprotected lay-bys on dual carriageways if at all possible. Unprotected lay-bys are those where there is no kerbed island between the main carriageway and the lay-by.

Many fatal incidents involving stopped vehicles on dual carriageways occur at these lay-bys. Try to find a protected lay-by if at all possible; you will be much safer there.

If you have to stop on a grass verge, take care as long grass could ignite from the heat of a catalytic converter.

You should also

- use your hazard warning lights and warning triangle or other warning device to warn others
- move your passengers to a safe position off the carriageway, well away from the vehicle
- go to the nearest telephone and arrange assistance
- keep animals safely in the car.

Punctures and blow-outs

If your car suddenly becomes unstable or you begin to notice steering problems, you might have a puncture or a blow-out (burst tyre).

Try not to panic.

- Take your foot off the accelerator.
- Don't brake suddenly.
- Try to keep a straight course by holding the steering wheel firmly.
- Stop gradually at the side of the road.
- Get the vehicle away from the traffic (onto the hard shoulder if you're on a motorway).

If you have to move the vehicle, do so very slowly to avoid further damage to the tyre or wheel rim.

Get the vehicle to a place of safety before attempting to change the wheel.

If you can't get off the road altogether, use your warning triangle, or any other permitted warning device, to warn other drivers, particularly if you're near a bend. Never use one on a motorway.

If necessary, wait for assistance.

On a motorway, never attempt to change a tyre yourself. Always use the emergency telephones to call for assistance.

If you do have to change a wheel and can do so safely, remember to

- secure the vehicle when changing any wheel by applying the parking brake and using chocks if available
- work on a level surface
- retighten the wheel nuts or studs after changing a wheel.

section **sixteen**

INCIDENTS, ACCIDENTS AND EMERGENCIES

This section covers

- The scene of an incident
- First aid on the road
- Fire and electric shock
- Tunnels

The scene of an incident

As we have seen in earlier sections, you can reduce the chances of being involved in an incident by driving defensively. Unfortunately road traffic incidents are always possible, even with the greatest care.

You might also come upon the scene of an incident. It could happen that you're the first to arrive and the safety of others, both the existing casualties and other road users, might be in your hands.

Knowledge and preparation can save lives. If you're involved in an incident, you **MUST** stop.

If you're the first or among the first to arrive at the scene of an incident, remember

- further collisions can, and do, happen
- fire is a major hazard
- both the victims and helpers are in danger.

What to do

Warn other traffic Do this by

- switching on hazard warning lights or other lights
- displaying an advance warning triangle (unless you are on a motorway)
- using any other means to warn other drivers.

Put out cigarettes or other fire hazards. Switch off your engine and warn others to do the same.

Call the emergency services if necessary.

Calling emergency services Give full details of the location and casualties. On a motorway, this could mean going to the nearest emergency telephone.

Mobile phones It can be very tempting to reach immediately for your mobile phone to call the emergency services.

Before you do, make sure you are able to tell them exactly where you are. This is particularly important on a motorway where imprecise details can cause great problems for the emergency services. Location details are given on marker posts located on the hard shoulder. Always check these before you make your call.

Dealing with those involved Move uninjured people away from the vehicles involved to a place of safety. On a motorway this should be away from the carriageway, hard shoulder or central reservation.

Don't move casualties trapped in vehicles unless they're in danger. Be prepared to give first aid as described later in this section.

Don't remove a motorcyclist's helmet unless it is essential to do so; for example, if they are having breathing difficulties.

When an ambulance arrives, give the crew as many facts as you can (but not assumptions, diagnoses, etc).

Dangerous goods

If the incident involves a vehicle containing dangerous goods

- switch off your engine and do not smoke
- keep well away from the vehicle
- call the emergency services and give the police or fire brigade as much information as possible about the labels and other markings. Do not use a mobile phone close to a vehicle carrying flammable loads
- beware of dangerous liquids, dust or vapours, no matter how small a concentration, or however minor the effects on you may seem.

Full details of hazard warning plates, such as the one shown below, are given in The Highway Code.

Passing the scene of an incident

If you are not one of the first to arrive at the scene of an incident and enough people have already stopped to give assistance, you should drive past carefully and not be distracted by the incident.

If the incident is on the other side of a dual carriageway or motorway, do not slow down to look. You may cause another collision on your side of the road or, at the very least, additional and unnecessary traffic congestion.

Always give way to emergency and incident support vehicles. Watch out for their flashing lights and listen for their warning sirens. Depending on the type of vehicle, the flashing lights used could be red, blue, amber or green (see rules 106, 107 and 219 in The Highway Code).

Police cones or vehicles If these are obstructing the road, do not drive round them, you should stop. They mean that the road ahead is closed or blocked for an unspecified time.

If you're involved in a road traffic incident

You **MUST** stop.

If there are injuries, ask someone to call an ambulance and the police. Ask them to return to you when they have made the call to confirm that they have made it. You should

- give whatever help you can. People who seem to be unhurt may be suffering from shock, and may in fact be unaware of their injuries

- ask yourself if you're hurt too. If in doubt, get a check-up at the hospital.

You **MUST** call the police

- if anyone's hurt
- if you've damaged someone else's property but can't find them to tell them.

If you hit a domestic or farm animal, try to find the owner to report any injuries.

For any incident involving

- injury to any person or animal
- damage to any vehicle or property

give your name and address, the name and address of the vehicle's owner and the registration number of the vehicle to anyone having reasonable grounds for requiring them. If this is not possible at the time of the incident, you must report the incident to the police as soon as possible and in any case within 24 hours. In Northern Ireland you must do this immediately.

If there has been an injury, you must also give insurance details to the police. If you can't produce the insurance documents when you report the incident, you have up to seven days to produce them at a police station of your choice.

Witnesses Note any witnesses and try to make sure they don't leave before you get their names and addresses.

Make a note of the numbers of any vehicles whose occupants might have witnessed the incident.

You'll need to exchange details and obtain

- the other driver's name, address and phone number
- the make and registration number(s) of the other vehicle(s) involved
- insurance details.

Find out the vehicle owner's details too, if different.

Information Gather as much information as you can, such as

- damage and/or injuries caused
- weather conditions
- road conditions
- details of other vehicles. Record all information: the colour, condition, whether the lights were on, and whether they were showing any indicator signals
- what was said by you and other people
- identification numbers of police involved.

Take photographs If you have a camera it can be useful to take photographs at the scene.

Draw a map Show the situation before and after the incident, and give distances

- between vehicles
- from road signs or junctions
- away from the kerb.

Note skid marks, where any witnesses were situated, street names, car speeds and directions.

Statements If the police ask you for a statement, you don't have to make one straight away. It could be better to wait a while, even if you don't appear to be suffering from shock.

Write your statement later. Take care with the wording, and keep a copy.

First aid on the road

The following information may be of general assistance, but there's no substitute for proper training.

Any first aid given at the scene of an incident should be looked on only as a temporary measure until the emergency services arrive.

If you haven't any first aid training the following points could be helpful.

Incident victims (adults and children)

It is essential that the following are given immediate priority if the casualty is unconscious and permanent injury is to be avoided.

Remember the letters **DR A B C**

D – Danger Check that you are not in danger.

R – Response Try to get a response by asking questions and gently shaking their shoulder.

A – Airway The airway must be clear and kept open.

B – Breathing Normal breathing must be established. If normal breathing is absent

C – Compressions Compressions should be administered to maintain circulation (see opposite).

Airway Place one hand on the forehead and two fingers under the chin, and gently tilt the head back.

Breathing Once the airway is open check breathing by placing your cheek over their mouth and nose, listen for breath, look to see if the chest rises and feel for breath. Do this for up to 10 seconds.

Compressions If they are not breathing normally, place two hands in the centre of the chest and press down 4–5 cm at a rate of 100/minute. You may only need one hand for a child. Give 30 chest compressions.

Then tilt the head back gently, pinch the casualty's nostrils together and place your mouth over theirs. Give two breaths, each lasting one second (use gentle breaths for a child).

Continue with cycles of 30 chest compressions and two breaths until medical help arrives.

Incident victims (infants under one year)

Use the same procedures as for adults and children, except

- use two fingers in the middle of the chest when delivering compressions
- to deliver breaths, make a seal over the infant's mouth **and** nose with your mouth. Breathe **very** gently.

Unconscious and breathing

Do not move a casualty unless there's further danger. Movement could add to spinal or neck injury. If breathing is not normal or stops, treat as recommended in the breathing section.

Don't attempt to remove a motorcyclist's helmet unless it's essential – for example, if the casualty is not breathing normally – otherwise serious injury could result.

If an adult or child is unconscious and breathing, place them on their side in the recovery position (as shown below).

- Place the arm nearest you straight out, move the other arm, palm upwards, against the casualty's cheek.
- With your other hand grasp the far leg, just above the knee and pull it up, keeping the foot flat on the ground.

- Pull the knee towards you, keeping their hand pressed against their cheek and position the leg at a right angle.

Make sure their airway remains open and that you monitor the casualty's condition until medical help arrives.

Bleeding

First check for anything that may be in the wound, such as glass. Taking care not to press on the object, build up padding on either side of the object. If there is nothing embedded, apply firm pressure over the wound to stem the flow of blood. As soon as practical, fasten a pad to the wound with a bandage or length of cloth. Use the cleanest material available.

If a limb is bleeding but not broken, raise it above the level of the heart to reduce the

flow of blood. Any restriction of blood circulation for more than a short time could cause long-term injuries. It is vital to obtain skilled medical help as soon as possible. Make sure that someone dials 999 or 112.

Dealing with shock

The effects of shock may not be immediately obvious. Warning signs to look for include

- rapid pulse
- pale grey skin
- sweating
- rapid, shallow breathing.

Prompt treatment can help to deal with shock.

- Don't give the casualty anything to eat or drink.
- Reassure the victim confidently and keep checking on them.
- Keep casualties warm and make them as comfortable as you can.
- Talk firmly and quietly to anyone who's hysterical.
- Don't let shock victims wander into the path of other traffic.
- Try not to leave any casualty alone.
- Don't move the casualty unless it's necessary.
- If a casualty does need to be moved for their own safety, take care to avoid making their injuries worse.

Burns

Check the casualty for shock, and if possible, try to cool the burn for at least 10 minutes. Try to find a liquid that is clean, cold and non-toxic with which to douse it.

Do not try to remove anything that is sticking to the burn.

Be prepared

Always carry a first aid kit – you might never need it, but it could save a life.

Learn first aid – you can get first aid training from a qualified organisation such as

- St John Ambulance and Brigade
- St Andrew's First Aid
- British Red Cross Society.

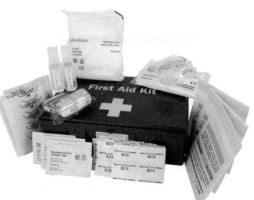

Fire and electric shock

Fire

Carrying a suitable fire extinguisher in your vehicle may help you to put out a small fire.

If you suspect a fire in the engine compartment

- pull up as safely and as quickly as possible
- get all passengers out safely
- summon assistance or get someone to dial 999 or 112
- **do not** open the bonnet
- you may be able to direct any available fire extinguisher through the small gap available when the release catch is operated.
- if the fire appears to be large **do not** try to tackle it; get well clear of the vehicle and leave it to the fire service
- **do not** take any risks.

Remember, fire can spread through a vehicle with alarming speed.

If you notice a strong smell of petrol, don't ignore it – investigate!

Electric shock

Some incidents involve a vehicle hitting overhead cables or electrical supplies to traffic bollards, traffic lights or street lights. Check before trying to get someone out of a vehicle in such cases.

Don't touch any person who's obviously in contact with live electricity unless you can use some non-conducting item, such as a piece of dry wood, plastic or similar – anything wet should not be used. You must not try to give first aid until contact has been broken.

A person can also be electrocuted simply by being too close to a high-voltage overhead cable. Contact the provider: their telephone number may be shown on a nearby pole, then follow their advice.

Tunnels

If you break down or are involved in a road traffic incident in a tunnel

- switch on your hazard warning lights
- switch off the engine
- leave your vehicle
- give first aid to any injured people, if you are able
- call for help from an emergency point.

If your vehicle is on fire and you can drive it out of the tunnel, do so. If not

- pull over to the side and switch off the engine
- leave the vehicle immediately
- put out the fire using the vehicle's extinguisher or the one available in the tunnel

- move without delay to an emergency exit if you cannot put out the fire
- call for help from the nearest emergency point.

If the vehicle in front is on fire, switch on your warning lights then follow the above procedure, giving first aid to the injured if possible.

section **seventeen**

ECOSAFE DRIVING AND THE ENVIRONMENT

This section covers

- What you can do
- Ecosafe driving
- Choosing a vehicle
- Vehicle maintenance
- Alternatives to driving

What you can do

Transport is an essential part of modern life, but we cannot ignore its environmental consequences – local, regional and global. There's increasing public concern for the protection of our environment, with the result that many motor manufacturers are devoting more time, effort and resources to the development of environmentally friendly vehicles.

But you, as a driver, can also help. If you follow the principles of ecosafe driving set out in the following pages, you will become a more environmentally friendly driver and

- your journeys will be more comfortable
- you could considerably reduce your fuel bills
- you could reduce those emissions that cause damage to the atmosphere.

More importantly, you will become a safer driver as you develop your planning, perception and anticipation skills to a high level.

Try to drive in an ecosafe manner at all times, whether you are driving for business or pleasure. Fuel, like all forms of power, costs money as well as having an impact on the environment. Minimising the fuel or power you use is always important, both for the planet and for your pocket.

However, although it is good to save fuel, you must not compromise the safety of yourself or other road users when attempting to do so. Road safety is more important than saving fuel. At all times you should be prepared to adapt to changing conditions and it may be that you have to sacrifice fuel-saving for safety.

The effects of pollution

Air pollution contributes to health problems for many people. In densely populated areas, traffic is the biggest source of air pollution. Road transport accounts for around 20% of all emissions and how we drive can make a surprising difference to local air quality.

The particular problem with emissions from vehicles is that they are at ground level and people with conditions like respiratory problems, heart or vascular disease are particularly exposed.

Motor vehicles account for most of the movement of people and goods. In addition, pollution also causes changes to communities and the landscape, including

- damage to vegetation
- deterioration and weakening of buildings and bridges
- the depletion of natural resources
- disruption of wildlife.

Fuel combustion produces

- carbon dioxide, a major greenhouse gas; transport accounts for about one-fifth of the carbon dioxide we produce in this country
- nitric oxides from traffic; these add nitrogen to the atmosphere, causing damage and disturbance to the ecosystem.

Catalytic converters in good working order reduce these emissions.

Information about air pollution is available on

- Air Pollution Recorded Helpline – freephone **0800 556 677**
- the internet at the following sites **http://uk-air.defra.gov.uk defra.gov.uk/environment/quality/air/ air-quality/**

What you can do to help The car has become a central feature in our lives, but it is still possible to drive in a manner more beneficial to the environment by taking a little care and thought with regard to how, and when, we drive.

We give some suggestions on the following pages about what you can do to help.

Ecosafe driving

Become an ecosafe driver and drive more efficiently. Ecosafe driving is a recognised and proven style of driving that contributes to road safety while also reducing fuel consumption and emissions.

One of the main factors in increasing road safety is the emphasis on planning ahead so that you are prepared in advance for potential hazards. By increasing your hazard perception and planning skills you can make maximum use of your vehicle's momentum, engine braking and engine torque. By doing this, you can reduce damage to the environment.

Hazard awareness and planning

You should be constantly scanning all around as you drive. Check into the far distance, midground and foreground, also check behind and to the sides by frequent use of your mirrors.

Early recognition of potential hazards is important, but just looking isn't enough, you need to act correctly on what you have seen.

This will mean you are able to anticipate problems and take appropriate action in good time to ensure you are travelling at the correct speed when dealing with a hazard. By doing this you will avoid

- late braking
- harsh acceleration.

Both of these actions lead to higher fuel consumption.

Keep a safe distance from the vehicle in front as this will help you to plan your driving. Don't always use the brake when the vehicle in front of you slows down. By just taking your foot off the accelerator, your vehicle will then slow down and fuel consumption will be reduced.

However, you may wish to use your brakes to advise vehicles behind you that you are slowing down.

If you plan early for hazards

- you will avoid causing other road users to bunch
- traffic will flow more smoothly
- you will use less fuel (see page 318).

Starting up

If your car is fitted with a choke and you need to use it to start the engine when it's cold, push it in as soon as the engine will run smoothly without it.

Driving away

Avoid over-revving your engine when you start your vehicle and try to pull away smoothly.

Do not leave your engine running unnecessarily. If you are stationary and are likely to be so for more than a few minutes, you should switch off your engine to reduce emissions and noise pollution.

Choosing your speed

Always drive sensibly.

Keep within the speed limit Exceeding a speed limit by only a few miles per hour will mean that you use more fuel but, more importantly, you are breaking the law and increasing the risk of serious injury if you're involved in a collision.

Slow down Vehicles travelling at 70 mph (112 km/h) use up to 30% more fuel to cover the same distance as those travelling at 50 mph (80 km/h). However, don't travel so slowly that you inconvenience other road users.

Cruise control When appropriate, use cruise control if it's fitted. Using cruise control keeps a steady setting on the accelerator, so not varying the intake of fuel. It can also help to maintain your speed within the speed limit.

Cruise control should not be used in heavy traffic or when driving on wet or slippery roads. Remember, when cruise control is activated, your feet may not be in their usual position in relation to the foot controls.

The accelerator

Try to use the accelerator smoothly and progressively. When appropriate, take your foot off the accelerator and allow the momentum of the car to take you forward.

Taking your foot off the accelerator when going downhill can save a considerable amount of fuel without any loss of control over the vehicle.

Wherever possible, avoid rapid acceleration or heavy braking as this leads to greater fuel consumption and more pollution.

Driving smoothly can reduce fuel consumption by about 15% as well as reducing wear and tear on your vehicle.

Selecting gears

It's not always necessary to change up or down through each gear; it is possible to miss out intermediate gears (this is known as 'block' gear changing). It helps to reduce the amount of time you are accelerating, and as this is when fuel consumption is at its highest, it will help you to save fuel (see page 310).

As soon as conditions allow, use the highest gear possible without making the engine struggle.

Check fuel consumption

Check your fuel consumption regularly. To make sure you are getting the most from your car, simply record the amount of fuel you put in your car against miles travelled. This will help you to check whether you're using fuel efficiently.

If you haven't changed your method of driving, or the conditions in which you're driving, an increase in the average consumption can mean you need to have your car serviced. Ecosafe car drivers are constantly aware of how much fuel their vehicles use.

If your car is fitted with a trip computer, it can help you check your fuel consumption.

Engine braking

With your foot fully off the accelerator the engine needs very little fuel, so take advantage of engine braking wherever possible.

Engine power

Modern cars are designed to deliver power even when engine revs are quite low. You'll find that you can make use of the higher gears at low speeds.

Route planning

Plan your route and avoid known hold-ups and roadworks. Always know where you're going – you'll use a lot of fuel by getting lost.

Plan your journey beforehand.

- Use a map.
- Check a route planner on the internet.
- Programme your satellite navigation system, if you have one.

Try to use uncongested routes. Continuous research has resulted in new methods of helping the environment by easing traffic flow (more information about avoiding congestion can be found on page 16).

If you're likely to be making a prolonged stop, for more than, say, two minutes at a level crossing or roadworks, you may consider it best to stop the engine.

Minimise drag

Avoid carrying unnecessary weight – save fuel by not carrying unnecessary weight in your car. If your car's roof rack is removable, take it off when it's not in use to reduce wind resistance. The drag on a roof box can increase the fuel consumption by more than 15%.

If air conditioning is fitted, use it only when you need to – running air conditioning continuously may increase fuel consumption by about 15%.

The alternative to air conditioning may be to open your windows but this will increase drag and consequently fuel consumption when you're driving.

Parking

Always try to reverse into a parking space so you can drive out of it.

Manoeuvring while the engine is cold uses a lot of fuel. When you park in a garage or car park and intend to stay for a long time, reverse the car into the space or garage while the engine is warm, and drive out forwards when it is cold.

A cold start in really cold weather could put additional wear on the engine.

Choosing a vehicle

When choosing a vehicle, try to bear in mind economy and emissions.

There are advantages and disadvantages to all types of fuel. To help you make an informed choice and understand the effect each has on the environment, some of the differences are explained below.

Petrol engines

The modern petrol engine has been designed to operate more efficiently to meet increasingly stringent emissions standards.

Key factors in this improvement in reducing exhaust pollution are

- fuel injection
- electronic engine management systems
- redesigned exhaust systems.

Ever stricter controls on exhaust emissions require catalytic converters to be fitted to the exhaust system of all new petrol-engined vehicles.

Catalytic converters These are exhaust treatment systems which remove up to 75% of carbon monoxide, nitrogen oxide and hydrocarbons.

The converter is a honeycomb-shaped filter with a total surface area about equal to a football pitch. This surface is coated with precious metals such as platinum, palladium and rhodium. These speed up a chemical reaction in the exhaust gases as the engine heats up.

The oxygen content of the exhaust is monitored and a sensor triggers controls to adjust the air–fuel mixture.

The converter only deals with toxic and polluting gases. Carbon dioxide is still produced.

Leaded petrol cannot be used in vehicles fitted with a catalytic converter. Even one tankful can permanently damage the system.

If you over-accelerate or exceed 3000 rpm the catalytic converter cannot clean up emissions completely, and will release some that are contaminated. Make sure therefore that you don't drive in such a way that this will occur.

Diesel engines

These engines are very fuel-efficient and produce less carbon dioxide (a global warming gas) than any other road transport fuel.

Compared with petrol-engined cars, they also emit less carbon monoxide and fewer hydrocarbons. They do, however, produce more emissions of oxides of nitrogen (NOx) and particulates that are bad for local air quality.

Newer vehicles have to meet strict new emissions standards aimed at reducing these pollutants, and all diesel vehicles can now use ultra-low sulphur diesel fuel to reduce exhaust pollution.

New fuels

There are alternatives becoming available to the standard petrol and diesel fuels.

City diesel and city petrol These fuels are now available at most filling stations. They have been formulated so that the sulphur content is very low.

Sulphur is the main cause of particulates in exhaust emissions, and it also produces acid gases. The lower sulphur content in these fuels helps to reduce this source of pollution.

Liquefied petroleum gas Vehicles powered by LPG are now commercially available and the number of fuel stations is increasing steadily.

This fuel is cheaper to use than petrol or diesel and the emissions cause less air pollution. However, LPG does produce more carbon dioxide per mile travelled than diesel.

Choosing a car

Try to choose a vehicle with low fuel consumption and emissions. The Vehicle Certification Agency produces a guide to the fuel consumption of new vehicles. This information can also be found on **direct.gov.uk/carfueldata**

Other points to bear in mind

- cars with automatic transmission use about 10% more fuel than similar models with manual transmission
- consider using ultra-low sulphur petrol which is available at most filling stations
- if you own a diesel car or van, use ultra-low sulphur fuel, such as city diesel, as it reduces harmful emissions of particulates.

Vehicle maintenance

Keeping your vehicle well maintained is important to ensure maximum economy and least damage to the environment.

You should make sure that your vehicle is serviced and maintained regularly.

Servicing

Have your vehicle serviced as recommended by the manufacturer.

The cost of a service may well be less than the cost of running a badly maintained vehicle. For example, even slight brake drag can increase the fuel consumption.

Make sure your garage includes an emissions check in the service.

Tyres

Make sure that your tyres are properly inflated. Incorrect tyre pressure

- results in shorter tyre life
- may create a danger as it can affect stability and braking capacity
- can increase fuel consumption and emissions in the case of under-inflation.

When replacing tyres, consider buying energy-saving types which have reduced rolling resistance. These increase fuel efficiency and also improve your grip on the road.

Engines

Use good quality engine oil – if you use synthetic engine oils rather than the cheaper mineral oil, you can save fuel.

Make sure the engine is tuned correctly. Badly tuned cars and vans

- use more fuel
- emit more exhaust fumes.

The MOT tests now include a strict exhaust emission test to ensure that cars are properly tuned. This means they operate more efficiently and cause less air pollution.

Recycling

If you do your own maintenance, make sure that you send oil, old batteries and used tyres to a garage or local authority site for recycling or safe disposal.

Don't pour oil down the drain; it's

- illegal and could lead to prosecution
- harmful to the environment.

Alternatives to driving

Try to help lessen pollution by using your car only when it is necessary. You should

- avoid using your car for very short journeys, especially when the engine is cold
- walk or cycle for short journeys
- use public transport when you can. Light rapid transit (LRT) systems, trams or 'metros' are being introduced in some cities and large towns to provide more efficient public transport which is also environmentally friendly as it uses electric power
- consider car-sharing if there is no suitable public transport. Consider sharing with a colleague or friend who is making the same journey (for example, to work or on the 'school run')
- avoid using your car when air pollution is high, if at all possible.

As well as the environmental effects of driving, consider also the relative costs, safety and travelling times of various forms of transport.

Costs When considering the costs of driving, remember that it isn't just the cost of fuel that you need to take into account, you also need to consider insurance, depreciation and road tax.

Safety Travelling by car (or motorcycle) incurs the highest road traffic incident risk of all forms of transport. Air, rail and water modes of transport incur the lowest risk, and buses and coaches have a similar incident risk to rail and water travel.

Travelling times Remember that it is sometimes difficult to estimate the time for a journey by car because of delays that can be caused by congestion, incidents and roadworks. These factors should always be taken into account, especially if it is necessary to travel at busy times.

315

section **eighteen**

AVOIDING AND DEALING WITH CONGESTION

This section covers
- Journey planning
- While driving
- Active traffic management
- Highways Agency traffic officers
- Urban congestion

Journey planning

The growth in car ownership and the associated increase in traffic has caused a level of congestion which can lead to frustration and longer journey times. This can affect both urban areas and higher-speed roads and motorways.

If possible, try to plan your journey to avoid busy times of day and congested routes.

Time of day Much congestion is caused by work and school-related travel. This causes delays in the early morning and late afternoon and early evening. If you don't have to travel at these times try to avoid them, thus

- allowing you to have an easier and more pleasant journey and one that is less likely to be delayed
- easing the congestion caused by traffic that is governed by work and school schedules.

Try to arrange appointments so that you avoid these times.

Plan your route Make sure you know where you're going by planning your route beforehand. If possible plan alternatives in case you find your original route blocked. This is particularly important if you are travelling alone on an unknown route.

If you have a satellite navigation system, enter the destination before you start your journey. This will plan your route for you. Otherwise plan your route before leaving by

- looking at a map. You may need to look at different scale maps depending on how far and where you're travelling

- consulting a motoring organisation or using one of the route planners available on the internet
- printing out or writing down the route, using place names and road numbers to avoid problems if a certain place is not adequately signed.

Try to avoid congested routes; consult websites such the Highways Agency information line on **highways.gov.uk/traffic** This can give you updated information about where there is, or is likely to be, congestion.

It is useful to build in additional time for your journey to take into account any congestion, incidents and roadworks, of which you may not have been aware, when planning your journey.

Leave plenty of time, especially if you're connecting with other forms of transport such as a plane or train. Concern about reaching your destination in time can lead to frustration and the increased tendency to take risks which could lead to an incident.

While driving

Delays and diversions

Carry a map with you so that you can check your position or identify an alternative route if you get held up or diverted.

If you are using a satellite navigation system

- always stop in a safe place if you need to reprogramme the system
- don't be distracted from making your own judgement about the safety of any manoeuvres
- before you turn, make sure it is permissible to do so by looking at any road signs.

Mobile phones A mobile phone can be useful in case of delays or breakdowns. However, remember that it is illegal to use one while driving, and this includes while you are waiting in a queue of traffic.

If you have a passenger, get them to make the call. When you're travelling alone and you need to call, find a safe place to stop first. If you are on a motorway, you must leave the motorway before using your phone.

Hazard perception

Looking well ahead to see what the traffic in front of you is doing will enable you to plan your driving.

If you see the traffic ahead slowing down, ease off the accelerator and gradually slow down rather than leaving it late and having to brake harshly. Plan your driving and slow down early – if you do this the traffic situation ahead will often have cleared by the time you get there.

Constant speed

When you can see well ahead and the road conditions are good, you should drive at a steady cruising speed. This is the time to use cruise control if it is fitted to your vehicle.

Whether or not you have cruise control, choose a speed which is within the speed limit and one which you and your vehicle can handle safely.

Make sure you also keep a safe distance from the vehicle in front. Remember to increase the gap on wet or icy roads. In foggy conditions you will have to slow down to the distance you can see to be clear.

At busy times, some stretches of motorway have variable speed limits shown above the lanes. The maximum speed limits shown on these signals are mandatory and appear on the gantries above the lanes to which they apply.

These speed limits are in place to enable traffic to proceed at a constant speed as this has been shown to reduce bunching.

Keeping traffic at a constant speed over a longer distance has been shown to ease congestion.

Your overall journey time normally improves by keeping to the constant speed, even though at times it may appear that you could have travelled faster for shorter periods.

Lane discipline

You should drive in the left-hand lane of a dual carriageway or motorway if the road ahead is clear. If you are overtaking a number of slower-moving vehicles it may be safer to remain in the centre or outer lanes until the manoeuvre is completed rather than continually changing lanes. Return to the left-hand lane once you have overtaken all the vehicles, or if you are delaying traffic behind you.

Don't stay in the middle lane. Remember that some vehicles are prohibited from using the right-hand lane, so if you remain in the middle lane they won't be able to get past you. If you stay in the middle lane an unnecessarily long time, you effectively turn a three-lane motorway into a two-lane motorway.

You must not normally drive on the hard shoulder but, at roadworks and certain places where signs direct, the hard shoulder may become the left-hand lane.

Using sign information

Look well ahead for signals or signs, especially on a motorway. Signals situated on the central reservation apply to all lanes.

On very busy stretches, there may be overhead gantries with messages about congestion ahead and a separate signal for each lane. The messages may also give an alternative route, which you should use if at all possible.

If you're not sure whether to use the alternative route (for example, whether you can reach your destination if you use the route suggested), take the next exit, pull over at the first available safe area (lay-by or service area) and look at a map.

On a motorway, once you have passed an exit and encounter congestion, there may not be another chance to leave and you could be stuck in slow-moving or stationary traffic for some time. Take the opportunity to leave the motorway when it arises; you can always rejoin the motorway if you feel that is the best course of action once you have had time to consider the options.

If you need to change lanes to leave the motorway, do so in good time. At some junctions a lane may lead directly off the motorway. Only get in that lane if you wish to go in the direction indicated on the overhead signs.

Motorway signals can be used to warn you of a danger ahead. For example, there may be an incident, fog, or a spillage, which you are unable to see.

Amber flashing lights warn of a hazard ahead. The signal may show

- a temporary maximum speed limit
- lanes that are closed
- a message such as 'Fog' or 'Queue'.

Adjust your speed and look out for the danger.

Don't increase your speed until you pass a signal that is not flashing or one that gives the 'All clear' sign and you are sure it is safe to increase your speed.

Active traffic management

Active traffic management (ATM) is a project to try to reduce congestion and make journey times more reliable.

ATM – also known as 'managed motorways' – features benefits including

- closed circuit television monitoring
- high-visibility driver information signs
- lighting to provide a safer driving environment at night and in poor light
- new emergency roadside telephones for use in an emergency or breakdown
- emergency refuge areas for vehicles to use in an emergency or breakdown
- use of the hard shoulder as an additional running lane under controlled conditions to manage traffic in peak congestion times or during an incident
- Highways Agency traffic officer patrols monitoring the motorway (see page 323).

Gantries The new gantries have been built about 500 metres apart. They feature a large message sign board and signal above each of the lanes and the hard shoulder.

Emergency refuge areas These are 100 metres long, wider than the hard shoulder and are located about every 500 metres. They are designed to be used in cases of emergency or breakdown. Features include

- sensors to alert the control centre that a vehicle has entered
- CCTV enabling the control centre to monitor the vehicles and send assistance as necessary
- new-generation emergency roadside telephones containing additional multilingual and hard-of-hearing support, and the ability to pinpoint your location
- additional space away from the main carriageway.

Driving in actively managed areas

As with driving on any motorway, you must obey the signals displayed on the overhead gantries. In addition to the normal signals which are used on any motorway (see page 225) there will also be a single red X without flashing beacons which is applicable to the hard shoulder only. When you see this sign don't use this lane, except in an emergency or breakdown.

There are three driving scenarios

- normal motorway driving conditions
- active traffic management without hard shoulder running
- active traffic management with hard shoulder running.

Normal motorway conditions When there is no congestion or incident, normal motorway rules apply. These are

- no speed limits shown on signals
- national speed limits apply
- hard shoulder for emergency and breakdown use only
- use emergency refuge areas in an emergency for added safety and increased distance from the carriageway
- use emergency roadside telephone for assistance.

Actively managed mode If there is congestion or an incident, ATM will manage the traffic to ease congestion. This means that

- all speed limit signals are set and must be obeyed
- driver information signs will provide information for road users
- a red 'X' over the hard shoulder means this lane must not be used, except in an emergency or breakdown

- use emergency refuge areas in an emergency or breakdown for added safety and increased distance from the carriageway
- use an emergency roadside telephone for assistance.

Controlling the traffic across all lanes with the right speed for the traffic conditions enables traffic to flow more smoothly and reduces congestion.

The system sets the same speed across the carriageway, which reduces the need for drivers to change lanes.

Hard shoulder running mode In the case of severe congestion or an incident in one of the normal running lanes, the hard shoulder may be opened between junctions which have a high volume of traffic.

Do not stop on the hard shoulder except in an emergency or if you are unable to reach an emergency refuge.

You should use the hard shoulder as a running lane, between junctions, when the signal above the hard shoulder is displaying a speed limit and not a red cross or a blank signal and

- you are intending to leave the motorway at the next junction; or
- you are joining the main carriageway from the previous junction.

Highways Agency traffic officers

Working in partnership with the police, Highways Agency traffic officers are extra eyes and ears on most motorways and some 'A' class roads in England only. They are a highly trained and highly visible service patrolling the motorway to help keep traffic moving and make your journey as safe and reliable as possible.

Traffic officers wear a full uniform, including a high-visibility orange and yellow jacket, and drive a high-visibility vehicle with yellow and black chequered markings.

Every traffic officer has a unique identification number and photographic identity card. They normally patrol in pairs. The vehicles contain a variety of equipment for use on the motorway, including temporary road signs, lights, cones, debris removal tools and a first aid kit.

Role of traffic officers They will

- help broken-down motorists to arrange recovery
- offer safety advice to motorists
- clear debris from the carriageway
- undertake high-visibility patrols
- support the police and emergency services during incidents
- provide mobile or temporary road closures
- manage diversion routes caused by an incident.

If you have an emergency or break down on the motorway the best action to take is to use an emergency roadside telephone.

Emergency roadside telephones are answered by Highways Agency control centre operators located in a regional control centre. Control centre operators are able to monitor any stranded motorists on closed circuit television screens and despatch the nearest available traffic officer patrol to assist.

Powers of traffic officers Unlike the police, traffic officers do not have any enforcement powers. However, they are able to stop and direct anyone travelling on the motorway. It is an offence not to comply with the directions given by a traffic officer (refer to The Highway Code, rules 107 and 108).

Extent of scheme Seven regional control centres, managed by the Highways Agency, are able to despatch traffic officers to any motorway in England.

Urban congestion

Congestion in urban areas leads to

- longer journey times
- frustration
- pollution through standing and slow-moving traffic.

London suffers the worst traffic congestion in the UK and amongst the worst in Europe. It has been estimated that

- drivers in central London used to spend 50% of their time in queues
- London lost between £2 million and £4 million every week in terms of wasted time caused by congestion.

Various measures have been introduced to try to reduce and alleviate the congestion and make traffic flow more freely. Red Routes and congestion charging are two of the schemes initiated in the London area. These are also being introduced into other congested towns and cities.

Red Routes

Red Routes keep traffic moving and reduce the pollution that comes from vehicle emissions. Stopping and parking is allowed only within marked boxes.

Overnight and on Sundays most controls are relaxed to allow unrestricted stopping.

There is a fixed penalty for an offence and illegally parked vehicles may be towed away.

There are five main types of Red Route markings.

Double red lines Stopping is not allowed at any time, for any reason. They are normally placed at road junctions or where parking or loading would be dangerous or cause serious congestion.

Single red lines Parking, loading or picking up passengers is not allowed during the day (generally 7 am to 7 pm). Stopping is allowed outside these hours and on Sundays.

Red boxes Indicate parking or loading is permitted during the day at off-peak times, normally 10 am to 4 pm. Some allow loading and some allow parking, the rules in each case are clearly shown on the sign.

White boxes Indicate that parking or loading may be allowed at any time, restrictions being clearly shown on the sign.

Red Route clearway There are no road markings but clearway signs indicate that stopping isn't allowed at any time apart from in marked lay-bys.

Congestion charging

Congestion charging is a way of ensuring that those using valuable and congested road space make a financial contribution. It encourages the use of other modes of transport and is also intended to ensure that journey times are quicker and more reliable for those who have to use the roads.

The London scheme requires drivers to pay if they wish to drive in central London during the scheme's hours of operation.

Extent of zone Traffic signs make it very clear when you are approaching, entering and leaving the charging zone. Advance information is provided on the main approach roads. These signs advise how far ahead the zone starts, the hours of operation and some give the amount of the charge.

As you approach the charging zone, directional signs indicate which routes take you into the charging zone and which you can take if you wish to avoid it.

As you enter and exit the zone, signs indicate the boundary of the zone. The sign on entry also gives hours of operation.

Paying and exemptions You can pay the congestion charge

- in advance or on the day of travel before, during or after your journey

- daily, weekly, monthly or even for the whole year.

To find out more about how to pay and where you can pay, visit **cclondon.com** or call **0845 900 1234**.

At midnight, images of all of the vehicles that have been in the charging zone are checked against the vehicle registration numbers of vehicles which have paid their congestion charge for that day. The computer keeps the registration numbers of vehicles that should have paid but have not done so. A penalty charge notice is issued to the registered keeper of the vehicle.

Not all drivers have to pay the charge. Some of those who are exempt are

- disabled people who hold a Blue Badge
- drivers of electrically powered or alternative fuel vehicles
- riders of two-wheelers.

Residents living within the zone obtain a reduced rate but are not exempt.

Some people may be able to claim reimbursement; for example, NHS staff, firefighters and patients too ill to travel to an appointment on public transport.

Transport strategy

This is only part of the London transport strategy. There is also a wide range of other measures designed to make public transport easier, cheaper, faster and more reliable.

If it isn't necessary to make your journey by car you might want to consider alternative forms of transport.

For London, the Transport for London (TfL) journey planner (**tfl.gov.uk**) can help you discover the quickest and easiest routes for your journey using public transport. Alternatively you can call TfL's Travel Information Call Centre on **0843 222 1234**.

section **nineteen**

TOWING A TRAILOR

This section covers
- Towing regulations
- Safety
- Driving techniques

Towing regulations

Most of the skills and precautions involved in towing a caravan are the same as those needed for towing a trailer. You must have a full category B* (car) driving licence before towing any size trailer or caravan.

Throughout this section reference is made to the maximum authorised mass (MAM) of vehicles and trailers. This should, in all cases, be taken to mean the permissible maximum weight – also known as the gross vehicle weight. You may not be planning to drive a vehicle, or a vehicle towing a trailer, at these maximum weights, but these are key factors that determine driver licensing requirements.

If you passed your test before 1 January 1997 You are generally allowed to drive a vehicle and trailer combination up to 8.25 tonnes.

If you passed your test on or after 1 January 1997 You may tow a trailer behind a category B* vehicle without taking a further test as long as the trailer doesn't exceed 750 kg.

If the trailer you wish to tow exceeds 750 kg you may tow it behind a category B* vehicle, provided that the vehicle and trailer combination doesn't exceed 3.5 tonnes and the MAM of the trailer doesn't exceed the unladen weight of the towing vehicle. If you wish to drive a category B* vehicle towing a trailer which exceeds that listed above, you will have to pass a practical category B+E test.

If you wish to drive a vehicle with a MAM exceeding 3.5 tonnes, for example a motorhome or recreational vehicle, you will need to pass a category C or C1 test.

Category B+E test

Details of the test and the minimum test vehicle and trailer may be found in *The Official DSA Guide to Learning to Drive*.

More detailed information about towing trailers can be found on DVLA factsheet INF30 'Requirements for towing trailers in Great Britain'. This also includes information about towing while driving a larger vehicle. DVLA factsheets are available from **direct.gov.uk/motoringleaflets** or free of charge from **0300 790 6801**.

Note
* A category B vehicle is a four-wheeled vehicle with a MAM not exceeding 3.5 tonnes which has not more than eight passenger seats (in addition to that of the driver).

Useful information on towing can also be found on the National Trailer and Towing Association Ltd website **ntta.co.uk**

From 2013, new European requirements will come into force that change towing regulations. New car and light van drivers wanting to tow trailers will be able to tow a slightly larger trailer on a normal car driving licence (category B) if they take a further test.

There will also be a restriction on the overall size of the vehicle/trailer combination that can be driven on a category B+E licence entitlement (car/light van plus trailer).

The combination

The vehicle handbook or the manufacturer's agent will normally have information on

- the maximum permissible trailer mass that can be towed by your vehicle
- the maximum noseweight that should be applied to the tow ball.

You should not exceed either limit.

There are separate and also legal limits on the laden weight of unbraked trailers. Make sure that you know what the limits are for your vehicle.

As a general rule, even if the vehicle manufacturer's limits are higher, you may be safer if the weight of the loaded trailer or caravan does not exceed 85 per cent of the kerbside (empty) weight of the towing vehicle. This applies particularly if you are not experienced at towing.

Remember that the overall length of the combination is generally double that of the normal family car.

Mirrors You will need to fit exterior towing mirrors so that you have a clear view along both sides of the caravan or trailer.

Stabiliser A good stabiliser fitted to the towbar can make the combination safer to handle, but it will not relieve you of the responsibility of loading the combination correctly. Neither will it cure instability caused by a poor towing vehicle/trailer combination.

The stabiliser will give you added security in crosswinds, especially when large goods vehicles overtake you on the motorway.

Riding in the caravan

Do not allow anyone to ride in the caravan when it's being towed.

If you stop for a break, always lower the jockey wheel and corner steadies of the caravan before entering or letting anyone in. Don't forget to raise them fully before you move off.

Safety

Weight distribution

The overall stability of both the caravan and the towing vehicle depends on correct weight distribution.

For example, heavy items should be loaded as low as possible in the caravan or trailer so that they are mainly over the axle(s).

Bulkier, lighter items, such as bedding or clothing, should be distributed to give a suitable 'noseweight' at the towing coupling. The noseweight should never exceed the vehicle manufacturer's recommendations.

If in doubt, the noseweight may be measured by using an inexpensive gauge available from caravan accessory stockists.

> **Remember,** the more weight you carry, the more fuel you use.

Safety checks

Any load must be carried so that it does not endanger other road users. It must be securely stowed within the size and weight limits for the vehicle.

The load needs to be secure so that it cannot move or fall from the vehicle when cornering or braking.

Before starting a journey, check that the caravan or trailer

- is loaded correctly, with the right noseweight on the towbar
- is correctly hitched up, with the breakaway cable or secondary coupling properly connected and the coupling head fully engaged and locked
- lights and indicators are connected and working correctly
- jockey wheel and assembly is fully retracted and in the stowed position
- braking system is working correctly
- windows, roof light and door are closed
- tyre pressures are correct.

In addition

- check the caravan or trailer tyres for tread depth, damage and cracking of the sidewalls. Even if the tread depth shows little wear or is above the legal minimum, the tyre may be suffering from the effects of ageing
- remember that tyre regulations also cover the tyres on your caravan or trailer
- a caravan that has to be left standing for long periods should be raised on supports that take the weight off the tyres. This will help prolong tyre life
- check that your caravan or trailer is fitted with tyres of the specified rating (see the vehicle handbook)
- check that you've secured and turned off all fuel supplies, such as liquid gas cylinders.

Driving techniques

If you haven't towed a caravan before, seek advice from one of the large caravanning organisations.

You should also consider attending one of their courses, which cover safety aspects such as loading, manoeuvring, and driving techniques.

You can find detailed guidance on all aspects of towing in the booklet *The Caravan Towing Guide*, which you can obtain from

**National Caravan Council Ltd
Catherine House, Victoria Road,
Aldershot, Hants GU11 1SS
Tel 01252 318251
Fax 01252 322596**

Manoeuvring

Experience of towing is desirable but not essential. Drivers without experience need to take great care, particularly when manoeuvring.

Don't be afraid to practise reversing in a quiet car park until you have mastered the technique.

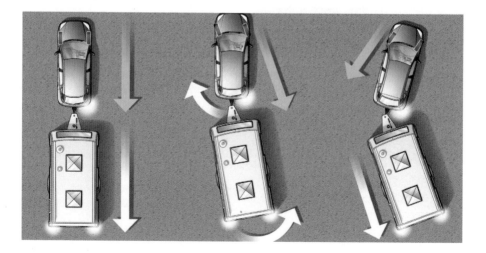

On the road

Always be aware of the increased weight, length and width of the combined vehicles.

You'll soon adjust to the different techniques involved in towing, so long as you remember not to hurry any manoeuvres and to plan well ahead. You should

- allow more time and brake earlier when slowing down or stopping
- give yourself three times the normal distance and time to overtake safely
- take account of the extra length, particularly when turning or emerging at junctions.

Snaking Never attempt to correct swerving or 'snaking' by increasing speed, steering sharply (zigzagging), or braking hard.

The safe technique is to

- ease off the accelerator slowly
- allow a certain amount of 'twitch' in the steering
- reduce speed until the snaking has stopped.

High-sided vehicles You need to take extra care when passing or being passed by high-sided vehicles.

Allow as much space as possible to avoid the affects of turbulence or buffeting.

Speed limits

Some speed limits are lower than normal when you are towing. Unless road signs tell you otherwise, you must not exceed

- 30 mph (48 km/h) in built-up areas
- 50 mph (80 km/h) on single carriageways
- 60 mph (96 km/h) on dual carriageways or motorways.

Reduce speed

- in high winds or crosswinds
- when going downhill
- in poor visibility.

Motorway driving

Caravans or trailers must not be towed in the outside lane of a motorway having more than two lanes, unless other lanes are closed.

> **Remember,** check your mirrors frequently. If you are holding up a queue of traffic, you should be prepared to pull in where it is safe to let other faster traffic pass.

section **twenty**

VEHICLE SECURITY

This section covers

- Security measures
- Parking

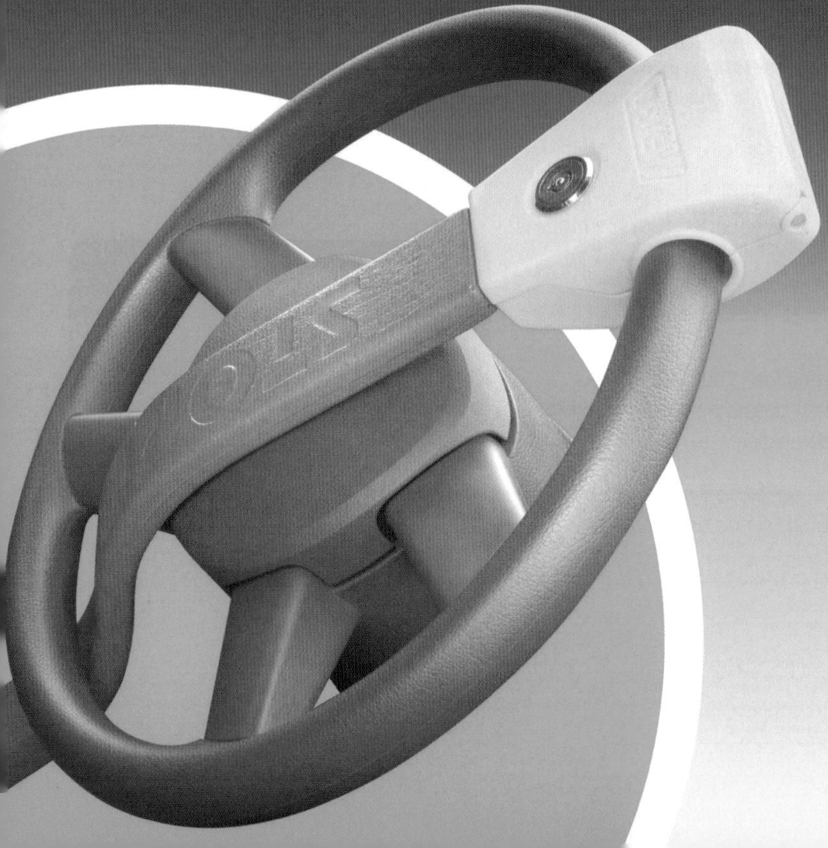

Security measures

Theft of vehicles, especially cars, has risen to unacceptable levels. In some urban areas, it has become an epidemic.

The thieves vary from opportunists to professionals who often work in gangs and target specific models for which they already have a buyer, sometimes in another country.

Even more common are thefts from private cars. Again, the thieves vary from opportunists who snatch valuables from unlocked cars to professionals who comb whole areas and steal car radios from poorly secured vehicles.

Having your vehicle stolen or broken into is at best an inconvenience and at worst very distressing.

While determined thieves would probably be able to steal or get into any vehicle, they are usually too busy with the poorly secured ones. If your vehicle is secured, and preferably alarmed and immobilised, they may well leave it alone.

This section deals very briefly with the precautions you can take to secure your vehicle.

Taking a vehicle without the owner's consent, or with the intention of driving it recklessly, is a criminal offence. Such actions sometimes end in death, often for other, innocent road users.

To make it more difficult for the would-be thief, particularly the opportunist, you can

- fit an anti-theft device (alarm and/or immobiliser)
- use a visible security device (to lock steering wheel, parking brake, etc)
- have the vehicle registration number etched on all windows.

Vehicle Watch

Join a Vehicle Watch scheme, if there is one in your area. This scheme reduces the risk of having your car stolen by displaying high-visibility stickers on the front and rear windscreens of your vehicle. There are two types of stickers

- **Vehicle Watch** By displaying these you are inviting the police to stop your vehicle if they see it in use between midnight and 5.00 am
- **25-plus** By displaying these you are also inviting them to stop your vehicle at any time of day if it is being driven by anyone apparently under 25 years of age.

Stickers and additional information about the scheme can be obtained from the crime prevention officer at your local police station.

Parking

Avoid leaving your vehicle unattended in poorly lit areas, which are known to be a high risk.

Whenever possible

- use attended and secure car parks
- at night, park in an area which will be well lit
- if you have a garage, use it.

When you leave your vehicle

- lock it
- remove the key
- engage the steering lock
- set the alarm or anti-theft device, if you have one
- close all windows completely (but don't leave pets in a vehicle with the windows completely closed)
- either remove all valuables or lock them out of sight
- never leave the vehicle documents inside.

Car parks

Using parking facilities that have won the Park Mark® Safer Parking award means that you are parking in an area that has been vetted by the police. They make sure that the site has measures in place to create a safe environment.

These facilities are run by responsible operators who are concerned with your safety and the safety of your vehicle, and who have done the best they can to reduce crime and the fear of crime on their site.

To find out where your nearest Park Mark® awarded site, visit **saferparking.co.uk** or **parkmark.co.uk**

Valuables

Car radios These are one of the prime targets for thieves.

Install a security-coded radio. This can deter thieves since the radio is likely to be of little use once removed from the vehicle.

Some manufacturers provide security coding for radios supplied in new vehicles.

An alternative is to install a removable radio. It looks exactly like any other radio, but it slides out of its housing. You can lock it away in the boot or take it with you.

Satellite navigation systems These are also becoming popular with thieves.

If you have a portable system, take it with you when you leave the car; also

- take the support cradle and suction pads
- wipe away any marks on the windscreen or dashboard which are left by the suction pads.

Don't leave the equipment in the glove compartment, as this is the first place thieves will look.

Soft-top vehicles

Never leave a cabriolet or soft-top vehicle where it will obviously be vulnerable.

Remember, lock it or lose it!

section **twenty-one**
EUROPEAN DRIVING

This section covers

- Travelling to Europe
- Planning your journey
- Driving in Europe

VOUS N´ AVEZ PAS LA PRIORITÉ

Travelling to Europe

Taking your car abroad, or hiring one in the country you're visiting, gives you freedom and mobility.

You can

- plan your holiday around your interests or business commitments
- travel at your own pace
- stop when and where you like
- visit places of interest on the way
- discover the more remote places
- carry extra equipment such as camping or sports gear, canoes, surfboards, etc.

This section summarises what you need to do to prepare for driving in Europe.

An extensive motorway network runs through most of Europe and there are regular ferry links from many UK ports.

You have more opportunity to choose routes which take you closer to your European destination.

The Channel Tunnel provides yet another link to continental Europe.

Planning your journey

If you're planning to take your car abroad, the major motoring organisations can help you to organise and plan the details of your trip.

They can

- save you time and money
- set up medical, travel and vehicle insurance
- provide equipment for minor repairs and breakdowns
- help you organise the correct documents for your car, trailer or caravan.

You can often make your trip much easier by using their facilities and experience.

Your route

Once you know which country you're going to visit, you can begin to plan your route.

If you have a satellite navigation system, it can now be used in most European countries.

Also, the motoring organisations can simplify this for you with

- computerised route guides
- summaries of motoring regulations
- details of tolls, etc.

They will recommend routes from continental ports or airports to specific destinations, using motorways for speed and convenience or scenic routes for pleasure.

Your vehicle

Before you travel abroad, have your car thoroughly checked and serviced. Checks to make include the spare tyre (make sure it's in good condition), your tool kit and jack (make sure all items are complete and in working order). Also make sure you have your spare car keys.

Lights Your lights will need to be altered for driving on the right. Deflectors are required in most countries. These prevent your dipped beam from dazzling drivers approaching on the left. Yellow-tinted headlights are no longer required in most countries. Always carry a set of replacement bulbs if appropriate.

Your mirrors Check your mirrors. You must have clear all-round vision. You will need to have exterior rear-view mirrors, especially on the left, for driving on the right-hand side of the road.

If you're towing a caravan or trailer, make sure you can see clearly behind down both sides.

Seat belts Check seat belts and child restraints, including booster seats. Make sure the fittings are secure and the belts and restraints are functioning correctly.

Emergency equipment In many countries emergency equipment must be carried. Check with motoring organisations to find out what is required in the countries you will be visiting. This equipment may include

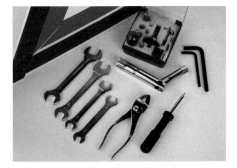

- emergency repair kits
- spares kit
- emergency windscreen
- emergency warning triangle
- fire extinguisher
- snow chains.

In some countries you may be required to carry skis, or anything else you carry on your roof, in a purpose-made box, securely fitted to your roof rack.

Precautions against breakdown Dealing with breakdowns abroad can be especially time-consuming and worrying without the help of one of the motoring organisations or breakdown services.

The best prevention is to have your car thoroughly serviced before you leave and to make regular checks en route. Make sure you're prepared for minor breakdowns.

You must have all the necessary documents before leaving. Again, the motoring organisations will be able to tell you what's required for each country.

Documents

Insurance Third-party motor vehicle insurance is compulsory in most countries. It is strongly recommended you contact your insurer to make sure you're adequately covered.

Most insurance policies issued in the UK automatically provide third-party cover in EC countries as well as in some others. They do not provide comprehensive cover unless you arrange this with your insurer, who may charge an extra premium.

Make sure you have the appropriate insurance certificate with you.

Certain countries require a bail bond as a security in the event of an incident. Consult your insurer.

Your driving licence You must carry your national driving licence when motoring abroad. Even if you need an International Driving Permit (IDP), take your national licence also.

If you want to drive a hired or borrowed vehicle in the country you're visiting, ask about minimum age requirements in case they apply to you.

In Italy, you must carry a translation with your licence. You can get this free of charge from the major motoring organisations. If you have a pink or pink and green EC-type UK licence, this translation isn't required.

International Driving Permit Many non-EC countries still require an IDP. To qualify for one, you must be 18 or over.

To apply you'll need

- your driving licence
- a passport-sized photograph
- a fee.

The motoring organisations can issue your IDP.

Note Seventeen-year-olds are not allowed to drive in most European countries.

Vehicle registration certificate You must carry the original vehicle registration certificate with you.

If you don't have your vehicle registration certificate, apply to a vehicle registration office for a temporary certificate of registration (V379). Apply through your local post office well in advance of your journey.

If you plan to hire, borrow or lease a vehicle, you must ensure you have all the relevant documents.

Blue Badges If you hold a Blue Badge you should take it with you. Many European countries recognise and allow special parking for any vehicle displaying these badges.

Passport/visa All persons travelling must hold an up-to-date passport, valid for all countries through which they intend to travel. **Carry your passport(s) at all times.**

Keep a separate note of the number, date and place of issue of each passport, in case they are stolen or lost.

Travellers need a visa for some European countries. Check well in advance with the embassies or consulates concerned. This is particularly important if you hold a UK passport not issued in this country, or the passport of any other country.

Medical expenses insurance You're strongly advised to take out comprehensive medical insurance cover for any trip abroad.

Most medical treatment can be obtained free of charge or at reduced cost from the healthcare schemes of countries with whom the UK has reciprocal healthcare arrangements. However, you should not rely on these arrangements alone.

European Health Insurance Card (EHIC) This is issued free of charge and can be used to cover medical treatment due to either an incident or illness within the European Economic Area.

The quickest and easiest way to get an EHIC is to apply online at **ehic.org.uk** For more information, visit **nhs.uk/healthcareabroad** You can also apply by phone on **0845 606 2030** or pick up an EHIC form from a post office.

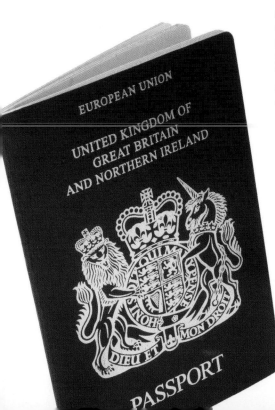

Driving in Europe

Regulations

Alcohol and driving Don't drink alcohol and drive. The laws and penalties abroad are often more severe than those in the UK.

> **Remember**, on-the-spot fines are imposed for most minor motoring offences. Make sure you know the regulations for each country you intend visiting and obey them.

Passengers Never take more passengers than your vehicle is built to carry. Make sure you use your seat belts and everyone is secure before setting out on any journey.

Speed limits There are speed limits in all countries, but they vary from country to country. A list of the speed limits can be obtained from the motoring organisations. Make sure you know the limits for those countries you will be travelling through.

Obey all speed limits. Many countries have severe on-the-spot fines for offenders, while others prosecute, and that could prove to be expensive.

Plates You need to display

- an identification plate if you're towing a caravan or trailer

- a nationality plate of the approved size and design at the rear of your vehicle or caravan or trailer.

Emergency equipment

Advance warning triangle The use of a warning triangle is compulsory in most countries for all vehicles with more than two wheels. Hazard warning lights should not be used instead of a triangle, but to complement it. Some countries require two advance warning triangles.

Spare bulbs Some countries require you to carry a spare set of bulbs in your vehicle.

Fire extinguisher A fire extinguisher is compulsory in some countries and strongly recommended.

First aid kit Make sure your vehicle carries a first aid kit. It is compulsory in some countries and strongly recommended in many others.

Checklist As part of your planning, make a checklist of equipment, documents and other items. If you're travelling through several countries, check against each item whether it's compulsory or strongly recommended.

Security

Don't leave handbags, wallets or other attractive items within obvious view inside the vehicle, even when you're inside too.

Never leave valuables in an unattended parked vehicle overnight. Loss of possessions, passports, tickets, cash and credit cards can be distressing and inconvenient when you're abroad.

When driving

It can take you time to adjust to driving on the right, especially if you are in a right-hand drive car. Mistakes can lead to incidents.

> **Remember,** hire vehicles will normally be left-hand drive. These may feel unfamiliar at first. Make sure you understand the controls before you drive.

Get into the habit of using all your mirrors before making any manoeuvre. This is particularly important before deciding to overtake. Remember to check the left exterior mirror. Don't attempt to overtake until you're used to driving on the right.

Don't let your attention wander. It can be dangerous to forget where you are, even for a moment.

- Each time you set out, remember that you're in a foreign country where you must drive on the right.
- Take special care after a rest when you have to drive on the road again.

Avoid driving for long periods and don't allow fatigue to set in.

Motorway tolls Find out about these. Include them in your budget and make sure that you carry change to use if you need to travel on any toll roads.

After your trip

Don't forget to adjust to driving on the left again as soon as you return!

Take extra care at roundabouts. Be aware of the changed priority.

Each time you move away, remember on which side of the road traffic will be approaching.

Make sure that you know the rules of the road; for example, in some countries you can turn right, with caution, at an amber filter light.

section **twenty-two**

AUTOMATICS AND FOUR-WHEEL DRIVE

This section covers
- Automatics
- Four-wheel drive

Automatics

Vehicles with automatic transmission have always been a great help to drivers with physical disabilities, because there's less work for the feet and hands to do.

They've become increasingly popular with all drivers, not least because of the easier control and convenience they offer, particularly in congested urban conditions.

This section deals with the extra knowledge and skill required when driving vehicles with automatic transmission and four-wheel drive.

Vehicles with automatic transmission have no clutch pedal. The transmission senses and selects the gear according to the road speed and load on the engine. This not only makes the physical job of driving much easier, but it also allows you more time to concentrate on what's happening on the road.

Automatic transmission usually changes to a higher gear as the road speed increases and to a lower gear as it falls.

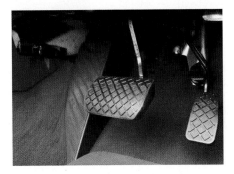

It will also change down to a lower gear going uphill as the load on the engine increases.

There are times – for example, when going down a steep hill – when you need to keep in a low gear, even if the speed is constant and the engine load is light. The system often tries to change to a higher gear in these situations. However, the driver is usually able to override the transmission by using the gear selector to remain in a suitable lower gear.

The gear selector

Virtually all automatics have a gear selector. A typical gear selector layout includes

P – (Park) This mechanically locks the transmission and should only be selected when the vehicle is stationary

R – (Reverse)

N – (Neutral) This is the same as neutral on a manual gearbox

D – (Drive) For driving forward

2 – (Second gear)

1 – (First gear).

Some automatics with four forward gears have third gear as an additional position that comes between 'D' (drive) and '2' (second gear).

These numbered gear positions enable you to prevent the transmission selecting a higher gear.

This is particularly useful

- in heavy traffic
- when manoeuvring
- when going down a steep hill.

There might be minor variations of the selector positions between different manufacturers.

With any automatic it's essential to study the vehicle handbook to understand the features of your particular model.

Kick-down

This is a device that provides quick acceleration when you need it; for example, to overtake.

Sharply pressing the accelerator pedal right down causes a quick change down to the next lower gear. To return to the higher gear, ease the pressure off the accelerator pedal.

The importance of the parking brake

Fully applying the parking brake whenever your vehicle is stationary is even more important on an automatic.

If the selector lever is in any position other than 'P' or 'N', it will move off under power if the accelerator is pressed (accidentally or on purpose), unless the brakes are on.

If the choke (manual or automatic) is in use, an even lighter accelerator pressure can move the vehicle away.

Creep

Creep happens if the tick-over, or slow running of the engine, creates enough power to move the vehicle. The brakes are necessary to prevent it moving.

Always check your vehicle for a tendency to creep excessively. Do this on the level (not uphill).

Never rely on creep to hold the vehicle on a hill – even though it doesn't move. The vehicle could roll back without warning if the engine stopped for any reason.

The safe rule is: apply the parking brake fully whenever you pull up.

Driving an automatic

Make sure you fully understand the procedure required before you attempt to drive a vehicle with automatic transmission.

- Although most automatics have a cut-out switch to prevent starting in gear, always check that the selector is in the 'P' (park) or 'N' (neutral) position and the parking brake is fully applied.

- For normal forward driving move the selector lever to the 'D' (drive) position.

The transmission will then change gear as necessary if there's enough pressure on the accelerator.

Alternatively, selecting one of the numbered gears will give the same flexibility as a manual gearbox.

Controlled use of the accelerator is essential when driving an automatic as it has such a direct effect when the selector is in any position other than 'P' (park) or 'N' (neutral).

Avoid heavy acceleration; it can

- cause the vehicle to surge forward (or backwards) out of control

- delay upward gear changes

- waste fuel and pollute the atmosphere.

Control

When carrying out manoeuvres at low speeds, use hardly any accelerator and only light braking; one foot on each pedal is often convenient and safer.

When driving, it's safer to use the right foot only for both accelerator and brake pedals, just as you do in vehicles with a manual gearbox.

This develops anticipation by encouraging the early release of the accelerator pedal and early and progressive braking. It cuts out

- the instability and wear and tear brought about by braking against acceleration

- the need to learn a different method if you change from an automatic to a manual or vice versa.

Points to remember

Apart from avoiding the danger of excessive creep you should also

- make sure the tick-over is not set too fast. This can make your road speed more difficult to control and you could, for example, find yourself approaching a junction much too fast

- avoid over-confidence and driving too fast for the road and traffic conditions

- be aware of the reduced effect of engine braking on automatics. Use the gear selector to hold a lower gear if necessary

- control your speed as you approach a corner.

Automatics sometimes change up as you approach a corner due to reduced pressure on the accelerator. To avoid this, slow down before you reach the corner then accelerate gently as you turn.

Four-wheel drive

Four-wheel drive (4x4) is an arrangement where both axles of a vehicle are driven. The system may be permanently connected, or drive to the second axle may be selected by the driver to suit the conditions.

Four-wheel drive has become much more widely available. There are three basic groups

- the original type
- the sport type
- the saloon.

The four-wheel drive vehicle was originally a military vehicle for use on rough terrain.

It was built to work in all weather conditions and on difficult surfaces. Vehicles of similar design and layout are now commonly used by farmers, contractors and public service authorities.

The centre of gravity tends to be higher and the wheelbase shorter than those of ordinary vehicles.

You don't need any extra skill to drive this type of four-wheel drive vehicle on the public road. However, you should be aware when driving these vehicles on public roads, that some 4x4s have very large blind spots which can easily obscure a group of pedestrians, a motorcyclist or even a small car.

Driving off-road

Always keep to safe driving principles.

- Remember to take into account the nature of the terrain – be wary on hilly terrain and soft surfaces.

- Don't overstep your mark, even if your vehicle feels strong enough to handle any difficult contour or surface conditions.

- Take corners at a steady speed. Remember that all the wheels are generally locked into the transmission system and revolve at different speeds. This could affect the stability of the vehicle if driven recklessly.

- Don't expect the vehicle to do more than it's capable of.

Look out for rocks which could either damage the underside of your vehicle or suddenly deflect the steering, causing loss of control.

Whatever type of vehicle you drive, if you take part in off-road activities, remember to

- avoid damaging walls, fences, paths, grassland, etc

- take care not to harm livestock or wildlife

- respect the countryside in general

- drive in a responsible manner at all times.

Defensive driving

When travelling diagonally downhill, always look for an escape route straight down the slope in case the vehicle strikes any object or if there is a danger of overturning.

Saloon cars with four-wheel drive

A few saloon cars are now fitted with four-wheel drive. This can be

- an optional extra when buying a new vehicle

- part of the overall design so that sensors in the vehicle's drive system automatically engage four-wheel drive.

Benefits The main benefit of four-wheel drive in a saloon car is improved traction under all weather or road conditions.

Limitations Saloon cars with four-wheel drive can deal with some off-road conditions.

However, because of low ground clearance they will not deal with very soft surfaces. Special off-road vehicles have higher ground clearance and, usually, off-road tyres.

The same applies to snow. A four-wheel drive saloon will deal very well with snow up to a certain depth, but not with very deep snow.

section **twenty-three**

DRIVING TAXIS

This section covers
- First steps to becoming a taxi driver
- Passenger care
- Professional driving
- Driving taxis
- Passengers with special needs

First steps to becoming a taxi driver

Professional hackney carriage and private hire drivers have a responsibility to ensure that their fare-paying passengers have a safe, comfortable and enjoyable journey.

As professional drivers, taxi drivers have a special responsibility to set an example to others by driving with courtesy and consideration. Many taxi drivers will have years of driving experience under their belt and be able to demonstrate a good standard of driving.

The principles of good practice are set out throughout this book. Study them to check that you haven't developed particular driving habits which may not be conducive to good driving practice.

Throughout this section 'hackney carriage drivers' and 'private hire drivers' will be referred to as 'taxi drivers' and 'fare-paying passengers' as 'passengers'.

If you wish to become a taxi driver you should contact your local authority to enquire about licensing arrangements in your area for both yourself as a prospective driver and your vehicle. Regulations differ from one local authority to another, whether you intend to drive a hackney carriage or private hire vehicle.

The main differences between hackney carriages and private hire vehicles are shown below.

A hackney carriage can be

- hailed on the street
- driven by any authorised licence holder when carrying a passenger.

A private hire vehicle cannot be hailed on the street.

The badging and licensing requirements for both hackney carriages and private hire are renewable and lie with the licensing authorities.

Regulations

Although regulations differ between local authorities, they all require a

- medical check which includes an eyesight test
- Criminal Records Bureau check
- current driving licence – even if you have penalty points on your licence, you may still be able to apply. Check with the licensing authority
- fee for the issue of the licence.

Many authorities require a driving test of some description. In some areas these are carried out by DSA driving examiners conducting special tests for taxi drivers.

Medical check Consult your doctor first if you have any doubts about your fitness. You may be refused a licence if you suffer from certain conditions including epilepsy, diabetes or do not meet the more stringent eyesight requirements (a full list can be found on the report form).

You'll need to send a medical report to your taxi licensing authority. The medical examination isn't free under National Health Service rules. Your doctor is entitled to charge the current fee for this examination, which will be your responsibility. You will have to submit this form within a specified time of completing it for it to be valid.

For more information on driving taxis, go to **businesslink.gov.uk/taxi**

Passenger care

Caring for your passengers is an important part of taxi driving. As the driver, you're responsible for the safety and comfort of your passengers as they get into and out of your vehicle as well as during the journey. Your job is to convey your passengers to their destination

- safely
- comfortably
- efficiently
- in a courteous manner.

It includes the care of your passengers as you pick them up and drop them off at their destination in a safe and convenient place.

Remember you are the representative of the licensing authority and how well you perform your role reflects on the authority.

Ask yourself the following.

- Do your passengers feel safe and comfortable during the journey? Are they getting a smooth ride? If they aren't, you may need to adjust your driving style to enable them to have a pleasant journey.
- Do they need assistance in getting in or out of your vehicle? Be aware of passengers with special needs, particularly when they are getting into or out of the vehicle (see page 360).

To help your passengers, you should

- look directly at them when you speak to them; it can help you to communicate effectively
- make sure they are comfortably seated before you move away.

In the event of a breakdown, show consideration towards your passengers' safety and the completion of their journey.

Passenger seat belts Passengers must wear seat belts where they are fitted.

- Adult passengers are responsible for their own actions.

- You are responsible for ensuring that children under 14 wear their seat belts. The only exception is where there is a fixed partition separating the front and the rear of the taxi, in which case you are not responsible.

It is unreasonable to expect the right child seat or booster to be available in a taxi unless a parent or carer has brought it with them. There is therefore a qualified exception which says that if child restraints are not available in a licensed taxi or licensed private hire vehicle

- a child under three years old may travel unrestrained but in the rear only – this is the only exemption for a child under three years old

- a child aged three years and above must use an adult belt in the rear seat only.

Any child up to 135 cm (approx 4 feet 5 inches) in a front seat of any vehicle must use the seat belts or child restraints available.

Dealing with lost property If you find any property in your vehicle after the passenger has left, you should normally hand it in to a police station as soon as possible.

Some licensing authorities run their own lost property section. If this is so you should hand it in there, again as soon as possible. Check with your licensing authority for the regulations in your area.

Professional driving

Professional drivers adopt a positive approach to driving. This means

- looking after your passengers, yourself and your vehicle
- planning well ahead – taking account of road and traffic conditions
- practising good observation
- keeping in control
- anticipating events.

It's essential that your vehicle is under control at all times. You must drive it with skill and plan ahead so that your vehicle is always travelling at the correct speed and ready for your next manoeuvre.

You need to develop your awareness so that you know what is going on around you at all times. This can be achieved through

- planning well ahead
- anticipating – experience will soon tell you what other road users are probably going to do next
- being in control. Always plan your actions.

You must show that your standards are high at all times by driving

- responsibly
- carefully
- considerately
- courteously.

Consider the environment You may often have to wait for a fare. If you have to wait more than a few minutes, turn off your engine to reduce emissions and noise pollution.

As a professional driver, you have a responsibility to use your vehicle in a manner which is sympathetic to the environment. Use your skills to set an example to other road users.

Seat belts It is always safer to wear a seat belt when driving; however, taxi drivers are not required by law to wear a seat belt at all times. Drivers of hackney carriages don't need to wear a seat belt when they are on duty, but private hire drivers are only exempt when carrying a fare-paying passenger.

Communication and in-car equipment
Don't allow the use of any such equipment to distract you from driving carefully and safely. It is illegal to use a hand-held mobile phone or other similar device when driving. Never use a hand-held microphone when driving. Find a safe place to stop before using such equipment.

If your taxi is fitted with a communications radio or telephone, you should only use it while driving if it's fitted with a hands-free microphone. However, even using hands-free equipment is likely to distract your attention from the road. It's far safer not to use any such equipment or to try to tune the radio while driving.

Tiredness and distractions

As a professional driver you may be driving for long hours. Even though your hours aren't restricted like those of a bus or coach driver, you should be aware that being on the road for a long time can be very tiring. You have a duty to yourself as well as your passengers not to drive when you're tired.

It's recommended that normally you should take a break of at least 15 minutes after every two hours of driving.

As a professional driver, you must make sure that you are always fit and able to concentrate for the whole of your shift.

If you know that you will have a long journey at the end of the day, such as an airport run, plan your day and your rest periods so that you can accommodate this journey.

Remember, if you're carrying passengers, you can't stop in the middle of a journey to take a nap.

There are particular problems associated with driving for long periods at night and the smallest lapses of concentration can lead to loss of control. Factors causing fatigue include

- time of day – natural alertness is at a minimum between midnight and 6.00 am
- lack of sleep
- continual glare from oncoming headlights. This is very tiring on the eyes and can lead to general tiredness
- limited lighting (street lights, pedal cycles) causing strain on the eyes when reading signs, looking for premises or seeing other vehicles.

Remember – tiredness can kill.

Be aware of distractions from your passengers when you're driving.

- Your passengers may be talking among themselves, so make sure you're not distracted by their discussions.
- Your passengers may try to engage you in conversation, especially if they're not familiar with the area and are trying to obtain local information – be polite, but make sure that you are not distracted and that you can concentrate on your driving at all times.

Driving taxis

All the advice about driving found in the rest of the book is relevant to you as a taxi driver. However, there are certain aspects of driving that you will have to carry out more frequently when driving taxis than you would when driving a private car. These are

- stopping on the side of the road
- turning in the road.

Stopping at the roadside

All drivers have to stop at the side of the road, but as a taxi driver you have to think of your passengers at all times and ensure that, when you stop, your passengers are able to get in or out of your vehicle safely and conveniently.

Make sure that

- you pull up within a reasonable distance of the kerb, in a position that is safe, legal and convenient
- you apply the handbrake and put the gear into neutral before your passenger opens the door
- your passengers can open the door fully and that their entry or exit is not blocked by trees or street furniture – lampposts, waste bins, signs, etc
- you are there to help if your passenger needs assistance with loading or unloading luggage or they are not able to get in or out without assistance
- all your passengers are comfortably seated before moving away.

Turning your vehicle around

As a taxi driver you're likely to have to turn your vehicle around more frequently than most other drivers – for example, if you have just dropped off a passenger and receive a call on your radio to pick up a fare in the opposite direction.

You should assess the situation and decide on the safest and most appropriate way to make the turn. You could consider

- making a U-turn within the width of the road
- using the mouth of a junction on the left or right in which to swing around
- turning in the road using forward and reverse gears
- reversing into a side road on your left or right.

Never drive into a side road with the intention of reversing out into the main road and don't use private driveways to make your turn. Make sure that you don't mount the kerb when you're turning around, as this could damage your vehicle.

Passengers with special needs

As a professional driver you should always be there to give assistance when it is needed, especially when your passenger has special needs.

Whatever vehicle you drive, be ready to give assistance when an older passenger, or one who has limited mobility, is getting into or out of your vehicle.

Some vehicles, especially black cabs, are fitted with special equipment to allow easy access for those who may otherwise find it difficult. If you have this equipment, make full use of it to improve your passenger's comfort.

Special fittings can include

- an intermediate step
- a swivel seat
- a ramp and wheelchair fittings.

Intermediate step It can be difficult for people with limited mobility to get into or out of some vehicles, including black cabs.

This can be because of the position of the seats and the greater distance between the floor of the vehicle and the street or pavement.

Assess your passenger's needs, and if you think it might help, offer to provide the additional step for them as they get into or out of the taxi. Use the following procedure.

- Remove the steps from the stowage compartment.
- Ensure the door is fully open and secured.
- Fit the step and ensure it is securely fixed before your passenger steps onto it.
- Once they are safely in, close the door and stow the step.

Swivel seat A person with limited mobility might also find the swivel seat helpful. Often this will need to be used in conjunction with the intermediate step. As they get into your vehicle, you should

- ensure the door is fully opened and secured
- pull down the seat and swing it outwards until it is locked
- help the person onto the seat if necessary
- swivel the seat back into the travelling position until it is locked
- offer to help secure the seat belt before closing the door.

Reverse the procedure once the journey is completed.

Ramp and wheelchair fittings If you have the facility to carry wheelchairs you must ensure that you are able to correctly load and secure the wheelchair so the passenger can be transported safely and then reverse the process at the end of the journey.

To load the wheelchair user you should

- prepare for your passenger. Fit the wheelchair restraint and make space available for the wheelchair. Ensure the door is fully opened and secured. Pull out the ramp and add an extension if necessary

- push the wheelchair user into the vehicle and stow the ramp. If you need to let go of the wheelchair to stow the ramp, make sure you apply the wheelchair brakes

- position the wheelchair so that it can be secured using the equipment provided by the vehicle manufacturer

- ensure that all straps and belts which secure the wheelchair and its user are fastened according to the manufacturer's instructions

- close the door.

To unload the wheelchair at the end of the journey, you should

- open the door fully and secure it

- release the restraining straps and belts

- pull out the ramp and fit the extension if it is needed. If you need to move the wheelchair to do this, make sure you apply the brakes before letting go of the wheelchair

- wheel out the wheelchair. Walk backwards for the safety of your passenger and so that you can retain full control

- remove the ramp and stow any equipment in the appropriate place

- close the door.

section **twenty-four**
FURTHER INFORMATION

This section covers
- Reviewing your driving
- Organisations providing advanced driving tests
- Mobility centres
- Recognising basic faults
- Index

Reviewing your driving

At the outset it was explained that this book is essential for every motorist, regardless of experience. Having read this book, and put it into practice, are **you** satisfied with your standard of driving? If you are, should you be?

It is an essential role of every safe and responsible driver to review and adjust their behaviour over their lifetime. However skilled and experienced you become, you and those around you will not remain as safe as you can reasonably be unless you keep up to date with changes and actively review your competencies.

As we progress through a lifetime of driving, there will be changes in circumstances. The context in which we approach driving alters, challenges change and we as individuals do too. For example, we are likely to experience changes

- to the law and to the rules of the road
- to vehicle and related technologies
- in our personal circumstances
- in the reasons why we drive
- in our health and physical condition
- in our attitudes and behaviours.

Safe and responsible drivers aim to maintain their driving competencies by reviewing their driving and continuously seeking to improve.

A conscious effort to learn from experience, avoid complacency and prevent the development of bad habits is necessary; as is the need to develop and maintain appropriate attitudes and behaviours.

The competent driver needs

- a sense of responsibility
- concentration on the job of driving
- good anticipation
- patience and confidence
- courtesy and consideration.

While experience tends to make you a safer and more responsible driver, you should also review your driving regularly.

A wide range of opportunities and initiatives exist to support drivers who want to review and to assess their driving, develop their competence and respond to changing circumstances. For example

- newly qualified drivers should seek to further develop their competence by completing the Pass Plus scheme and practising with or without an accompanying driver
- a periodic session with an approved driving instructor (ADI) should become the norm for **all** drivers. This enables them to refresh their knowledge, understanding and skills, keep up to date with changes to rules of the road, legal requirements and maintenance requirements. This may need to be focused on specific elements if our driving requirements change.

For those who find the context of their driving has changed, it is important to review and assess their skills and knowledge in the new environment.

Additional learning and/or training, or other support, may be necessary.

Driving with young children Those who drive with young children in the vehicle may face increased distractions while driving. Preparation and planning become increasingly important. It is sensible to devise and review strategies for coping with unforeseen circumstances and situations.

Driving for work Those required to drive for work, or to drive a van regularly, face a significant change to the circumstances, challenges and pressures they face while driving. Conflicting commitments, legal obligations and the potential impact of stress and/or fatigue all need to be considered.

All drivers All drivers need to be alert to changes in their physical or mental condition. Ill-health or relevant age-related changes can have a significant impact on driving and should be considered and addressed.

So make sure your aim is 'safe driving for life'.

Organisations providing advanced driving tests

The Institute of Advanced Motorists
510 Chiswick High Road
London W4 5RG

Tel **020 8996 9600**
Fax **020 8996 9601**
iam.org.uk

DIAmond Advanced Motorists
Safety House
Beddington Farm Road
Croydon CR0 4XZ

Tel **020 8665 5151**
Fax **020 8665 5565**
diamondam.org

RoSPA Advanced Drivers and Riders
RoSPA House
28 Calthorpe Road
Edgbaston
Birmingham
B15 1RP

Tel **0121 248 2127**
Fax **0121 248 2050**
roadar.org.uk

Mobility centres

A current list of mobility centres can be found at **mobility-centres.org.uk/find_a_centre** or telephone **0800 559 3636**.

Belfast

Disability Action
Portside Business Park, 189 Airport Road,
Belfast BT3 9ED

Tel **02890 297 880** Fax **02890 297 881**
Email **mobilitycentre@disabilityaction.org**
Website **disabilityaction.org**

Birmingham

Regional Driving Assessment Centre
Unit 11, Network Park,
Duddeston Mill Road,
Birmingham B8 1AU

Tel **0845 337 1540** Fax **0121 333 4568**
Email **info@rdac.co.uk**
Website **rdac.co.uk**

Bodelwyddan

North Wales Mobility and Driving Assessment Service
Disability Resources Centre
Glan Clwyd Hospital, Bodelwyddan,
Denbighshire LL18 5UJ

Tel **01745 584 858** Fax **01745 535 042**
Email **mobilityinfo@btconnect.com**
Website **wmdas.co.uk**

Bristol

Living (formerly the Disabled Living Centre)
(West of England)
The Vassall Centre, Gill Avenue,
Fishponds, Bristol BS16 2QQ

Tel **01179 653 651** Fax **01179 653 652**
Email **info@thisisliving.org.uk**
Website **thisisliving.org.uk**

Cardiff

South Wales Mobility and Driving Assessment Service
Rookwood Hospital, Fairwater Road,
Llandaff, Cardiff CF5 2YN

Tel **0292 055 5130** Fax **0292 055 5130**
Email **helen@wddac.co.uk**
Website **wmdas.co.uk**

Carshalton

Queen Elizabeth's Foundation Mobility Centre
Damson Way, Fountain Drive,
Carshalton,
Surrey SM5 4NR

Tel **02087 701 151** Fax **02087 701 211**
Email **mobility@qef.org.uk**
Website **qef.org.uk**

Derby

DrivAbility (Derby Regional Mobility Centre)
Kingsway Hospital,
Kingsway,
Derby DE22 3LZ

Tel **01332 371 929** Fax **01332 382 377**
Email **driving@derbyhospitals.nhs.uk**
Website **derbydrivability.com**

Edinburgh

Scottish Driving Assessment Service
Astley Ainslie Hospital,
133 Grange Loan,
Edinburgh EH9 2HL

Tel **0131 537 9192** Fax **0131 537 9193**
Email **marlene.mackenzie@nhslothian.scot.nhs.uk**

Leeds

The William Merritt Disabled Living Centre and Mobility Service
St Mary's Hospital, Green Hill Road,
Armley, Leeds LS12 3QE

Tel **01133 055 288** Fax **01132 319 291**
Email **mobility.service@nhs.net**
Website **williammerrittleeds.org**

Maidstone

South East DriveAbility
Cobtree Ward
Preston Hall Hospital, London Rd,
Aylesford,
Kent ME20 7NJ

Tel **01622 795 719** Fax **01622 795 720**
Email **wk-pct.sedriveability@nhs.net**

Newcastle upon Tyne

North East Drive Mobility
Centre for Neuro-rehabilitation and Neuro-psychiatry
Walkergate Park, Benfield Road,
Newcastle upon Tyne NE6 4QD

Tel **0191 287 5090**
Email **northeast.drivemobility@ntw.nhs.uk**
Website **ntw.nhs.uk**

Oxford

Oxford Mobility Centre
c/o Regional Driving Assessment Centre
Unit 11, Network Park
Duddeston Mill Road,
Birmingham B8 1AU

Tel **0845 337 1540** Fax **0121 333 4568**
Email **info@rdac.co.uk**
Website **rdac.co.uk**

Southampton

Wessex DriveAbility
Leornain House, Kent Road,
Portswood,
Southampton SO17 2LJ

Tel **023 8051 2222**
Email **enquiries@wessexdriveability.org.uk**
Website **wessexdriveability.org.uk**

Thetford

East Anglian DriveAbility
2 Napier Place, Thetford,
Norfolk IP24 3RL

Tel **01842 753 029** Fax **01842 755 950**
Email **info@eastangliandriveability.org.uk**
Website **eastangliandriveability.co.uk**

Truro

Cornwall Mobility Centre
Tehidy House, Royal Cornwall Hospital,
Truro, Cornwall TR1 3LJ

Tel **01872 254 920** Fax **01872 254 921**
Email **mobility@rcht.cornwall.nhs.uk**
Website **cornwallmobilitycentre.co.uk**

Welwyn Garden City

Hertfordshire Action on Disability Mobility Centre
The Woodside Centre, The Commons,
Welwyn Garden City, Hertfordshire AL7 4DD

Tel **01707 324 581** Fax **01707 371 297**
Email **driving@hadnet.org.uk**
Website **hadnet.org.uk**

Wigan

Wrightington Mobility Centre
Wrightington Hospital, Hall Lane,
Appley Bridge, Wigan, Lancs WN6 9EP

Tel **01257 256 409** Fax **01257 256 538**
Email **mobility.centre@alwpct.nhs.uk**

Recognising basic faults

Symptom	Probable cause	Remedy
Brakes		
Vehicle pulls to one side when braking	Incorrect adjustment	Seek qualified assistance
Warning light shows	Undue wear in pads/shoes	Seek qualified assistance
	System fault	Seek qualified assistance
	Low brake fluid level	Check level
	Brake light failed	Replace bulb
Brakes inefficient on good road surfaces	Possible component failure	Seek qualified assistance
	Brakes require adjusting	Seek qualified assistance
Parking brake will not hold vehicle	Cable adjustment or replacement needed	Seek qualified assistance
Lights		
Light does not come on	Bulb failure	Check and replace
	Fuse failure	Check and replace
Indicator flashing irregularly	Possible bulb failure	Check and replace
	Relay failure	Check and replace
Main/dip beam not lit	Part failure of unit	Check and replace
Tyres/steering		
Steering 'heavy' or erratic	Puncture	Change wheel and repair or replace tyre
	Power-assisted steering unit	Seek qualified assistance
Vibration in steering at specific speeds	Front wheel out of balance (check for loss of balance weight or bulge in tyre)	Seek qualified assistance or change tyre

Symptom	Probable cause	Remedy
Engine		
Misfiring or won't run	Fuel or electrical fault	Examine connections
		Seek assistance
	Defective spark plugs	Examine and replace if necessary
Fails to start	Out of fuel	Check gauge
	Damp in electrical circuits	Use anti-damp spray
Starter doesn't operate	Battery discharged (flat)	Change battery
		Jump start
		Push start
Starter or solenoid clicks	Starter motor jammed	Rock vehicle backwards and forwards in gear with ignition **off**
		Turn 'square' end on starter with a spanner
Squealing noise from engine area	Fan belt or alternator belt slipping	Adjust or replace
Overheating	Fan belt snapped or hose leaking	Replace belt or hose
		Tape hose for temporary repair
	Fuse blown on electric cooling fan	Replace fuse

Index

Where can I find out more?

Whether you're learning to drive, helping others to learn or improving your skills, make sure you're using the official Driving Standards Agency materials for expert information from the people who set the tests. For the full range of official DSA titles, go to tsoshop.co.uk/dsa

Did you know you can:

- book your theory test
- book your practical test

and much more by visiting: direct.gov.uk/drivingtest

or call customer services on 0300 200 1122

twitter To join the conversation on Twitter
follow @Liz_DSA or @John_DSA

Find out what to expect when you take your theory and practical driving tests by visiting DSA's YouTube channel:

You Tube youtube.com/dsagov

Become a fan on Facebook for hints, tips and news for learners:

f facebook.com/mydrivingtest

* scan to become a fan (needs a phone with a QR code reader app)

The Official DSA Theory Test for Car Drivers and
The Official Highway Code

Book ISBN 9780115531828 £14.99
Downloadable PDF ISBN 9780115531842 £14.99*

Every official theory test revision question plus full DSA explanations of the answers and references to the source material throughout so you can get all the help you need to fully understand the answers. Includes a FREE Theory Test Extra eBook download.

The Official DSA Theory Test for Car Drivers and The Official Highway Code

CD-ROM ISBN 9780115531286 £12.99
Interactive Download ISBN 9780115531590 £9.99*

The closest experience you can get to the multiple choice part of the theory test. Contains every official theory test revision question, practice for case studies on all topics, references from each question to the source material and a digital version of The Official Highway Code. Includes a voiceover option.

The Official DSA Complete Theory Test Kit

CD-ROM & DVD ISBN 9780115531309 £19.99

Ideal preparation for both parts of the theory test, includes The Official DSA Theory Test for Car Drivers CD-ROM and Hazard Perception DVD. The Theory Test CD-ROM contains every official theory test revision question and answer. Save £8.99 on individual prices.

The Official DSA Guide to Learning to Drive

Book ISBN 9780115530913 £9.99
Downloadable PDF ISBN 9780115530623 £9.99*

Fully explains the standards required to pass the practical driving test. Includes information on independent driving and advice for those helping learners to practise.

* for instant access from tsoshop.co.uk

TSO is proud to be DSA's official publishing partner.

Six easy ways to purchase

Online Visit tsoshop.co.uk/dsa
Email Email your order to dsa.merchandising@tso.co.uk
Telephone Please call 0870 850 6553. Please quote reference CQD when ordering
Fax Fax your order to 0870 243 0129
Post Marketing, TSO, Freepost, ANG 4748, Norwich NR3 1YX (no stamp required)
Shops Available from all good high street and online book stores. For interactive products please also visit selected computer software retailers.

Prices, cover images and publication dates are correct at the time of going to print but may be subject to change without notice.

 Visit our Facebook page at **facebook.com/learningtodrive**

Follow us on Twitter **twitter.com/DSA_Publishers**